Someone I Love
Lives Here

Someone I Love Lives Here

A story about looking for love and acceptance in all the wrong places, and finally finding it within myself.

Justine Moore Sloan

gatekeeper press™

Columbus, Ohio

Someone I Love Lives Here: A story about looking for love and acceptance in all the wrong places, and finally finding it within myself.

Published by Gatekeeper Press

2167 Stringtown Rd, Suite 109

Columbus, OH 43123-2989

www.GatekeeperPress.com

The interior formatting, typesetting, and editorial work for this book are entirely the product of the author. Gatekeeper Press did not participate in and is not responsible for any aspect of these elements.

Library of Congress Control Number: 2021938824

ISBN (hardcover): 9781662908309

ISBN (paperback): 9781662907784

eISBN: 9781662908903

Contents

Introduction   17

Part I: The Problem   27

Part II: Problem Areas   73

Part III: The Plan   179

Part IV: The Phoenix (Healing)   269

4-year-old me, joyfully surrounded by my beloved stuffed cats.

Dedicated to my parents, Kelly and Janet.

*Thank you for raising me to believe that
I am smart, special, and can be anything
I want to be (including an author!)*

*I know parts of this book may be hard
for you to read, just as parts of my life
may have been hard for you to watch. I'm
eternally grateful for your unconditional
love, support, and acceptance.*

*Thank you for the tremendous gift of
letting me forge my own path.*

Disclaimers

The diet and exercise programs and regimens printed in this book are meant to give the reader a deeper look at the psyche and lifestyle of the author at an earlier time. In no way does the author recommend or condone these methods as safe or effective.

This publication is meant as a source of information for the reader, however it is not meant as a substitute for direct expert assistance. If such level of assistance is required, the services of a competent professional should be sought.

Author's Note

All of the stories in this book are true, but some details may not be entirely factual. I have changed names of people, identifying details, and some locations to protect the privacy of the people involved. For the sake of narrative coherence, some incidents have been edited down or left out. In cases of dialogue, I am telling my story to the best of my memory, though they are not written to represent word-for-word transcripts. Rather, I've written my story to convey the feeling and meaning of what was said. In all instances, the essence of the dialogue is accurate.

11 Unspoken Rules of Being A Woman

1. **Unspoken Rule #1:** Lose weight to feel great.

2. **Unspoken Rule #2:** Be the right size, as determined by society.

3. **Unspoken Rule #3:** Do whatever you need to do to eradicate your "Problem Areas."

4. **Unspoken Rule #4:** Do not trust your hunger. Magazines and diets will tell you how much to eat.

5. **Unspoken Rule #5:** THIN is more important than healthy.

6. **Unspoken Rule #6:** The purpose of exercise is to get thinner. Exercise as much as possible, and as hard as possible.

7. **Unspoken Rule #7:** Your value is directly correlated with how desirable you are to men.

8. **Unspoken Rule #8:** Other women are not your friends. They are your competition and your enemies.

9. **Unspoken Rule #9:** Pretty girls are "taken." It is better to be in a toxic relationship than to be single.

10. **Unspoken Rule #10:** There is a limited supply of attention, success, and resources available for women. You will constantly have to strive to come out on top.

11. **Unspoken Rule #11:** Keep your feelings to yourself to ensure others are comfortable. The uncomfortable things that happen to you are yours to carry alone. In silence.

Introduction

"All I could say was, 'I don't know what to do.' I remember her taking me by the shoulders and looking me in the eye with a calm smile and saying simply, 'Tell the truth, tell the truth, tell the truth.'"

~Elizabeth Gilbert; Eat, Pray, Love

I was seven years old when I first learned my body was wrong.

I sat there wide-eyed at the doctors' office and began to determine who I was in this world as a woman, and who I would need to be in order to be accepted and loved.

Children are like sponges, and even when they're not *told* things, they feel things. They see things modeled to them, and they inherit old beliefs passed down from previous generations. They absorb energy and emotions, and they intuitively know their place in the world. They know what they need to do to ensure they maintain safety, love, and belonging.

I was *told* I could be anything I wanted to be. Yet I *saw* that the *most* important thing to be as a woman was thin, flawless, and desirable to men. The significance of jean sizes, makeup, and hair was clear throughout my childhood. I became deeply entangled in a spiderweb of both subliminal and explicit messages from a patriarchal culture.

Through these messages, I pieced together the rules of being a woman. More than anything, I wanted to learn the rules, and then, I wanted to *win*. For me, winning would verify that I was good enough. Behind the trophy-chasing was a desperate longing to prove my worthiness. Winning would indicate that I was lovable and valuable.

As trapped prey in this spider web of lies throughout my pre-teens, teenage years, and young adulthood, I unconsciously attracted relationships and experiences that reflected back to me all of the beliefs about the "rules" I had formed at such a young age.

It wasn't until I was physically sick, mentally unwell, and spiritually bankrupt that I began to free myself from the web— one sticky, binding piece at a time. I realized the cost of winning at the game I was playing wasn't worth it. The stakes were far too high.

After hitting my "rock bottom," I set forth on a path of examining every corner of my life, and transforming all the parts that weren't serving me. I began to unlearn everything I was taught by a world that doesn't prioritize the well-being of girls and women. I began to reject the rules, and then, through a tremendous amount of healing and inner work, I began to write *my own* rules.

Rejecting the rules that were so deeply ingrained in me was a grieving process— I denied, I cried, I screamed, and I even broke stuff (including an innocent iPad, in a sudden fit of rage.) But eventually, I came out on the other side, feeling empowered for the first time in my life, all the while still unlearning, and still feeling mad as hell that this is the way of the world.

Writing this book has been the most challenging undertaking of my life, and throughout the process, I've asked myself countless times, *WHY? Why write this? Why should I tell my story? Why does MY story matter?*

Writing a book— especially a memoir— is no easy feat, so to do the work, you'd better have an answer to the question of, "Why does this matter?" That answer needs to be powerful enough to pull you through hundreds of hours of laboring over your keyboard, and hundreds more spent exploring the darkest corners of your psyche. That WHY has to be big enough to possess you to dive deep into the most painful memories of your life and transmute them into something meaningful on the pages.

So here is my answer to the question, *"Why should I tell my story?"*

In Stephen King's book "On Writing," something struck me regarding the chapters about his youth. King shares how early his writing journey began— writing his first original story around 7 years old, and submitting stories to publications regularly by his early teens.

I thought about how I too had written my first original stories by the time I was 7 years old. To this day, I have six actual "books," with writing and illustrations I lovingly added to a professionally bound blank book, all completed by the end of the third grade.

I even went on to take first place out of my entire elementary school in a writing contest in sixth grade, which scored me a full day field trip to the Milwaukee Art Museum to refine my craft. But then it stopped.

Unlike King, I didn't send my creative work to publications in my teens, because I didn't do any. I simply stopped being creative. Following the unspoken rules became a crucial part of my existence and replaced the creativity I once held so dear. More "important" ways to spend my time took over my life, like being thin, being liked, and being seen as desirable to the opposite sex. I mean, who has the time and energy to use their imagination to craft original works of art when you are busy trying to perfect your physical appearance? The quest to physical perfection is exhausting, and devastatingly all-consuming.

This hurts my soul on the deepest level, because I know I am not the only woman whose creativity and talent were stifled in the meaningless chase of physical perfection. My generation was raised with a sense of hopefulness that things could be different for girls, but sexist attitudes and overtones that had been present for centuries still dominated our culture. While boys were encouraged to hone in on their strengths and talents, girls were encouraged to hone in on their looks to attract the boys.

It is far too easy to fall into this trap of obsessing over your appearance, and getting stuck there for years. Or worse, some fall into this trap and never come out.

In my coaching career, I've worked with women in their late sixties who are still berating themselves on a daily basis for their "fat thighs," or "jiggly arms." Oh, how my heart aches when they share things like this! How much precious life goes down the drain because of thighs that are thicker than what society told you is acceptable, or whatever other physical imperfections ail you most?

This trap— this sticky web of lies— can hold you hostage for years, decades, and even lifetimes, because the pursuit of perfection never ends. It is forever a carrot dangling in front of you that you can never reach.

You are convinced that when *this* happens, *then* you'll move forward and do *this*.

"When I lose these 20 pounds, *then* I'll go on online dating sites and look for my soul mate…"

"When I'm happy with how I look, *then* I'll launch the website and blog…"

"When I feel more confident, *then* I'll go after that promotion…"

"When I like how I look on camera, *then* I'll step up as a leader and share my story…"

"I feel fat right now, so this will have to wait. When I lose the weight, it'll be different…"

"I feel ugly today, so I'm not going to do that thing I wanted to do. Maybe tomorrow…"

But tomorrow never comes. You never reach the place where you feel perfect enough, thin enough, or pretty enough. Your dreams go on the back burner as you buy that next thigh cream, or hire that trainer, or start that diet your friend told you about, or whatever that seemingly "next right thing" may be in your quest to be good enough to start actually living your life.

You think looking good enough will give you that permission slip you long for. The permission slip that deems you "ready" to go after what you really desire. But the permission slip never comes.

You wake up and realize you spent your entire life chasing something unattainable. And something that is meaningless, and illusory, as even the most physically "perfect" humans in the world grow old. Looks fade; that's inevitable. But we get distracted by chasing beauty and perfection for so long, we forget to create meaningful moments in our lives that don't fade.

I have so many "what ifs" about my life. I wouldn't call them regrets. I just have a genuine curiosity about what could have been different for me. I wonder what I might have done with my time, energy, resources, and brainpower if I wasn't playing by the unspoken rules for two decades. For the first 27 years of my life, it was all about that carrot I was chasing— thinking I needed to be what everyone else wanted me to be.

Now looking back, I recognize that no one actually wanted me to be onstage "competing" in bodybuilding shows, with clear plastic heels, a spray tan, and plastic surgery. I must admit that I took these unspoken rules to the extreme, and I won. I went after these rules and conquered them, because I thought winning at the game of being a woman would make me finally feel like I was enough. Having a body that others thought was "perfect" was what I thought was most important to put my energy into— and I crushed it. I attained *all* the things I was striving for, and then some. The trophies, the brand endorsements, the 1.9 million followers on Facebook— I had it all. I did an excellent job pursuing these meaningless, dead-end goals, until it all exploded and crashed and burned.

If all that energy, passion, and natural ability had been redirected into a different goal, or trying to prove that I was smart, kind, and generous, I may have ended up in a very different place when I was 25 years old. I often think about how much woman-power is being wasted on the "I need to look perfect *first*" mentality. I wonder how many other women have wasted their time and energy chasing a similar dangling carrot.

How do we change this for future generations? How do we rewrite the rules to encourage fuller lives, and more *meaningful* values, to pass onto our daughters, and their daughters?

I don't have a clear answer to that, but I believe it starts here. I believe it starts with sharing our stories. Voicing our truth. Having the hard conversations, with ourselves and with others.

Nothing can change without first being seen and acknowledged. I hope my story serves as a testament to a very real problem that affects the majority of girls and women, with an astounding 97 percent of women reporting they have negative body image. (CBSnews.com, 2011) I hope my story gives you the insight and willingness to explore your own story, and the courage to share it with others.

We suffer because we think we are separate and alone in our problems, when in fact, we are all so very similar, and so very connected. Sharing our truth is tremendously healing, for ourselves and for the world.

Parts of this book may trigger you. It might awaken things within you that you don't want to look at. I'm inviting you to dive into those shadowy places within yourself.

The parts that trigger you are actually the most powerful gateways to your own transformation and awakening. I encourage you to explore those parts more deeply and ask yourself: *What do I believe? Where did I first learn that? Is it true? Is it what I want to continue believing? What do I want to believe NOW?*

Through my coaching education, I've learned that creating choice is how you empower someone. When we have no choice, we are a victim— a victim to other people's actions, a victim to society, and a victim to our circumstances.

When we *have* choices, we get to be the creator of our own world. We get to choose, and if we don't like it, we get to choose again. And that's what I want you to know, most of all— that the painful and fucked up beliefs you've adopted over the years are not *yours*. You didn't create them, and you don't have to keep them. You can choose again at any moment.

You get to decide which rules you follow and play by, and which ones you don't. You get to hit the "unsubscribe" button on anything that makes you feel less than worthy. You get to decide which dangling carrots you chase after. And if you get tired of chasing, please know you can grab that carrot and take a bite out of it. Bake it into a carrot cake, if you'd like.

I want you to know that the power is yours, my darling. The power has always been yours.

11-year-old me, fishing in the Gulf of Mexico on a family vacation to Florida.

Part I: The Problem

"Girls are taught to view their bodies as unending projects to work on, whereas boys from a young age are taught to view their bodies as tools to master the environment."

~Gloria Steinem

In the US, over 80 percent of girls report they've been on a diet by the age of 10. *(Miller, 2015)*

February 1995; age 7

I sat in the doctor's office waiting room, a Phil Collins song playing softly in the background. Next to me sat my effortlessly beautiful mom— dainty, petite, and pulled together— consuming the latest issue of *Good Housekeeping*.

My mom was rarely caught without her signature Mary Kay lipstick— a fierce shade of hot pink that so few women could pull off. But even in a pair of Lee high-rise jeans and a T-shirt, she pulled it off.

Emulating her, I quietly read a copy of *Highlights* magazine, which always sparked my creativity. I tried to distract myself with brain teasers in the magazine like, "What's Wrong in this Picture?" but I couldn't shake a feeling of uneasiness, knowing the reason why we were here.

In the years prior, I was a happy, playful child, who adored music and animals. I enjoyed drawing, reading, and writing, and all of my teachers loved me. Every March, my mom would invite every girl in my class to my birthday party, and we'd always have a big turnout. I knew I was loved, and felt free to be myself. My smile was big and genuine. My eyes were sparkly, always imagining my next book, art project, or experiment. Most importantly, though, my body was small. I loved eating all kinds of food and never worried about having too much dessert— twice a day, if it called to me. All was right in the world.

Things started to change when I was seven years old, because my body started to change. My face started getting rounder. My porcelain skin started to freckle in the sun, which I despised, because it made me different, and when you're a kid, anything that makes you different feels insufferable. I could no longer play outside all day without the consequences of these little sunspots spattered across my face.

My baby teeth fell out, and my front teeth re-entered my mouth at a tragic angle. They were practically horizontal, sticking straight out, hovering above the others, much to my despair. I wished I could give my $2 back to the Tooth Fairy in exchange for an acceptable-looking smile.

I gained a whopping 13 pounds in 9 months when I was in second grade, causing my mom a great deal of uneasiness. She figured something must be very wrong with me, so she took the first appointment she could get with our pediatrician.

A door opened, and a pretty blonde nurse wearing Winnie-the-Pooh scrubs glanced down at her clipboard.

"Justine?" she called out. My mom and I followed her back into a hallway filled with exam rooms. She led us over to a corner that housed a scale and stadiometer for measurements.

"Let's get you weighed and measured. Stand here against the wall, and stand up straight," she told me, motioning toward the sliding headpiece and ruler attached to the wall. I backed myself into the wall and stood up straight. She slid the headpiece down until it rested on my little 7-year-old head.

"49 inches," she announced, noting it on her clipboard. "Now take off your shoes and step on the scale."

I removed my little white Keds sneakers, and stepped onto the platform of the scale. The nurse began sliding the large counter weight over, over, and over some more. The beam remained in place, in front of my face, resting down to the left, unchanged. Something about this made me feel even more unsettled. She edged it over a bit more, notch by notch, until finally the beam lifted up and settled at rest in a straight, horizontal line.

"68 pounds," she said quietly, recording this new information onto my files.

The nurse led us into one of the exam rooms and instructed me to undress, put on a paper gown, and sit on the exam table to wait for the doctor.

I handed my mom my stretchy pastel pink leggings and my favorite oversized sweatshirt, with a big, fuzzy appliqué of a gray cat on it.

Growing up, I freaking *loved* cats. From the moment I began speaking and expressing my tiny toddler thoughts, I was requesting all things cats. Unfortunately, my parents weren't as enthusiastic about felines, so a pet cat was out of the question. I had to settle for cat clothing, imaginary cat friends, cat decor in my bedroom, and stuffed cats. At my cat-collecting peak, I was the proud owner of over 100 stuffed cats. One of them came with me on the car ride to the doctor's office that day for moral support.

I climbed up onto the exam table and waited. My little legs dangled below me.

Dr. Ross entered the room and greeted us. She was an attractive woman with a soothing voice and a cordial smile. After taking my vitals and assessing my records, she turned to my mom to discuss The Problem.

"Justine is in the 90th percentile for weight," Dr. Ross informed my mom, speaking as if I wasn't sitting three feet away. "That means she weighs more than 90 percent of children her age. Have there been any changes in her eating habits?"

My face and body instantly grew hot. I felt my chest and throat tighten. Dr. Ross and my mom continued to discuss my eating habits, my activity level, and different tests we could run to see if something was physically wrong with me— perhaps a thyroid issue, or something like that. The conversation continued, but I was no longer listening. It all blurred together as Dr. Ross's statement kept replaying again and again in my mind.

She weighs more than 90 percent of children her age, I kept repeating. My brain raced to make sense of it— to sort through this new information and what it meant about me, and my body.

I weigh too much. I am heavier than all the others. I am fat.

This is precisely where the narrative was formed— a narrative that would shape *so* many moments in my life. This defining moment in 1995 was embedding itself into my brain, my beliefs, and my identity. It lodged itself deep into the very DNA of who I was on this Earth, and would stay there for decades to come.

August 1995; age 8

My big brother Ryan and I sat at the breakfast counter together, crunching on my favorite cereal—sugary, delicious Reese's Peanut Butter Puffs, with two percent milk. It was like dessert for breakfast, which was ideal, because my love of desserts knew no bounds. In first grade, I had three pet hermit crabs who I named Cocoa, Cheesecake, and Chocolate Mousse. I was not playing around.

We finished eating, rinsed our bowls in the sink, and got dressed for the day. It was a big day— back-to-school clothes shopping for the upcoming school year. I headed to my mom's bathroom for our daily hair routine.

Every day my mom would style my thick, reddish-brown, shoulder-length hair. As a baby, I'd been bald for so long that well-meaning women felt the need to assure my mom, "When her hair does finally come in, it's going to be extra thick and beautiful!!"

They were right. My eight-year-old self had been cursed with many physical flaws, but hair wasn't one of them. My mom and I regularly rotated through different looks— ponytails, half-up, braids, the works. That morning, I requested a slicked-back ponytail. Sensible, for shopping, you know.

My mom wielded the fine-toothed comb through my thick hair, wrangling it back to make a perfectly smooth, bump-free ponytail.

"*Ow*, Mommy!" I protested.

"Beauty is pain, baby," she replied, and we laughed.

With my ponytail in check, my mom, Ryan, and I headed out the door.

The medical tests I'd taken earlier that year had come back negative for a thyroid issue, or any other red flags. Dr. Ross assured my mom I was a perfectly healthy little girl, just going through a "growth spurt." Since the appointment in February, I'd gained another *4 pounds*, much to both my mom's and my implicit horror.

In the girls' department at Kohl's Department Store, my mom and I browsed the back-to-school selection. Looking through the aisles, I saw denim, velvet, and corduroy overalls. Floral and plaid shirts, and polka dot skirts lined the rows of clothes. We pulled items from the rack and made our way to the dressing room.

My mom took a seat on the bench in the corner to perform her motherly duties of undoing each item from its hanger, handing it to me to try on, then neatly putting it back on the hanger to separate the "keepers," from the "no's."

I eagerly began my little fashion show, pulling a pink-and-blue-striped turtleneck over my head, along with a pair of light denim jeans. The turtleneck clung tightly to my arms, chest and belly. The jeans wouldn't zip. Instantly I felt a lump in my throat, as I gritted my teeth to hold back tears.

They don't fit me. I'm too big. I'm too big. I'm too big.

My mom scrambled to find similar items in the next size up. Hurriedly, she took a different pair of jeans off the hanger.

"Here, try these instead! These are cute!"

She handed me a pair of jeans with flowers embroidered on the pockets. I took the jeans from her, noticing the tag. Size 12, it read. I yanked the first pair of too-tight jeans off my body, and noticed the tag for the first time. Size 10.

I pulled on the flowery Size 12 jeans with ease, and could comfortably zip and button them. But the bottoms of the jeans bunched up around my feet, drooping across the floor, visibly 4 or 5 inches too long for my legs.

I stared at my reflection in the full-length mirror as those bright, unforgiving fluorescent lights blared down on me. My full face and my chubby cheeks looked like a fat little pig. My stumpy, thick legs looked disgustingly large. My round, pudgy belly stuck out much further than little girls' bellies are *supposed* to stick out. I felt embarrassed, ashamed, and confused as I studied my inconveniently shaped body.

"Hmm, those are a bit long. Why don't you try these on, baby?" my mom gently said, handing me a pair of denim overalls with sunflowers embroidered on the chest. "And here, try them on with this shirt!"

The overalls had a relaxed, roomy fit— *praise the Lord*— so they fit my growth-spurting, 8-year-old body without being noticeably too long. My mom and I breathed a sigh of relief in unison.

"Oh now, *this* outfit is a keeper!" my mom exclaimed, and I just nodded. I forced a little smile. I took the clothes off and handed them to her to hang on a separate rack, starting our pile of "keepers."

This continued on for what felt like an eternity. I noticed my mom didn't hand me all of the clothes we had selected from the racks. She was attempting to do damage control, carefully prejudging which items seemed to have the highest likelihood of fitting my problematic little (or not-so-little) body. I was grateful for her efforts to protect my self-esteem, but I knew exactly what was going on. We managed to successfully find three new outfits that fit me.

On the car ride home, I sat in the backseat and stared out the window. TLC's "Waterfalls" played on the radio, and normally

I'd sing along enthusiastically, because that was my *jam*! But I was silent, lost in my thoughts. I thought about the other 8-year-old girls from school, and imagined *their* shopping trips must be quite different. I was sure their slender little bodies easily fit into anything they desired.

Size 8, Size 10, Size 12. It wasn't hard for me to crack the code. There was only one perfect, right size to be—and my body didn't fit the mold. Not by a long shot.

October 1995; age 8

By the time I was in third grade, my dad earned a more-than-comfortable living, and since my only sibling was a boy, I never really wore hand-me-downs. But for some reason unbeknownst to me, I did inherit one distinct pair of pants from my brother.

They were bright red pajama pants Ryan had worn the previous Halloween, when he dressed up as a "Little Devil." They were cotton and stretchy, with elastic around the waist and ankles.

I liked the pants so much that I'd often change into them after dinner to watch TV or play games with my family. The pants fit me quite differently than they fit my brother, who was small for his age, and everyone seemed to be amused by this, except for me. My parents began fondly referring to the pants as the "sau-seeege pants," which was a funny way of saying the word "sausage."

I'd emerge from my bedroom proudly wearing the red pants, and my parents would catch sight of me and exchange glances. They'd giggle, trying to hold back tears of laughter.

"Justine's wearing the saus-eeege pants again!" someone would remark, and my mom, dad and brother would erupt into a fit of laughter.

I tried to smile and laugh with them, because it's no fun to be left out of a joke. But what I hid haunted me for years. Although I knew it was "just a joke," I didn't realize until many years later how much this joke hurt me. Even at 8 years old, I laughed at my own body. I was a mockery, best resembling a stuffed sausage. I deeply resented my body for growing too big, too fast, and I wished I could somehow make myself smaller.

April 1996; age 9

After school one day, I opened the refrigerator door to look for a snack. There's a solid chance I wasn't hungry; I just really liked consuming food, because it's delicious. There are two types of people in the world: people who *like* food, and people who *love* food. I'm the latter.

Something new caught my eye on the top shelf— six cans of SlimFast.

I picked up a can and studied it with intent. The aluminum can was thicker and sturdier than a soda can. The label was shiny and sleek, laminated with bold, bright red font jumping out at me, reading, "Lose Weight, Feel Great!"

The flavor was, "Rich Chocolate Royale," which sounded sophisticated and delicious. The lower corner of the can read, "Healthy Shake. 99% Fat Free."

I held the can in my hand, taking it all in. The cool aluminum on my skin. The enticing promises of this magical elixir.

Without a second thought, my fingers popped open the can. I felt a thrill rush through my body. I took my first sip; the cool, creamy beverage slowly hit the taste buds on my tongue. It was thicker than chocolate milk, but less sweet, and a bit chalky. I closed the refrigerator door and took the can with me to the counter. Just then, my mom walked into the kitchen smiling, and stopped in her tracks when she noticed the SlimFast can in my hands

"Oh," my mom said with a pause, searching for the next right thing to say. For a moment I felt embarrassed, like I'd been caught doing something bad. "Do you like that?" she asked, my embarrassment quickly fading away upon recognizing her calm, reassuring tone.

"Yeah, it's yummy!" I responded, taking another drink to demonstrate my fondness of this promising new tool.

I hope she'll let me drink this stuff, I thought, longing for this to be a solution to The Problem that had been tormenting me the past two years.

"Okay," my mom said, smiling at me and brushing my hair back gently with her hand. "If you like it, you can help yourself to it. Let's keep it a secret though, okay baby?"

I smiled back at her and nodded enthusiastically. I liked that it got to be a secret. I felt like I'd just accessed some grown-up lady superpower, a trick for manipulating my body, to lose weight and feel great, and my mom was allowing me to be in on this grown-up secret.

My mom has always been naturally thin and strikingly beautiful. With her huge blue eyes, delicate bone structure, and warm, inviting smile, people have always been drawn to her. But despite her beauty and petite body, my mom often lamented to me about her flaws— the stretch marks from two pregnancies, the tiny varicose veins on her legs, and most of all, her "fat thighs."

She didn't suffer from the same weight struggles her sisters faced, but she had decided at an early age that her thighs were simply unacceptable. She told me a classmate once pointed out how huge and fat they were, and she'd accepted that girl's opinion as truth. Comments can have that kind of effect.

My mom had bought the Slimfast for herself, hoping to remedy her "fat thighs." But now that I'd stumbled upon it, she was willing to share this body-slimming tool with her only daughter. It felt like a rite of passage— like I was mature enough to partake in the female ritual of obsessively trying to get thinner.

I felt hopeful that day, drinking my new secret weapon. I figured this magical chocolate beverage would soon fix all of my problems, by helping me become slim, *FAST*!

May 1997; age 10

While I excelled in all of my schoolwork, art, and music, I found sports to be terribly boring, and I knew I was downright rotten at them. I was painfully slow, clunky, and uncoordinated. When I'd attempt to join games of kickball at recess, I was always picked dead last by the team captains. It was humiliating, so I usually just did my own thing, wandering around the playground to pass the time instead.

Year after year, my mom would sign me up for softball, swimming, and other activities that still haunt my dreams to this day.

I never spoke up, because I believed it was something I *should* do— something I *should* like. Plus, I sensed my mom secretly hoped the extra activities would help me shed some pounds to fix The Problem. I secretly hoped so too, since the SlimFast had failed me. Perhaps I was doing it wrong, by *adding* it to my hearty diet of sugar-filled cereals, Toaster Strudels, and loads of frozen custard, without actually *replacing* anything. After all, this was my first diet. I'd get better, with years of practice.

My humiliation attempting to demonstrate athleticism extended beyond organized sports. I voluntarily entered into countless kickball and baseball games with my brother and the neighborhood kids, because being bad at sports was better than being left out. These backyard games were less painful, though, because, bless my big brother Ryan's heart, he always picked me first for his team, and coached me throughout the game so I didn't do anything horrendous.

Ryan was the oldest kid in our neighborhood, so he had that advantage over all of us. His age and athletic talent balanced out my shortcomings, so the Moore Team typically came out victorious.

One backyard baseball game, I was up to bat. I already had two strikes against me— one from swinging and missing, and one from watching a good pitch sail right past me.

Billy, our outspoken next-door neighbor who was one year younger than me, was pitching. He turned his faded Milwaukee Brewers baseball cap backwards and spit before he wound up to deliver the next pitch.

He launched the ball toward me. I clenched the bat tightly and swung as hard as I could, trying not to close my eyes and duck for cover, which has always been my natural instinct when an object is flying at me.

Whoosh! The ball flew past me again.

"Strike 3!" Billy yelled. "You're out, you hippo!"

I froze. The past three years, I'd known I was heavy, but no one had ever actually *called* me fat. Sure, it had been implied at times, but usually everyone spoke in polite code, referencing percentiles and growth spurts, or making clever jokes, in the case of the "saus-eeege pants." I felt a lump in my throat immediately, and I tried to choke it back as hot tears started welling up in my eyes.

No one said a word. My eyes caught my brother's. He quickly darted his gaze away from me, and down to the ground. I wanted so badly to melt into the grass and disappear.

I set the bat down, and turned away, walking from home plate to the back corner of the yard. My brother stepped in and picked up the aluminum baseball bat. I continued to go through the motions until the game was over, but my mind was racing, and my heart ached. I was finally rescued when my mom called to us from the back patio, "Ryan and Justine! Time to come in for dinner!"

I hurried away from the scene of the humiliation, trying to bury the whole episode deep down, where it wouldn't sting so much. I needed to make everyone else comfortable around me, by hiding my own pain.

That night, after brushing my teeth before bedtime, I stared at my reflection in the mirror. I lifted my Hello Kitty pajama shirt up and inspected my stomach with disgust. I pinched the fat on my belly and wondered why my body was this way. I thought about my brother, the other kids in the neighborhood, the other kids at school. We all ate similar cereals and snacks, and drank similar drinks. They were all so naturally skinny.

Why am I so different? What's wrong with me?

I made my way down the hallway and crawled into my twin bed. My mom came into my room to tuck me in, as she did every night. She'd scratch my back and sing me lullabies. When she sat down on the edge of my bed that night, I burst into tears.

"I'm fat!" I cried, reaming my blankets up to my neck, wrapping myself in a protective cocoon.

My mom looked surprised; her heart visibly broken for me. She didn't argue the point, or ask why it was coming up now. I never told her what Billy said, because I was too ashamed to repeat it. She gently stroked my hair, wiped my tears, and finally replied, "You're just going through a growth spurt, sweetie. It's just baby fat. You'll grow out of it."

She stayed at my bedside a little longer that night, until my tears subsided. I yawned, exhausted from the meltdown and all the painful emotions of the day. I let my eyelids slowly flutter shut.

"Good night. Sleep tight. Don't let the kitties bite. Sweet dreams. I love you," Mom whispered, as she did every single night, and kissed my forehead.

May 1998, age 11

Overcompensating for my chubbiness became a way of life for me. I figured I sure as hell wasn't cute, so at least I'd better be smart, funny, courteous, and obedient.

When a police officer took our class through the *D.A.R.E.* program to educate us on the dangers of drugs in fifth grade, I won the "Good Citizenship Award." I won lots of awards throughout elementary school, mostly for writing, and one for my epic stamp collection in fourth grade. Yes, stamps, like postage stamps. Don't laugh. Okay, you can laugh a little. I won first place in a city-wide competition for my nautical-themed stamp exhibit, entitled "See It By The Sea." My mom snapped pictures of me as I proudly posed next to my first-place ribbons, wearing my favorite cat vest, with a cardigan over it to complete the whole child-librarian vibe I had going on. "Champion of Champions," the ribbons read. You bet I was.

I stayed busy with after-school activities like Stamp Club, Art Club, and Recycling Club. I was most definitely a little nerd, but I was a conscientious little nerd! My mom was still deeply concerned with my weight, but she was oh-so-proud of all of my accomplishments.

All of my overachieving, people-pleasing ways couldn't help me in gym class. Of all of the memories of my childhood, few are worse than my memories of the mile run. Running has always been, and probably always will be, the bane of my existence.

The mile run consisted of four timed laps around a giant field to be performed in less than 10 minutes, ideally. I'd push my clunky little body as hard as I could, feeling my "baby fat" jiggle with each painfully slow step. I'd gasp for air, feeling a burning sensation and a metallic taste in the back of my throat. Finally, I wouldn't be able to jog another step, so I'd allow myself to walk. I was always dead last to finish, clocking an astoundingly poor time of 15 or 16 minutes. Humiliation always clung to me in gym class, like flies swarming around a carcass, but the mile run branded my psyche with feelings of inadequacy. I'd look down at my pudgy little legs and curse my body for betraying me—for not being able to do what all the other kids could do. The fastest, most athletic kids would lap me, and I'd watch them do so with both horror and awe, admiring their gazelle-like bodies effortlessly breezing through the air.

Why can't I be like that? I'd wonder over and over again.

My fifth-grade gym teacher, Mr. Webster, showed no mercy when it came to my struggles with physical fitness. When I brought home my spring report card, my mom and I opened it together to bask in the glory of my A's.

I'll never forget the shock and horror of seeing a "D" jump off the page, tarnishing my straight-A status. Mr. Webster had given me a "D" in gym class, for effort. "D," which must have stood for Disappointment. It might as well have been graded an "E" for Embarrassment, or an "F" for Fat-Ass.

The very next day my mom marched up to that school and gave Mr. Webster a piece of her mind. She fiercely defended her child, like a lioness defending her cub. She explained that I *was* trying my hardest, and it wasn't *my* fault I wasn't naturally gifted with speed, agility, or athleticism.

He didn't change my grade. He probably didn't give it a second thought after my mom was out of sight. It was the last quarter of the school year, so I didn't have another chance to improve, or prove to him I *was* trying my best.

To him, this was a meaningless grade for an 11-year-old's level of effort in gym class. But to me, it felt malicious. I felt attacked for being chubby. A scrawny, rude little neighbor kid calling me names was one thing, but an adult pointing out my shortcomings held so much validity. I'd been raised to respect adults, and now this callous grown man seemed to be preying on my weakness— a weakness that felt completely out of my control.

April 1999, age 12

Growing up, my brother and I were blessed— or to put it bluntly, we were spoiled. My dad's unmatched work ethic had paid off, affording our family an abundant lifestyle. We vacationed three or four times every year, and my favorite place to visit was Florida.

I loved every minute of it— the sunshine, the beach, Disneyworld, the wildlife parks with manatees and other critters, the boat rides, and the tiny lizards that roamed freely, which I would catch, befriend, and then release back into the wild.

We often stayed with our friends, Jack and Sue, who owned a big home right on the Gulf of Mexico. They had no children— just a big fluffy cat, Smokey, whom I loved. They also had a giant pool, where my brother and I would spend countless hours splashing, swimming, and perfecting our underwater handstands. I loved being in the pool. I felt weightless and free.

The only part of these trips I did not enjoy were our visits to Hooters, a restaurant chain that hired ample-chested waitresses, and dressed them in child-sized clothing.

The waitresses all looked like sex on a stick, and everyone just pretended they were there for the hot wings. It felt like that horribly uncomfortable feeling you get watching a sex scene in a movie with your parents, cringing every second, praying for the scene to be over. Being an overweight, pre-teen girl dining at Hooters made me feel icky, self-conscious, and painfully aware of how much I did *not* resemble these perfect female specimens. I'm sure we were there for the exquisite culinary experience, but it felt like a little slice of hell for me. Every time a perfectly tanned, toned, top-heavy waitress passed by in her tiny orange short-shorts and skintight Hooters tank top, I felt myself sink a little lower into my chair.

Nothing goes better with humiliation and shame than a bacon cheeseburger, and a side of curly fries with ketchup. Highly recommend. Oh, and a Sprite, please!

I politely placed my order with our blonde waitress, Brittany, who didn't look a day over nineteen.

"Justine is going through a bacon cheeseburger phase," my mom announced to the table, although my physique made it clear I was no stranger to bacon cheeseburgers. I wasn't sure if the announcement about my current "phase" was to justify my order or to defend my body, but it only added to the discomfort of the experience.

The food came out quickly, much to my relief, and I buried the feelings of hot, icky embarrassment in my plate of greasy food. I finished up quickly and looked around the open-air restaurant. I noticed a dock to the side of the restaurant, jutting out over the water, and I could see schools of fish circling below. I asked to excuse myself so I could go feed the fish, taking the last few remaining curly fries off my plate.

My mom joined me, tossing in tiny pieces of fries to the hungry fish below us. I wondered if she too felt quietly humiliated having to eat lunch at a restaurant called "Hooters," where the main focus was obviously not the food. And if she did, I wondered why she pretended it was okay.

I couldn't stop thinking about Brittany that day. I imagined her life must be *perfect*, and everyone must be so nice to her all the time. I wondered what it would feel like to have a body like hers, like a real-life Barbie doll. I secretly hoped that someday I could be like her, and get all that attention from guys.

May 2000; age 13

Middle school started, and in the blink of an eye, a darkness crept into my mind, heart, and soul. Creativity was replaced with conformity. Playfulness was traded in for popularity. An innocence was stripped away, never to return.

The fun-loving, imaginative, bright-eyed little girl was replaced overnight with a desperate girl, longing for love and acceptance from the outside world. I threw out all of my copies of *Ranger Rick* magazine, and replaced them with issues of *Teen People* and *Seventeen*. I couldn't be bothered to care about animals and the environment when I so badly needed to figure out how to be pretty and popular.

Magazines provided an extensive education on how to achieve perfection as a woman. Countless hours were spent cutting out articles I planned to revisit— things like "Easy Breezy Summer Makeup Tips," and "6 Moves for A Super Flat Tummy!"

I'd carefully cut the articles out and then organize them in folders and 3-ring binders as study material to return to, when schoolwork wasn't absorbing my time. Every article felt like a little golden ticket that held the secrets of looking thin, pretty, and perfect, which I was convinced was the key to a life of happiness.

Over the course of seventh grade, I completely transformed my look, from a 12-year-old stamp-collecting cat enthusiast, to 13-going-on-20. Feeling ugly and chubby undoubtedly sucked in grade school, but once I got to middle school, it was intolerable.

I'd examine my peers carefully, dissecting what the pretty, popular girls were doing so I could follow suit. They looked older than me— polished, wearing makeup and more grown-up, sensuous clothing that showed off the curves of their bodies, and flashes of skin with smooth, shaved legs.

I begged my mom to let me start wearing makeup, and when she caved, I started drawing a thick line of white eyeliner across my upper eyelid every day— a weird and horrible trend we can only pray never comes back in style, like so many other trends from the early 2000s. I also convinced my mom to let me start shaving my legs.

"This feels too soon. You're still so young," she said wistfully, but she gave me her blessing and some pointers anyway. Growing up, she had been teased about the clothes her mother made her wear, and for *not* shaving her legs, so she was determined to never put her children through the same experiences.

As refining my appearance became my number one priority, I finally began to grasp a basic understanding of what made my body gain or lose weight. The low-fat craze of the '90s was phasing out, *thank God*, and the nutrition trends of the new millennium were on my side. In the '90s, the food pyramid suggested a diet rich in grains— but now, there was a discussion of "good carbs," and "bad carbs," and a bigger focus on protein and nutrient-dense foods. This information was seemingly everywhere, from mainstream magazines like *Women's Health* and *Self*, to segments on shows like *The Today Show* and *The Oprah Winfrey Show*.

My mom and I gobbled up this information like a snack we'd been craving for years. She started buying nutrition books, including one called, "Eat This, Not That." It's a little guidebook of sorts that shares tips for trading in high-calorie foods for sensible, low-calorie options. You know, like "instead of a Big Mac, how 'bout some carrot sticks?!" Stuff like that.

I studied every page of that book, and anything else I could get my hands on that provided tools and secrets to shrink and reshape my body. Slowly I began to piece it all together, and at the first indication that my body was responding, I knew I'd struck gold.

I studied every food label that entered our home. When foods came without a label, I'd look up their caloric value in a nutrition book. By my thirteenth birthday, I knew how many calories were in just about every type of food.

For breakfast, I swapped sugary cereals, like Lucky Charms and my favorite Reese's Peanut Butter Puffs, for more nutritious choices, like oatmeal with berries, or a piece of whole grain toast with a protein shake. My mom began to incorporate more salads and vegetables with our dinners, and reduced the portions of our starch intake as a family.

I started running, by *choice*. I loathed every second of it, but my newfound awareness of "calories in, calories out," meant I needed to burn as many calories as possible. From what I read in magazines; running was the best way to do so.

I even joined the Butler Middle School Track & Field team, although my speed and agility still left much to be desired. I felt like the "Least Valuable Player" when we'd do relay races, but I didn't let that stop me. I was burning calories and fitting in, participating in team sports with the popular girls. Being popular was worth the pain.

The meticulous calorie-counting and the torturous hours I spent forcing myself to run eventually paid off. Oh, happy day, *finally* it paid off. I donated every single one of my oversized cat sweatshirts, and packed up my stuffed cat collection to store in the closet. I got rid of everything that elementary school Justine stood for, hoping to eradicate my identity as the chubby girl.

Every pound that came off felt like sweet, sweet victory, and it also prompted me to double down and keep going. Four pounds down felt great, but I figured six would feel even *better*. A raw, primal determination took over, and morning, noon and night, I was constantly thinking, *how can I lose more weight?*

Over the course of ten months, I shed eight pounds of "baby fat," while growing an inch taller. My body looked completely different. The dressing room became a happier place. I easily fit into a juniors' Size 4, like the other girls on the Track & Field team. The ultra-low-rise jeans that were growing more popular by the day actually *worked* on my figure, dare I say they even *looked good* on me.

I was unspeakably relieved to have finally demystified weight loss. I missed my sugary cereals and bacon cheeseburgers, but I knew the outcome of eating salads would be worth it in the long run. The sick feeling of immense shame over something that was out of my control vanished from my life. Now, I realized, I *could* control my body. I looked in the mirror and was pleased with what I saw in the reflection. I vowed to myself, *never again will I let myself be the chubby girl.*

June 2000; age 13

My family and I were back in our old neighborhood for a backyard barbecue. We had moved the summer before, into a massive brick house my dad's company built from the ground up. I loved our new home, but even better, my parents finally caved and let me get a cat after moving. I named him Milo after one of my favorite childhood movies, *Milo and Otis*.

I hadn't seen our old neighbors since the previous summer, so I wondered what they'd think of my new, more grown-up look. I imagined everyone would be very impressed with my transformation. I proudly wore my Tommy Hilfiger denim short-shorts, a crisp white tank top from Express, and flat leather sandals.

When it was time for dinner, I approached the back of the assembly line to wait my turn for food. Hot dogs, burgers, and bratwursts, hot off the grill, along with various salads and sides that other families had brought to share filled the table to make a glorious potluck spread.

I grabbed a Styrofoam plate, plastic utensils, and a paper napkin as I eyed up my choices. I spotted the salad I'd helped my mom prepare that day— a vegetable salad, marinated in fat-free Italian dressing. I spooned a sensible portion onto my plate, grateful for a low-calorie option to fill up on.

Let's see, about a half cup of the salad is around 25 calories. Plus, a bratwurst with mustard and just half of the bun, that's about 270 calories, so I'm still under 300 calories total. Maybe just a little fruit salad too?

As I was doing math equations on how much food I could have for dinner, our former next-door neighbor Bruce joined me at the back of the line.

Bruce was Billy's dad, and I'd known him since I was five years old. He had an outgoing, tell-it-like-it-is personality, and a boisterous, recognizable laugh.

"Justine! Look at you!" Bruce exclaimed, holding his hand up to give me a high five. "You got skinny!"

I froze. He stood before me, in his faded black Harley Davidson T-shirt and khaki cargo shorts, arm outstretched, waiting for me to slap him five.

Instinctively I felt self-conscious. Here was the attention I'd been seeking, but this type of praise and commentary felt foreign and scary to me. Bruce had never really spoken to me directly, and the sudden focus on my body made me squirm. I wondered who else was looking at me now.

I looked at my mom who was standing within earshot, and she just smiled. I quickly regained my composure, realizing this was a *compliment*, so I should accept it graciously. I shifted my plate into my left hand, and reached up to meet Bruce's hand to complete the high five.

Bruce wasn't the only one to praise my weight loss that summer. Glowing reviews about my transformation streamed in from relatives, friends, and members of our church. Even people who had never acknowledged me in any way found it imperative to share their approval of my slimmer, prepubescent body. The consensus was clear: my weight loss was an *achievement,* worthy of praise at 13 years old. The people had spoken, and all I heard was, *Smaller is better. Your appearance is everything.*

I replayed these compliments over and over in my head when I was pushing myself through an after-dinner jog, or declining a second slice of pizza at a birthday party. These words of affirmation were my fuel to continue refining my body into a smaller, thinner, more ideal physique.

My mom and dad never commented on my weight loss, and did their best to simply gloss over other people's comments. But deep down, I sensed my parents were relieved when the pounds came off. It is no secret the world can be very unkind to women in larger bodies, so no one wants the chubby girl as a daughter.

There was never any discussion of what I was doing to lose the weight, or my rapidly changing body. Although my family was extremely close, we never really discussed the "hard" stuff life threw at us. Without heart-to-heart conversations about body image and body size, I was left to make my own observations, carefully assessing comments from others regarding my appearance.

January 2001; age 13

"It's your turn, Justine!" my friend Tara exclaimed from the other side of the Spin-The-Bottle circle.

Hostile rap lyrics from Eminem barked out of the stereo system as nine eighth graders sat in a circle on an old, musty rug. We were in Nick Moreno's dark basement, which reeked of mothballs, but his parents never bothered us, so it was a cool place to hang out.

I was excited to be there. The invitation to hang out with popular kids let me know that my trendy clothes, caked-on makeup, and thin body were paying off.

Tara slid the empty plastic Mountain Dew bottle over to me. "What are you waiting for? Spin it already!" she said with a smirk. Tara was effortlessly cool and confident, and a good friend to have because the boys in school always wanted to hang out with her.

All eyes were on me. I reached for the bottle and gave it a spin, holding my breath. It landed on Nick. My palms sweat and tiny butterflies danced in my stomach as I waited for what would happen next. Nick was popular and cute, with shiny black hair, dark eyes, and smooth, caramel skin.

Will he reject me? I wondered, with fear and anticipation surging through my body. I desperately hoped he would kiss me to confirm I was not some misfit loser, there by accident. Part of me feared I was only there as an accessory to Tara. I longed to know I'd been *chosen*— I'd been deemed good enough.

I watched with relief as Nick slid his body across the floor toward me, meeting me more than halfway for our kiss. I leaned forward, closed my eyes, and felt his warm lips press up against mine. I felt electricity course through my veins as I tasted his wintergreen gum. After a couple of seconds, Nick pulled away slowly, leaning back and smiling at me, before smoothly sliding back to his place in the circle. I melted, holding his gaze and wanting to freeze time. This was my very first time kissing a boy, and it occurred to me that perhaps he actually *wanted* to kiss me. *Wow! I'm skinny enough that a cute, popular boy actually likes me!*

This new idea that I might be acceptable, and maybe even *desirable* to boys thrilled me. The voices inside that constantly screamed, *Pick me! Choose Me! I NEED you to tell me I'm good enough!* quieted down for the rest of the day. The experience sent validation to the chubby little girl who still lingered inside of me, giving me hope that I, too, could be popular with the boys.

April 2001; age 14

Growing up, my friends and I loved to choreograph dances to popular songs. In elementary school, we'd dance around to the Spice Girls, Backstreet Boys, and the Grease soundtrack. The suggestive lyrics soared over our heads as we had some innocent fun. In middle school, we graduated to more explicit lyrics and sexier, more scandalous dance moves beyond our age.

At sleepovers with Tara, we made up dance routines to hip hop songs like, "What's Your Fantasy?" by Ludacris, and "You Can Do It, Put Your Ass into It," by Ice Cube. We'd show off our sexy dance moves to the boys at our next co-ed hang out, or the upcoming middle school dance.

The Friday night of the Spring Dance, I spent an hour curling and pinning my hair into an intricate updo, finishing it off with a hefty coat of Herbal Essences hairspray. Remember that stuff? The women in the TV commercials would moan and scream "Yes! Yes! YES!" to depict a fake orgasm, insinuating the hair products were *that* good.

I spent another hour applying my makeup, meticulously following instructions from an article in *Seventeen* magazine titled, "How to Get Britney Spears' Look from the (You Drive Me) Crazy Video."

The night before I had applied a thick coat of Neutrogena self-tanning lotion to my fair, Irish skin. Self-tanner was a hot new product on the market. It had a distinctive, yeasty odor that made you sort of smell like cat pee, and it would stain your clothes and sheets. But I was totally into it, because I recognized that tan, glowing skin was attractive, and my pale, freckled skin was *not*. I watched gorgeous pop stars like Britney Spears, Christina Aguilera, and Jennifer Lopez shimmy and shake on the TV screen with their tan, glowing skin and perfectly toned bodies.

Tan was the goal, but the self-tanner resulted in more of an orange color that stained my palms dark brownish-orange for weeks. I looked like a human Cheeto, but I thought it looked fantastic.

I put on a tight, baby blue tube top from Abercrombie & Fitch and low-rise jeans. To complete my look, I rolled body glitter onto every square inch of my Cheeto-colored skin, until I sparkled enough to be spotted from space.

Dances were held in the school cafeteria, with the tables folded up and pushed against the walls to clear space for hundreds of seventh and eighth graders to dance, grinding and rubbing up against one another. The lights were off, and the air was sticky and steamy, filled with sweat, lust, Axe body spray, and raging hormones.

My friends and I rolled up our shirts, tucking them into our bras to expose our midriffs. Then we stuck to the center of the crowd to avoid having the chaperones see and insist we roll our shirts back down.

Boys noticed me in my rolled-up tube top and low-rise jeans, and without a word they'd start grinding up against the back of my body, dry humping me. I felt a thrill from being an object of desire, combined with a disconcerting sense of shame, as though I was doing something naughty.

The music stopped abruptly at 9:30 p.m., and all the lights were turned on, leaving us shamefully exposed after hours of thrusting and grinding in the darkness.

Tara and I hurried outside to the front of the school to look for my mom's new light blue BMW sedan. There she was, in the front of the pack of parents, waiting to pick us up.

Inside the car, we were quiet. In my mom's saint-like presence, I felt dirty after dancing seductively with boys all night. I was sure she'd be horrified with my suggestive dance moves, if she had seen them.

"So, how was the dance, girls?" my mom asked cheerfully, breaking the silence.

"Good," Tara and I responded sweetly in unison.

"I'm glad you had fun," my mom said smiling. "Tara, your parents know you're spending the night, right?"

"Yes, Mrs. Moore," Tara replied. We waited until we were in the privacy of my upstairs bedroom to erupt into excited conversation about the night.

"I think Nick likes you!" Tara gushed.

"Really?!" I asked, my heart beating a little faster at the possibility of a popular boy actually liking me. *Justine Moreno has a nice ring to it,* I thought to myself. "Ben couldn't keep his hands off of you!"

"I know," Tara said, dreamy-eyed, replaying the night in her mind. Then she paused and turned to me, lowering her voice. "I've decided I'm going to give Ben a blow job. On Monday, after school!"

My eyes grew wide. None of my friends had given blow jobs before, to my knowledge, I didn't have the slightest clue how one would even perform this "job."

I felt foolish and juvenile for not being as mature as Tara. It felt like scary territory I wasn't ready to enter, but I didn't want Tara to think I was an immature prude. Finally, I whispered back, "Really, Tara? Are you *sure*?"

"Um, yeah!" Tara said nonchalantly. "I really like him, and he's totally hot."

We whispered into the early hours of the next morning until we fell asleep, still covered in body glitter.

***

That Monday after school, I joined Tara and a few other friends as we walked to Ben's house. Ben's house was the coolest place to hang out. His parents were never home, and he had a hot tub in his basement.

I had packed a swimsuit and a change of clothes in my backpack that morning, along with a couple of tampons. The day before, my mom had taught me how to insert a tampon for the first time so that I could go in the hot tub with my friends. I'd only been getting my period for a couple of months, and I was still pretty out of touch with my anatomy "down there."

"Do you want me to come in there and help?" my mom called out from the other side of the closed bathroom door.

"No!" I yelled back, mortified. Just before I threw in the towel and committed to using maxi-pads for life, I got that thing in, referencing that frightening diagram that came inside the box.

The whole ordeal was so horribly awkward, and left me feeling embarrassed and icky about menstruating, like it was a curse rather than a miraculous biological process responsible for all human evolution. Getting my period felt like a nuisance, so I was relieved that I'd at least figured out how to use tampons.

That day in the hot tub I felt like a grown woman, tampon securely in place. We were playing Truth or Dare, and it was Tara's turn.

"Dare," she said confidently, smirking and raising an eyebrow at the boys.

Ben's best friend Steve pounced on the opportunity. "I dare you to give Ben a BJ!"

He must have been in on Tara and Ben's agreement to go to "third base" that day.

Tara and Ben grinned at each other. Tara made the first move, boldly climbing out of the hot tub and toweling off, before handing a towel to Ben. The two of them disappeared down the hallway together, into a back room. Steve and another boy looked at each other laughing, and high-fived.

I looked at my friend Chelsea, who was as wide-eyed as I would have been, if I hadn't already been mentally prepared for this moment.

I wondered what was going on in that back room and how long it would be before *I* was in a back room with some boy. I desperately *wanted* to be wanted, *wanted* to be chosen, *wanted* to be popular and liked, but venturing into this new terrain of sexuality felt scary, gross and confusing.

October 2001; age 14

My high school had a clear hierarchy, laid out according to class. If high school was ancient Rome, the seniors were Gods— even the nerdy ones. Juniors were royalty. Sophomores were patricians— the upper class, who had paid their dues. And freshmen were plebeians, or peasants— the lowest class— until proven otherwise, by being "chosen" by upperclassmen. So naturally I was smitten with every older guy who would give me the time of day.

When I was a freshman, my brother was a senior, much to his horror. He played varsity volleyball, and as the supportive little sister that I was, I attended every game. It didn't take long for his teammates to notice me. They'd yell out, "Moore's sister is hot!"

"Moore's sister." That's what they called me.

I was so delighted that upperclassmen boys knew I *existed* that it never occurred to me how stupid this nickname was, since I too was a Moore. Or how insulting it was that they didn't bother to learn my name.

***

The bell rang to signal the school day was over, but my day was just getting started.

I hurried to my locker and gathered my things, then walked to the main entrance of the building to meet Sean, a senior from my drama class. He needed more art credits to graduate, but instead of taking an interest in the theater, he had taken an interest in me.

Sean would call me after school and say things that made me blush and *pray to God* my mom wouldn't pick up the other end of the landline.

"Hey cutie," Sean said, sliding his arm around me. "Let's go."

Sean had invited me to come to his house after school. Somehow, I managed to ask for permission from my mom in a cool-and-casual-enough way to not raise any suspicion.

I was floored as I thought to myself, *I'm walking with a SENIOR! To his CAR!*

Cars were pure kryptonite for freshman girls who couldn't drive yet but were too cool to be carted around by their parents. On the short drive to Sean's house, I was especially quiet. I felt terrified and excited, all at once.

"Chop Suey!" by System of a Down came on the radio and Sean turned it up. Like *way* up.

"I love this song!" he shouted over the music, drumming his hands on the steering wheel. I smiled in order to appear enthusiastic about the song, but I'd been expecting him to sweetly ask about my day, or my favorite color, or something like that. I thought of this as somewhat of a date, so I expected him to be all sweetness and charm, the way I'd seen in movies.

Relax, Justine. Just loosen up and be cool. Guys like girls who are laid back and cool, I told myself.

We arrived at Sean's house and I noticed we were the only ones there. He wasted no time giving me a tour, or offering me a beverage or an after-school snack.

"Let's go to my room," he said leading the way to the end of a hallway and into his bedroom. His room was neat but plain, with bare walls except for a Green Bay Packers 1997 Super Bowl Champions poster hanging over his bed. He turned on the stereo and cranked up the volume. More blaring rock music.

I stood in the center of the room wondering what I should say or do next. Before I had time to decide, Sean took over.

He stood facing me, and put his arms around my waist. He seemed so much taller now, standing this close.

"Relax, you're so nervous," he laughed, softly touching my cheek. I smiled a little, without showing my teeth. I still had braces and I hated them because they made me look like the fourteen-year-old child that I was, when I desperately wanted to be seen as a sexy, grown-up adult woman.

Sean touched the bottom of my Abercrombie & Fitch baseball tee and pulled it over my head.

I stood in my lacy pink bra and jeans, frozen. Sean's fingers knowingly unzipped my jeans and slid them to the floor. I stepped out of them. I felt exposed standing there in nothing but my bra and underwear. My heart was pounding so hard I could hear it in my ears. Sean pushed me onto the bed and climbed right on top of me.

Without hesitation, he started kissing me and touching me, his hands all over my body. He seemed to know exactly what he was doing. It felt good, but also weird and dirty and confusing. Then he pulled his boxers off. I could feel the color drain from my face. For the first time he paused, noticing the look of shock and disgust on my face.

"You've never seen a dick before?" he asked, laughing again and I quickly shook my head no. I hadn't.

Sean pressed his body against mine and whispered in my ear, "Let's have sex."

"I— I'm not ready," I blurted out.

"I get it. You're scared," he said, clearly annoyed, making me *feel* my age. He begged and pleaded for maybe five, ten minutes. I didn't budge. He quickly lost interest once he realized he wasn't going to get what he wanted. "Whatever. Thanks a lot for giving me blue balls. I guess I'll drive you home."

Sean was 18 and I was 14, but that didn't strike me as inappropriate at the time. I didn't feel taken advantage of. I felt *chosen. Anointed.* Like I was one of the popular, thin and pretty girls—one of the girls that the guys wanted. I felt like it was an honor that guys wanted my body— it validated I was doing everything right in terms of molding my appearance— but I wasn't ready to go all the way. Growing up Catholic, my mom had always preached that sex was for marriage. I wanted to be cool and popular, but I also wanted to be a good girl. I was determined to at least wait until I was in a real relationship, believing my first-time having sex should be special.

I assumed my willingness to share my body with Sean, even without having sex, would inevitably make me his girlfriend, or at the very least, score me a date to Prom that year. I didn't realize that wasn't how it worked. Two weeks later Sean *did* have a girlfriend, but it wasn't me. It was Amber—a skinny, blonde sophomore who would glare at me in the hallways and in the cafeteria.

I felt rejected and hurt, and continued to obsess over Sean from a distance until he graduated later that year, and we never spoke again.

January 2002; age 14

In my quest to make myself as desirable as possible to the boys at school, I'd been blissfully unaware of how it would be received by other girls. During my freshman year of high school, I realized how Rules 7 and 8 intertwine.

Unspoken Rule #7: Your value is directly correlated with how desirable you are to men. **Unspoken Rule #8:** Other women are not your friends. They are your competition and your enemies.

I discovered these rules are layered: Be desirable to men, but the more you achieve this, the more other women will resent you, and try to take you down.

The more I worked on my physical appearance, the more attention I received from boys— and girls, too. I basked in the glory of upperclassmen guys knowing my name, but soon realized the older girls knew my name too, and were not pleased I was mingling with "their men."

"Look who it is! Justine Moore! The prettiest girl in the whole school!" Taylor, a popular sophomore would sarcastically remark as I walked past her locker on my way to AP Geometry.

"Skank!" she'd yell, and her minions would erupt into a fit of laughter, cackling at me. This became a daily occurrence, making me wish there was any other route I could take to get to class. Some days, I'd purposely sneak into class at the very last minute, almost making myself late, just to avoid Taylor and her squad of venomous sophomore girls.

My friendships with other girls were as unpredictable and inconsistent as a Madonna look. I'd get super close to one friend for a few months, then the friendship either fizzled out for a new one, or worse— it would end in a catty fight, or some sort of backstabbing. My friend Tara had gone to a different high school, and we didn't stay in touch after that.

In my mind, I was always competing with other girls— in a race I *did not* want to run, but just like gym class, I felt I had no choice in the matter. If my friend was pretty or skinny, that made me uglier and chubbier. If a boy liked my friend, it meant he was *not* attracted to me, and I was the runner-up. No one wants to be the runner-up in high school, but there can only be one winner. The rest of us were left to battle it out— not through force, or violence— but through gossip, snide remarks, backhanded compliments, and rumors.

We seemed to inherently know there was a limited amount of space for women at the top. Another girl's demise was an opening for a coveted spot in the winners' circle. I found myself perpetually hungering for more. More attention, more validation, more supremacy… not to mention, more to *eat*, since competing for popularity involved keeping my waistline small and my food intake to a minimum.

I knew very well the unspoken rules for women who wanted to be on top. Our desires and appetites were not to be trusted— with messaging around food eerily parallel to messaging around sexual gratification. Satisfying my appetite was a surefire way to lose power. Maintaining my composure with guys was similar to depriving myself of food. I always left them hungry; wanting more. I was allowed to be sexy, but not slutty. I was allowed to be appealing, but not easy.

***

I started hanging out with Dana mid-way through my freshman year. She was a sophomore, which instantly made me feel cooler by association. But it didn't take long for me to recognize that Dana and I were in fact fierce rivals, disguised as friends.

We stood in front of the large bathroom vanity at Dana's house, primping for a night out at the Friday night basketball game. Basketball games were *THE* place to go and be seen.

"Why are you putting on more makeup?!" Dana snarled at me. I looked up from adding a second coat of mascara to my long, thick eyelashes.

"Huh?" I asked, caught off guard by her accusatory tone.

"Why are you putting on more makeup? You know you're already prettier than me!" Dana snapped.

I said nothing.

But inside I felt complimented that she thought I was prettier than her. A triumph in the battle I was in, against my peers.

Dana would drill me about which guys I had crushes on, then usually would tell me how gross or lame the guys I liked were. She'd also probe me for information about my sexual history. One night at a sleepover, I divulged the details of my encounter with Sean, the senior guy from drama class.

"Promise you won't say a word to anyone," I begged her. "Sean's girlfriend already hates me. I can tell."

"I promise," Dana responded sweetly.

April 2002; age 15

I was over at my friend Crystal's house, making up a dance to "Hot In Herre" by Nelly. We took a break from dancing to see which of our classmates were hanging out on AOL instant messenger, or AIM, as we called it back in the day.

We sent a couple messages, and started looking at away messages and profiles. On AIM you could create a profile with any text you wanted, as long as it fit within the 1024-character limit. Your AIM profile needed to be as carefully manicured as your real-life image.

As Crystal clicked through her list of friends, a girl named Cassie's away message caught our attention: "New profile—important!"

Cassie had transferred to our school halfway through the year, with salacious rumors following her. She was very developed for a freshman girl, and looked about five years older than the rest of us. Her curvy body, sophisticated demeanor, and "newness" at our school made her an instant hit with the most popular upperclassmen guys. She hung out with Marissa, the captain of the junior varsity dance squad. Cassie and Marissa had never been particularly nice to me, but they never really bothered with me either. Until now.

My eyes grew wide with disbelief as Crystal and I read Cassie's "very important" profile update: "Justine Moore is a dirty, gross SLUT. Justine Moore? It should be Justine WHORE."

The profile continued on, attacking me with atrocious insults and broadcasting details about my hook-up with Sean. A knot of regret formed in my stomach, and I immediately knew Dana had blabbed my secret.

What a bitch. I should have never trusted her, I thought, wondering how many people she'd told.

Crystal and I stared at the words on the computer screen, silent and motionless. Time stood still for a few minutes.

Everyone in school can see this. Everyone in school WILL see this, I realized, feeling anxiety take over my body as I pictured myself going to school the next day.

My mom picked me up from Crystal's house shortly after, and I was silent on the ride home. I felt ashamed, believing I had brought this upon myself, from the incident with Sean. I was afraid that if I told my mom what those girls wrote about me, she might wonder why they wrote it. Or worse, she might believe it's true. So I said nothing. I decided it was my fault, and this pain was mine to carry, alone, in silence. Once again, I believed making others comfortable was more important than my own feelings.

The next day at school, I was convinced everyone was laughing at me, and whispering behind my back. I felt like I had a scarlet letter plastered onto my forehead for all to see.

That day I stopped eating in the cafeteria for good. Instead, I began buying my lunch from the school store, run by the extracurricular business club. And by "lunch" I mean a Diet Mountain Dew and some candy. That was my lunch every day, and after the AIM profile incident, I began eating it on the floor in a quiet hallway, away from the drama, the rumors, the backstabbing, and the social climbing. I felt like high school had chewed me up and spit me out, so I decided to keep to myself to protect myself from any further pain, disappointment, and humiliation. I couldn't control who would spread gossip and rumors about me. But I could control where I ate lunch, what I ate, and who I trusted from now on.

17-year-old me, posing for a picture before my Junior Prom.

Part II: Problem Areas

"Do girls abandon our bodies because that's where we're shamed and boys abandon their emotions because that's where they're shamed?

Little boys: Don't feel.

Little girls: Don't hunger."

~Glennon Doyle; Love Warrior

April 2003, age 16

Sophomore year of high school, I pulled away from my peers, studied hard to earn straight A's, and kept myself on a tight workout regimen, which included dance classes and daily workout videos.

Getting boys to notice me was just icing on the cake, but that wasn't my main motivation anymore. What I cared about most now was fixing my Problem Areas. That's what magazines called them. Any fleshy parts you *don't see* on a Barbie doll or supermodel counted as Problem Areas. And I had numerous amounts of these unsightly, jiggly bits of body fat. I was determined to remedy and correct these through a methodical combination of the right exercises. I observed my thighs were too thick; my tummy wasn't tight enough, or flat enough; my arms were too soft, and my face was too round, especially if I gained a few pounds. I wanted to perfect every inch of my exterior as a thick coat of armor to protect me from hurtful words, or rejection.

My brother had enlisted in the Marines the previous summer, so I used his vacant room as my Pilates studio. I'd fire up one of Mari Winsor's Pilates DVDs and go to town on my saddlebags. Our Siamese cat Milo would follow me in to watch, his crystal blue eyes darting up and down with every side kick. I welcomed the distraction of trying to perfect my body.

Ryan's absence left a gaping hole in our family unit, altering the dynamic of our family forever. The four of us became the three of us, creating a sorrowful void I constantly felt around my mom and dad. My mom turned to wine to cope with the heartache of her oldest child flying the coop. And exercise became *my* way to cope, and a way to tune out the emptiness.

When I wasn't side-kicking my saddlebags into oblivion with Mari Winsor, I was jogging, or performing strength-training routines I'd cut out of magazines. I was diligent in my quest to eradicate all Problem Areas from my body, engaging in some type of exercise every day.

"Baby? Can I come in?" my mom called from the other side of my closed bedroom door. It was 9 p.m. on a school night, and I was face down on my bed.

"Yeah," I murmured, not lifting my head up as she entered.

"What's wrong?" she asked, rushing over with concern. I raised my head to display my tear-soaked face. I took a shallow breath in through my mouth, since my nose was too snotty to breathe through.

"I couldn't work out today. I had to finish a paper for AP English, and between that and voice lessons, I ran out of time," I explained through my tears.

"Oh baby, it's just one day! You can work out tomorrow! This is no big deal," my mom assured me, laying down next to me and rubbing my back.

But it felt like a big deal to me. I didn't like the way my mom brushed it off, because in my mind, she and I were different. She didn't exercise regularly, because she didn't have to work at keeping her weight down. I did.

She doesn't get it. She doesn't even have to work out. She's just naturally thin, I thought. *Exercise is the key to burning off the food I eat— otherwise I'll get fat again!*

I was thoroughly convinced my weight was a special burden that had been placed on me— a constant battle that I had no chance of winning unless I stayed vigilant, every single day.

September 2004; age 17

My friend situation temporarily stabilized the last two years of high school. My best friend was Emily, who was soft spoken, and as sweet as syrup. She shared my sense of humor, laughing hysterically at all of my jokes.

Emily was physically perfect in every way. Her Problem Areas were nonexistent. She had straight blonde hair, huge glittering brown eyes, long eyelashes, and flawless golden skin.

Emily and I were inseparable. We stayed away from all the high school drama and focused on perfecting ourselves simultaneously.

In the summertime, we'd spend our days baking in the sun. We'd douse our skin in enough baby oil to lube up a Slip 'N Slide and lay out all day, sipping zero-calorie Crystal Lights and listening to the hip hop station on the radio. Emily always ended up sun-kissed and golden, while I ended up bright lobster-red.

On school days, we'd leave together and go to the mall, the nail salon, or the tanning salon. We even dressed alike, calling each other almost every night to plan coordinated outfits for the next day.

Two weeks before homecoming, Emily and I went dress shopping with my mom. Emily was practically family at this point— she vacationed with my family, I vacationed with hers. We scoured the racks for the perfect dresses to wear to our last homecoming dance.

We struck gold when we came across a black glamorous, strapless gown, fitted through the body, flaring out at the bottom. The side panels of color came in turquoise or light pink, perfect for Emily and me, as our signature colors were pink and blue, respectively.

We found a large fitting room and went in together. I took the Size 2 off the hanger and climbed into it. I could pull it all the way up, but the zipper would not go past my hips and butt. I climbed out of the dress and looked over at Emily, who had fully zipped her dress and was admiring herself in the mirror.

"What size is that?" I demanded. Emily looked down and found the tag.

"A 2," she said, unaware of the impending meltdown I was about to have. My chest tightened, and a giant lump formed in my throat.

"Everything okay in there?" my mom called to us from right outside of the fitting room.

"No!" I said, feeling my face get hot. "I need a different size. I need a 4."

My mom vanished for a few minutes and came back with the black and turquoise dress in a Size 4. She tossed it over the dressing room door for me. I took it off the hanger and climbed in once again. This time the zipper went all the way up.

"Oh girls!" my mom exclaimed. "You look fantastic. These dresses are stunning on you!"

Emily twirled in the mirror smiling, but I just stood there motionless. Tears began to form in my eyes and I swallowed hard, trying to choke them back.

"What's wrong, baby?" my mom asked, noticing my mood had dramatically changed since we'd entered the fitting room.

"Nothing!" I snapped as the tears began to pour down my cheeks. Emily looked at me with concern and confusion, but remained silent.

"Did something happen?" my mom asked, perplexed as she put her arms around me in an embrace.

"I don't fit into the size 2! I'm a 4! And I'm bigger than Emily!" I sobbed into my mom's soft cashmere sweater.

"Oh honey," she said, stroking my long, highlighted brown hair as I continued to cry. "Who cares about that? No one can see the size! You look absolutely gorgeous in this dress. Come on, change back into your clothes and let's go check out."

She left Emily and I to awkwardly change out of the gowns and back into our ripped jeans, baby tees, and fitted fall jackets. I brought the Size 4 up to the counter for my mom to pay for it. I remained somber and quiet the entire car ride home. It didn't occur to me that I was over two inches taller than Emily, so it was only natural for me to wear a size up. It only occurred to me that I was *bigger*— and that felt unacceptable.

The whole car ride home, I couldn't think about anything other than how I could get smaller. I vowed to myself that I'd work out an extra twenty minutes every day, and I'd stop eating the peanut butter M&M's I loved so much. That would do the trick. I would be as thin as Emily.

But of course, giving up my favorite candy wasn't enough. Nothing was ever enough. Within the next six months, my weight loss obsession would hit an all-time high.

***

Over the course of writing this book my mom gave me my old journals and hundreds of photos of me growing up, for "research purposes." We came across pictures of me in this aforementioned Size 4 dress— all glammed up for the homecoming dance. I was shocked to see how thin I was at the time.

I thought I needed to lose weight here? How? Where?

It felt like I must be looking at the wrong girl, or maybe my mind had made this whole story up, but it didn't, and my mom can confirm the details of the dressing room meltdown.

How could this girl ever think she was fat? I asked repeatedly with disbelief, staring at the photographs searching for answers, heartbroken for this younger version of myself. It is absolutely ludicrous that someone in *that* body could have ever believed she was fat, but I clearly remember feeling it. And that's just it— "feeling fat" is in fact a *feeling*. It's emotional. It's not about a size, or a number on the scale, or any concrete metrics whatsoever. It's all internal. It's a corrosive condition of the mind.

Body dysmorphia is like looking in a funhouse mirror, all the time. It's deceptive. It's illogical, irrational, and demented from the outside looking in. But inside the mind of someone who is afflicted, it is *so* convincing— so very real. It is devastatingly powerful.

October 2004; age 17

When the idea of college arose, I immediately set foot in the nearest Barnes & Noble to purchase college guide books, fixed upon making the "right decision."

Back at home, I began to pour over my options.

"Finding some good ones, baby?" my mom asked, interrupting one of my intense highlighting sessions as she plopped herself down next to me on the couch.

"Yeah, I guess," I replied, not taking my eyes away from the daze of statistics. Choosing a college was a daunting decision for a teenage girl who could hardly choose a drink at Starbucks without consulting a friend or a magazine article to confirm she was making the right choice.

"Maybe something in Wisconsin?" she asked jokingly, with a big smile, taking a sip of her Earl Grey tea.

"Yeah, right. Very funny, Mom," I said sarcastically. "I'm looking at Boston and New York."

"Oh?" she replied. "I thought you had your heart set on California."

She was right. For years, I'd dreamt of moving to California, where I imagined I could surf, sing, write music, and spend my days soaking in sunshine and the warm ocean breeze. But when it came time to send in those applications, my insecurities about my appearance stopped me. I had this image in my mind of what girls were like in California, based on what I had seen in the movies. I imagined these college campuses were overflowing with perfectly tan, blonde, gorgeous girls, with flawless, thin bodies. Basically, a whole sea of Emily's. I didn't believe I could handle being surrounded by modelesque California girls and movie stars.

I would never live up to their standards, or my own, if I moved there.

My fear of not feeling like I was "enough" for an *entire state* ran deep enough to stop me from applying to a single school there. How many other choices were influenced by my insecurities about my body and appearance? And how many other women can say the same—that the things they do and don't do, the chances they take (or don't take) are influenced by their insecurities?

"Yeah, I did," I responded quietly, leafing through my notes, ensuring my eyes stayed close to the page. "I just haven't found any that feel right. So I'm thinking the east coast might be better."

My mom set her tea down on a coaster on our large glass coffee table. She rubbed my back, and I immediately relaxed into her touch.

"Whatever you decide, your dad and I will be here to support you," she promised, and pulled me in for a kiss on the forehead.

I believed her wholeheartedly, because my parents had always supported me, and trusted me enough to make my own decisions. Little did I know that four months later my perfect little family would be torn to shreds.

May 2005; age 18

"Let's talk about why you're not eating," my therapist said, leaning forward in her black leather armchair, notebook in hand. The look in her eyes gave just the right amount of sympathy.

There are moments where your life is forever altered in a matter of seconds. Moments where your brain fights to process new information, and you know with every fiber of your being that life will never be the same. It's as if you become a whole new person, separate and disconnected from the person you were before that moment your life changed forever.

"I'm eating," I replied, scanning the carpeted office floor, chomping on my Orbitz Bubblemint gum. I'd developed a serious gum habit. I'd chew an entire pack every day, as a tactic to help me forget how little food I was eating. "I'm just not that hungry lately."

"Your mom says you've been losing a lot of weight. Twelve pounds in one month is dangerous, especially for someone your size."

She paused.

"Does this have to do with your dad leaving?"

I winced at the mere mention of my dad leaving. The knife that was lodged into my heart on the morning of February 17th twisted deeper, foregoing my past sense of reality.

My mind replayed the past months' pivotal events over and over again, like a tortuous movie. I recalled the exact moment I decided to stop eating. I was sitting at the kitchen counter, my arms resting on the cool granite countertop. Three days prior, my brother had been shipped off to Iraq. The day after, my dad dropped the bomb that he was leaving my mom for his secretary, who was a close family friend. I vividly remember my mom breaking the news to me, in complete shock, a shell of the woman she'd been the day before.

I brought my attention back to the window in the therapist's office, swallowing and shifting on the couch. Trying to get comfortable when you're stick-thin is no easy feat.

I couldn't just confess that I was *purposely* starving myself for some sense of control in my now unstable life. I couldn't explain that my hunger pains for food were a welcome distraction from the unbearable ache of my broken heart.

"Is it okay if we talk about that?" Dr. Williams asked.

Nothing is okay, I responded in my head. *Nothing has been okay since that morning! I am not okay, and I need people to see that I am not okay.*

I couldn't even begin to process or express the pain I was in, so I decided to let my body speak for me. I decided to turn my body into a desperate cry for help. I'd hoped to earn the comfort and attention I was craving from my parents, but instead, my efforts landed me in weekly therapy sessions with an uptight stranger saving the world one troubled teen at a time.

I was terrified to openly talk about my feelings. I've always felt things very deeply, and would experience confusing, dark emotions I didn't understand, even before our family unit exploded.

Now my emotions were more than I could bear. I was afraid if I let myself fully drop into what I was feeling, it might consume me forever. I was afraid to acknowledge the pain, because that would solidify my reality.

I still clung to the hope that my dad would change his mind. There was a part of me that truly thought my parents would work things out, and he'd move back in. We would put this behind us and live happily ever after.

"I guess we can talk about it," I said as I grabbed the fluffy cream-colored pillow next to me and pulled it tightly over my skeletal chest. "That's why I'm here, right?"

"Everyone just wants what's best for you, Justine. Your parents know this isn't easy for you. They only want to help," Dr. Williams said.

It didn't feel that way to me.

Every morning I'd wake up, and for a few fleeting seconds I felt *okay*, until I became conscious again of my new reality. I'd feel the ache creep back into my heart and a knot form in the pit of my guts, and I'd remember. I'd catch a glimpse of morning sunlight before consciousness set in, suffocating me again in darkness.

The denial phase would only last for a hot second before anger set in, ripping my body apart. I couldn't get a handle on my emotions, but I could control my body. I had control over how much I ate, what I consumed, and how much I worked out.

I knew that losing weight always felt so good in the past. I clung to that feeling of normalcy. Denial, anger, and depression are three separate stages of grief, but it felt like they'd joined forces, hanging out simultaneously in my insides at every waking hour of the day.

"Yeah, sure. Whatever," I said quietly, hugging the pillow a little tighter and wondering when the hell I could leave this office to go home, cry, and run, in that order.

"What's bothering you most, Justine?" she prodded, pushing her straight blonde hair behind her ear.

I wanted to laugh at the ridiculousness of her question.

Where to begin?

I took a deep breath in, smirking, and made full eye contact with Dr. Williams for the first time that day.

"What's bothering me most is that my family is never going to be the same. *Nothing* is going to be the same. Holidays and vacations will never be the same. We'll never have a family dinner together, ever again. I never thought we'd be one of those divorced families. I thought we were happy. And my dad didn't just leave my mom— he left *us*. He left *me*."""

My eyes welled up with tears as I continued.

"I'm so pissed off all the time. My dad's the one who left, but I feel like I lost my mom too. She's not the same person at all. She doesn't even get out of *bed* most days. And I'm the one left to pick up the pieces. I just want things to be the way they were. My friends don't even like me anymore. Emily, who was supposed to be my best friend, told everyone to stop inviting me to hang out. She said I'm too depressing to be around. And it's true. I *am* depressed."

I paused for a moment, swallowing hard.

"There is constantly a lump in my throat from wanting to cry," I explained slowly, feeling my eyes grow more watery with every word I spoke. "I feel like no one understands me. I feel lost and helpless. I've never felt so alone in my life."

A single tear made its way down my cheek, and then a few more followed. The floodgates had opened. I grabbed a handful of tissues and began to delicately blot my face, so as not to smudge my mascara.

"Thank you for sharing this with me," Dr. Williams said softly. "Have you told you parents any of this? Have you expressed your hurt and anger with your dad?"

"No," I told her. "I can't. I can't tell him I'm angry."

"Why not?" she asked.

"I don't know. He's my *dad*," I responded instinctively, not bothering to contemplate why I couldn't express my feelings outwardly.

That's just what good girls *do*. They don't make trouble. They don't disturb the peace. They bottle up their own discomfort for the sake of keeping everyone else comfortable, and they look pretty, smile, and act like everything is *okay*.

"I guess I don't want to hurt his feelings."

"I understand," Dr. Williams said.

She didn't understand. Not even close. No one understands what it feels like to be someone else, ever. It's not comforting when someone says they understand. It's rude, and lazy, and infuriating.

"I don't think there's such a thing as a *good age* to experience your parents getting divorced, but I can tell you, eighteen really sucks," I said.

Dr. Williams started scribbling down notes, visibly pleased with herself for getting me to open up. I decided to indulge her and just continue to spill it all.

"Everything I've ever known, everything I had believed about marriage, life, family, and what my future will look like— it was all destroyed overnight. I never saw it coming. And temper tantrums are frowned upon when you're considered to be an adult. So instead of kicking and screaming and crying and beating my fists against the floor, I feel like I'm kicking and screaming on the *inside*, with no way to let it out."

"So you're using food to cope? To feel in control?" Dr. Williams prodded.

Exactly, I thought. I bottled up all the fury, the frustration, the anger, the sorrow, the heartache. I stuffed it way down, suppressing my emotions along with my appetite.

"Yeah, I guess. It's like a thrill for me. I get a rush from seeing how little I can eat, or when people tell me I'm skinny. Those comments feel so satisfying, it's like I don't even care about food anymore," I confessed. "Plus, it's good for me to concentrate on anything other than what's going on. I think about calories all day, and how I can eat less, so I don't have to think about all the shit going on at home."

"Oh! Sorry, Justine, we've run out of time." My therapist looked at the clock, awaiting her next patient. "But let's pick this back up next week, shall we?"

I froze, and held the rest of my feelings inside. I realized this was just a transaction to her, and I mentally lumped her with all of the other adults in my life that let me down.

Before she packed up her notebook, she sent me off with a script to see a psychiatrist.

"I want to get you some help for the feelings of depression you're experiencing," she explained.

"Okay, fine, whatever," I said, climbing back into my emotional shell. I highly doubted a pill could wash away the grief I felt from my family falling apart, but I didn't have the energy to argue, and I didn't care enough to advocate for myself.

"Take care of yourself, Justine," she said, wrapping her arms around me for a phony embrace.

I hurried out of her office feeling confused, emotional, and teary-eyed again. As soon as I reached my car, I let out a scream and began to sob hysterically.

Two weeks later, a psychiatrist wrote me prescriptions for Xanax, for anxiety, and Zoloft, for clinical depression. One Bachelor's Degree in psychology later I'd argue my "clinical" depression was *situational*, but what do I know? Besides, working through my feelings and challenging life events the old-fashioned way— unmedicated— was so 2000-and-late.

June 2005; age 18

I was working at Hollister, a trendy clothing store for preppy, upper-class teens who want to look like effortlessly cool, sun kissed California surfers.

The previous summer I'd been shopping there when I was recruited and hired on the spot. It made me feel like a supermodel, getting discovered on the street. Hollister, like its sister company, Abercrombie & Fitch, is a store where only good-looking, skinny people get hired.

I loved that job. I felt special and chosen, like I was one of the beautiful people. And I relished the fact that no one knew about my family situation at work, unlike at school. Here, I could be a totally different person, and forget all about my real life for a few hours. Being at Hollister was another escape from my reality, besides my food intake, or lack thereof.

Also, I had a massive crush on one of the managers, making the workplace environment the only place in the world I wanted to be. I'd go to the store on my days off, using coy excuses like "I'm picking up my check," or "I'm just here to shop!"

Every cent of my paycheck went directly back to the store, and then some, as I had to have the latest styles in every collection that came in.

One Saturday after finishing up my shift, I punched out and decided to do a little shopping. I went to the front room to gather up the newest items on the floor— including these heavily destroyed, light denim jeans with silver paint purposefully splashed across them. They were *so* cool. I grabbed a Size 0 and a Size 00— just in case. Size 4 was ancient history to me by now.

Once in the fitting room, I pulled on the Size 0 and didn't even need to unbutton the jeans to get them on. I was swimming in them.

I quickly pulled them off and tossed them to the side of the fitting room, grabbing for the pair of Size 00 jeans— the smallest size the store carried. To my astonishment, they were also too big on me. They hung off my hip bones, pronounced and jutting out from my skinny little body.

I paused, at first amazed, and then oh-so-pleased with myself. I smiled proudly, looking at myself in the mirror, soaking in the moment. I pulled off the jeans, sliding them down my legs while they were still buttoned up. It didn't occur to me to be disappointed that I wouldn't be wearing these fabulous jeans anytime soon. Instead, I felt like I just won the lottery of womanhood—*I am too thin to wear Size 00! I am officially too thin for this store!*

I left the dressing room empty handed, feeling triumphant. That chubby little girl people once laughed at and teased was finally vindicated. At least for one day.

It felt like all of my hard work, sacrifice, and dedication had paid off. All of those minutes clocked breathlessly jogging when I wanted to stop. All of those sit ups and lunges and sidekicks. All of the times I told my friends I wasn't hungry, or "I already ate," when my stomach was growling for sustenance—it was all worth it now.

I treated myself to a Diet Mountain Dew from the vending machine before leaving the mall, and drove home in my bright, yellow Mustang convertible, with the top down and the new Fall Out Boy album blasting, feeling victorious.

August 2005; age 18

The summer after high school graduation, I got my wish—I moved the hell out of Wisconsin. I was eager to create a whole new life for myself, since the one I thought I had was blown to smithereens.

I'd earned an academic scholarship to Hofstra University, a private school in Long Island, New York. Despite my headspace being largely consumed with thoughts of perfecting my body, I was wicked smart, and scored so well on my ACT that I received multiple scholarship offers from prestigious universities. As big of an honor as this was, looking back, I realize I didn't really acknowledge myself for these academic achievements. It was hard to appreciate my intelligence, when in my mind, I still had so many physical imperfections to correct.

That's the thing about being a perfectionist—anything you do right, or do well, gets glossed over, while your brain highlights anything you did wrong, or any area where you're still not good enough. There's *always* more work to do.

I had just built my college Facebook profile and under "favorite quote," I cited Salvador Dali, saying, "Have no fear of perfection—you'll never reach it."

I thought it made me sound edgy and deep, but looking back, it is achingly ironic, given my mental state at the time.

Moving to New York felt like moving to a different planet in a different galaxy, far, far away. I felt so out of place, like a weird alien who stood out like a sore thumb. For the first time, strangers didn't bother to say "hello" to me on the street. In fact, I kept getting pushed out of the way. People talked differently. They drove differently. They dressed differently. They listened to different music and called sub sandwiches "hoagies" and "heroes." The Hollister clothes that had earned me the title of "Best Dressed" in high school felt cheap and childish next to the chic designer clothes the East Coast college girls were wearing.

Thankfully, my four suitemates were friendly and made me feel more at ease. But one of them in particular had a strange fascination with my tiny, underweight physique.

"How much do you *weigh*?" she'd inquire, with a sense of admiration and awe.

"I don't know," I'd tell her, brushing it off. But I did know. *Of course* I knew. I always, always, *always* knew what I weighed.

When it came to my weight and my eating habits, I didn't like to divulge the details with people. I reveled in the attention I got for being so thin, but the behind-the-scenes drama of my eating disorder felt intensely personal. I wanted people to believe I was just naturally thin— hashtag *#blessed*—like that annoying girlfriend everyone has who stays super skinny no matter what she eats.

One afternoon, I was weighing myself on the digital scale we shared in the suite bathroom. At this time, I was weighing myself twice a day, every day. I didn't realize I had left the door open behind me.

"Oh my GOD, you're so skinny!" my suitemate squealed, peering over my shoulder. She had crept in without my knowing, and now she had her answer.

100.4 pounds, the scale read. With clothes on. In the middle of the day.

Just a few weeks later, that number changed drastically, and I never hit 100.4 pounds again. Prior to college I never drank alcohol, but now, nearly a thousand miles away from home, it became my new way of life.

My suitemate Rachel, from Boston, taught me everything I needed to know. We'd walk to a nearby liquor store and buy Smirnoff raspberry vodka with a fake ID. Her ID said she was 28 years old and Hispanic, when in fact she had long red hair and fair skin like mine, but those minor details didn't matter to the liquor store clerk. We'd mix the flavored vodka with Sprite Zero to "pre-game," before walking to the college bars.

Once out, Rachel knew how to capitalize on my lack of experience. I was painted to be the wholesome, sheltered girl from the Midwest. When I'd tell people I was from Wisconsin, they'd usually ask something like, "Did you live on a farm?" when in fact the suburb I grew up in had four high schools and a population of 70,000.

"She's from Wisconsin! She never drank before this!" Rachel would announce to random guys near the bar. Some guy would always take the bait. He'd turn to face me, look me up and down approvingly, and lean in.

"For real? You've never gotten drunk before?" he'd yell into my face, breath smelling like Jägermeister and chewing tobacco. *Delightful.*

"Yeah! I never drank before college!" I'd shout back.

"That's fucking crazy! Let me buy your drinks! What do you want?" he'd holler into my eardrums while wrapping his arm around my waist, resting his hand on my lower back. I'd inhale his Axe body spray and place my order.

"Malibu Bay Breeze! One for my friend too, please!"

I'd discovered a Bay Breeze is, hands-down, the tastiest of all alcoholic drinks. Rachel and I would sip our drinks and dance around to blaring songs by 50 Cent and the Ying Yang Twins before moving onto the next bar to pull the same stunt with another guy.

We didn't pay for a single drink throughout the first month of college, which meant we always had enough cash left to buy pizza at the end of the night. We'd stumble home drunkenly and sit on the fluffy gray shag carpet in Rachel's dorm room, devouring an entire large cheese pizza together, night after night.

I'd usually top it off with whatever chocolate I had in my dorm room, polishing off entire bags of almond M&M's in one sitting. And by "entire bags" I don't mean single serving, or even King Size. I mean the big party-size bags, with 38 servings, *allegedly*, if you happen to possess the self-control to stop after 32 pieces.

It felt glorious and gratifying. After six years of depriving and starving myself, I was like a ravenous, wild animal who just escaped from the zoo. The pleasure and thrill I'd been getting from seeing how thin I could get was replaced by the deep satisfaction of feeling full. I hadn't let myself eat past fullness in *years*, and it felt profoundly cathartic and comforting.

The next morning I'd feel shitty when I'd see the empty wrappers. I'd grab a Diet Coke and dry Kashi cereal to eat during my first class of the day, determined to "make things right," but my willpower would dwindle as the day rolled on. By evening I'd find myself indulging with my carefree suitemates again.

Like a pendulum, the intention behind my daily habits swung back hard as I ditched all rigidity around food and exercise that first year of college. Like the unchaperoned child that I was, I lived on chocolate chip muffins, sugary Frappuccinos, bagels, pizza, Pop Tarts, and booze. I didn't see the inside of a gym once that year, and sit ups and jogging went out the window.

Instead of the infamous "Freshman Fifteen," I gained a hefty "Freshman Thirty."

By second semester, I was too big for all of my jeans, and could barely even zip the newer, larger sized jeans I'd bought to accommodate my weight gain. Low rise jeans were still a thing, and mine burrowed into the fat that had recently taken up residence on my hips, causing the disgusting appearance of what magazines call a "muffin top."

After working so hard to eliminate all of my Problem Areas the years prior to college, I had officially let myself go. The Problem was back.

By the time final exams came around, I was mortified with the damage I'd done, and horribly disappointed in myself. I despised the larger body I found myself in—*again*—and I hated myself for losing control.

Alcohol had the power to silence my inner critic, which haunted me whenever I was sober: *I can't believe you ate all of that last night. You eat too much. What is wrong with you? You're fat again. You need to lose some weight. Restrict your calories today. Ignore your hunger.*

Without that voice, my body would become primal. I'd gorge myself while I could, reveling in the rare feeling of being *full*, knowing damn well that cruel voice of deprivation would be back in the morning, so we'd better get it in while we can.

January 2007; age 19

I had an uncanny ability to attract guys who would sniff out my deepest insecurities, then use them against me.

Anthony was the first to do so. He was my first real boyfriend. We met in Italian class, on my very first day at Hofstra University. I'll never forget the way he shamelessly leaned over his desk from the other side of the room to stare at me, with a gleam in his eyes and an uninhibited smile plastered to his face.

He was one year older than me, called me "Princess," and lived in the same dorm, which met all of my criteria for "boyfriend material" at the time. He smoked cigarettes and tons of weed—both of which disgusted me. But I was especially desperate for male attention after my dad left, so nasty habits were easy to overlook.

I lost my virginity to Anthony after a fire drill in the middle of the night. It was not the romantic escapade my younger self had dreamt of, but I had given up on fairytales by that point anyway. My parents' divorce left me feeling cynical about love and relationships, so I figured I might as well just get it over with. Anthony took me out for dinners, proudly introduced me to his parents and all of his friends, and bought me a gold "I Love You" necklace for Christmas (clearly to mark his territory.) Years later, I still cringe when I remember that necklace.

I made light of Anthony's atrocious temper and jealous, overbearing behavior. Whenever we were apart, he'd call and text me nonstop, demanding to know where I was at all times and accusing me of cheating on him.

When I first started gaining weight freshman year, he was supportive.

"You look good with a little more meat on your bones!" he'd tell me.

That concept was new to me, and it felt good to have a break from my demons who promised me the *less* I weighed, the more people would praise me. It felt as if I was free to enjoy college life, *and* I could gain a little weight while still being validated by the man in my life.

Unfortunately, the fun and freedom I let myself experience freshman year had consequences. When I packed on thirty pounds in nine months, the rapid weight gain created new stretch marks on my hips, butt, and lower back. I'd developed a few tiny stretch marks in adolescence from losing weight, but these new stretch marks were deep, prominent, and way more noticeable.

Even an expensive laser treatment couldn't help me. My mom paid for it the summer after my freshman year, and it made zero difference. Plus, the treatment hurt like hell. The unsightly, stretch-marked zones of my body quickly became the bane of my existence—the most problematic of all Problem Areas.

After a year of bickering with one another, Anthony and I broke up. We fell apart in a dysfunctional, volatile way, which pretty much summed up our entire relationship. He first broke it off with me and I wanted *him* back, right up until he wanted *me* back, and by then I had moved on. The first semester of sophomore year I was initiated into a popular sorority, after six long weeks of being hazed, which we called "pledging."

Of all of the unpleasant or regrettable times in my life, those six weeks are the ones I would least like to re-live. Sleep deprivation, public humiliation, eating garbage off a dirty floor, and being screamed at by "sisters" of the sorority were just a few of the tactics used to get me to prove my commitment and loyalty to Greek life. Every day I wanted to quit, but I'd heard horror stories about girls who "de-pledged" and had to transfer to a different school because the harassment that followed was unbearable.

Once I earned my letters, I started exercising my right to mingle with fraternity boys. My newfound sorority life made me feel superior to Anthony, and I no longer wanted to be burdened by the drama of our relationship. When I rejected Anthony, he became furious and distraught.

"I'm going to kill myself," he texted me late one night after we'd been fighting. I raced out of my high-rise dorm to his building next door. I got to his suite and started banging on the door.

"It's me! Let me in!" I shouted through the door, continuing to pound on it. The door opened and Anthony backed away to let me in. His face and eyes were red and bloodshot from crying. He glared at me, seething. His eyes looked dead behind his cold stare.

"Listen, I'm sorry I don't want to get back together. But I still care about you. I don't want you to do anything stupid," I pleaded.

"Did you hook up with that frat guy I saw you with at the bar?" Anthony asked through his clenched jaw. I glanced down at the floor and shifted uncomfortably. I've always been a very bad liar.

Before I could muster a word, Anthony came at me and took hold of my arms. With one swift motion, he slammed my body up against the cold, steel door. His hands were gripped so tightly around my arms, digging into my flesh as he pinned me against the door. Terror overtook me as he held me firmly in place, his icy stare sending chills through my body. He was unrecognizable— this person I'd known for over a year, and had shared so much with. I'd seen his temper so many times, but never like *this*. He was like a rabid animal gone mad.

"I never want to see you again, you *whore*," Anthony growled at me. "Who would want your chubby, stretch-marked ass?"

He released his grip and my body dropped down a few inches from where he had pinned me against the door. I regained my footing as he turned away. I didn't bother to catch my breath before I tore out of that suite, out of the building, and back to the safety of my dorm room.

I locked the door and flung myself face down onto my bed and began hysterically sobbing into my leopard print sheets. I vowed I would *never* be alone with him again, to protect myself physically. But emotionally, I felt wounded and raw. The old scars of my past had been sliced open, and I'd become the chubby girl again.

March 2007; age 19

I put my relationship with Anthony behind me and tried to focus on the good in my life. I was single for the first time since I started college, and being newly initiated into Greek life opened up my options. At Hofstra, the guys in the most popular frats only dated girls in the most popular sororities. Mine happened to be one of those sororities.

I still felt chubby and insecure from that horrendous night in Anthony's room, and a stupid decision to bleach my dark hair blonde the previous year left my hair short, brittle and broken. I was terribly self-conscious about my hair and body, but wearing the Greek letters I'd worked so hard to earn helped me feel more confident. I used their acceptance as validation that I wasn't completely hopeless.

Still, my insecurities were loud as hell, so I picked up my old habit of drowning them out with booze. One of the rules of being a new sorority sister included "mandatory bar nights" on Tuesdays. We were required to be at the bar wearing our Greek letters no later than 10 p.m., and then were expected to stay until the DJ played our sorority's chosen song, "We Are Family," which usually happened around 1 a.m.

There I was in black leggings, suede knee-high boots, and a tight sorority t-shirt at the Dizzy Lizard Saloon. (Yes, that was really the name of the bar and yes, it was as classy as it sounds!)

I was an hour into guzzling down vodka tonics in little plastic cups when I first saw him. In a split second, I determined that he was the most physically perfect specimen I had ever laid my eyes on— tall, muscular, dark hair, and gorgeous bone structure. He was wearing a black Sigma Chi hoodie, perfectly tailored designer jeans, and crisp, white Chuck Taylors. His big, sparkling brown eyes met mine, and to my amazement, he gave me a cocky, adorable little smile with a head nod.

My knees grew weak as I practically started drooling all over myself. The vodka helped me stay cool enough to hold his gaze, instead of looking away awkwardly. It felt like staring into the sun. I sensed this guy would burn me, but he was so shiny, bright, and beautiful; I just couldn't help myself.

With liquid courage and Greek letters on my side, I confidently made my way through the crowd and walked right up to him.

"Hey," I said casually, with a smile. "I'm Justine."

"I'm Josh," he said, grinning back at me. I can only imagine what it felt like for him to be admired by me the way that I was admiring him. It was shameless. I was already smitten then and there, gazing at this frat boy like a God of Gods, who could do no wrong.

After a few more hours downing rail liquor in mass quantities, my sorority's song played, and I was free to leave.

"Wanna come back to my room?" Josh asked me. I felt like I might faint.

Is this really happening? I thought. *Damn, being in a sorority is awesome!*

Once in Josh's room, I drunkenly slept with him. I hoped he'd like me more for doing so, but figured he'd probably never speak to me again. My virginity was gone— and I wanted to be liked so badly by men that I was willing to ignore my better judgment for the payoff of cheap validation. Josh was so good looking that I was convinced he would never *date* a girl like me, so I should be grateful for this one drunken night we'd shared.

I felt like I'd died and gone to heaven when he invited me to see a concert with him the following week. We had similar taste in music, with a love of indie rock, along with an appreciation of many genres.

"The Shins play at Madison Square Garden tomorrow. Wanna go?" he texted.

"Yes!! I love the Shins!" I wrote back immediately.

The next day I wore my cutest jeans, a tight sweater, and Van's sneakers.

"We'll get tickets when we get there," he said on the train ride into Manhattan. "I do it all the time, and I always get the sickest deals."

Sure enough, we arrived at the Garden and scored an amazing deal on tickets. We spent the next three hours drinking and dancing, smiling at each other, touching and kissing. Every time Josh's lips touched mine, I thought, *I can't believe this is happening! I can't believe* HE *likes* ME*!*

Jumping around in a sweaty crowd works up an appetite, so after the show, we made our way across the street to a diner.

"I'm starving! I haven't eaten since lunch!" I said looking at the menu. It was almost 11 p.m. at this point. "I'm thinking I'll get a Ruben or the Patty Melt."

"You should get a salad," Josh said, without looking up from his menu. "You could really stand to lose seven or eight pounds."

His words stunned me like an electric shock.

Seven or eight pounds. Seven or eight pounds.

His voice echoed over and over in my head. The blissful, dreamlike state I'd been living in the past week evaporated.

I knew it was too good to be true, I thought. *He thinks I'm fat. How silly I've been to think a guy like Josh would want me exactly as I am. How naive and stupid.*

My mental spiral was interrupted when the waitress showed up to take our order.

"I'll have a burger— medium-well, no cheese, no onions. Sweet potato fries. And an iced tea," Josh ordered, handing the waitress his menu. He looked over at me, unsympathetic about the bomb he just detonated in my head.

"I'll have the chopped salad, with chicken. Dressing on the side please," I responded on autopilot. "And a Diet Coke."

I said nothing to Josh about his comment on my weight. I didn't defend myself, or call him out for being so thoughtless and hurtful with his words. I did the same thing I always did when someone criticized my appearance—I agreed with their judgment and got to work on fixing myself.

I do *need to shed some pounds,* I thought, excusing his behavior. *Maybe then he'll ask me to be his girlfriend.*

April 2007; age 20

Over the next few weeks, I went back into my big bag of get-skinny-fast tricks. I knew how to be in diet mode. By now, I'd been dieting on and off for half of my life. I was a pro.

I started going to the gym every single day, forcing myself to stay on the elliptical machine until I burned exactly 500 calories, which usually took an hour. I replaced bagels and pizza with egg white omelets and salads. My favorite blended mocha frappes were replaced by black coffee with Splenda. I chewed sugar free gum incessantly to diminish food cravings. I replaced my beloved vodka tonics with lower-calorie vodka seltzers, even though I thought they tasted like shit. After drinking enough of them, I couldn't tell the difference anyway, and I required a *lot* of them to drown out the cruel, critical voices in my head.

Three weeks later, I showed up to our sorority's "Crush Party" with Josh on my arm and exactly *eight* fewer pounds on my body. I wore a skintight, purple mini dress and black ankle boots to show off my slimmer physique.

"Sick body, Justine!" one of my sorority sisters complimented me as we walked in.

Josh hadn't commented on my progress, but he was there with me, as my *date*, so I figured he must have thought I was acceptable enough to be seen with, in front of all of Greek life.

A week later I realized he was not impressed by my progress.

"I'm going to the gym," he said, switching off the TV and getting up from the futon we'd been sitting on in his dorm room. He pulled his Ed Hardy T-shirt over his head and changed into a sleeveless workout tank from H&M. I ogled his beautifully sculpted chest, chiseled abs, and muscular arms. "Wanna come with?"

"I already went this morning," I responded proudly.

"Well, what did you do?" he asked.

"I did 60 minutes on the elliptical."

Was he being curious or incredulous?

"See, that's your problem." He rolled his eyes in annoyance. "You only do cardio. You need to lift weights too. Go upstairs and change. I'll let you do weights with me today."

For a few seconds I was unable to think, speak, or move. It felt like the wind had been knocked out of me. All I heard was, *YOU'RE STILL NOT GOOD ENOUGH.*

I collected myself and left Josh's room. I took the four flights of stairs up to my dorm room instead of the elevator, to burn the extra 17 calories. I dug through my drawers looking for workout clothes I hadn't already worn this week— or *this morning.*

Once at the gym, Josh barked orders at me, as I struggled to keep up.

"Between sets I want you to do lunges to tone your butt and legs. I want you to keep your heart rate up the whole time, to burn more fat," he said callously.

Josh was basically all of the critical, fat-phobic voices in my head, personified. I did exactly what he told me to do. I lunged, robotically and silently, eager for the burning sensation in my quads to distract me from the aching in my heart.

I wanted this arrogant frat boy to like me so much that I willingly sacrificed my dignity, tolerated his verbal assaults, and let him tell me where to go, what to do, and how much weight I needed to lose. I obliged, because I wanted—no, *needed*—him to want me. I voluntarily became his doormat thinking that someday, if I was a thin-enough, pretty-enough doormat, then I could be his girlfriend.

June 2007; age 20

Before moving back home to Wisconsin, I called my mom to express the importance of having an adequate place to work out.

I had my mind on one thing and one thing only—obliterating my body's Problem Areas before I saw Josh again. He had graduated from Hofstra and moved back to Philadelphia for the time being, but he promised to visit me that summer.

"I need to be doing cardio *and* weights," I informed my mom.

Translation: *I need Josh to want me.*

"I've got you covered, baby," she promised. "I got you a membership at my new gym for the summer. You'll love it. And I know you're all about Josh right now, but there are lots of cute guys there."

One of the "cute guys" she was dying to introduce me to was Chad. He was tall, muscular, and good-looking, and you never saw him without a baseball cap on backwards. Chad quickly became my training buddy at the gym, who happened to flirt with me constantly. After months of following Josh around like a puppy, it felt so good to have this hot guy interested in me.

Before long, Chad started inviting me to hang out after our workout sessions with his friends and on group outings. Then the two of us began spending time together alone, which I liked. But I was still smitten with Josh. We'd text every day, and in July, Josh booked a flight to Milwaukee to visit, as promised. We'd be going to Lollapalooza in Chicago while he was in town. I couldn't believe he was actually flying out to see me.

I was pleased with the progress I'd been making in the gym, but Josh's upcoming trip added a new level of pressure and urgency to get as fit as possible. I somehow believed if I was svelte, toned and beautiful enough, he would surely realize he was smitten with me, too, and he'd ask me to be his girlfriend.

"How do you get leaner fast?" I asked Chad one day as we were laying on his bed watching true crime shows on TV, after our daily trip to the gym.

"Increase cardio, and drop your carbs," he responded without hesitation. "Why though? You look great, and you've made a lot of progress already this summer."

"I want to get leaner before August," I said, ignoring his compliment. Deflecting compliments was my default—I'd let praise roll off my back, unlike criticism, which I'd internalize and cling to.

"I can do extra cardio with you after we train. And I can help you with your diet, if you want," he offered as he turned his body to face me directly, lying next to me. "But there's something more important I want to talk to you about."

I swallowed uncomfortably.

"Okay," I said, turning to face him as well. He grabbed my hands and held them in his.

"I really like you, and I want you to be my girlfriend."

My face grew hot and my heart started beating faster.

Josh is visiting in a month and Chad has no idea. This is turning into a hot mess.

I searched for the right words, to let Chad down gently.

"I really like you too, but I don't live here. By September I'll be back in New York."

"So? I can visit you. And you can visit me too. People make long distance relationships work all the time," Chad argued, a bit agitated.

"I just— I'm not sure. Can we just keep hanging out the way we are now?" I asked, not wanting to lose my training partner and summertime fling just yet.

"Sure, whatever," Chad said, dropping my hands and turning away from me, obviously insulted and hurt.

"I'll think about it, okay?" I offered, trying to buy myself time before I'd ultimately have to let him down. I felt guilty for leading him on— but also flattered. Here I had *two* attractive, older guys interested in me. My ego was throwing a real rager, with confetti and everything.

Chad pulled away after that conversation, but we continued seeing each other at the gym. The day before Josh arrived, Chad found me on a treadmill.

"What are you up to this weekend?"

"Going to Lollapalooza in Chicago," I replied, bracing myself for whatever questions would follow.

"Oh, cool. With who?" Chad asked.

"My friend who's visiting from Hofstra."

"That's fun. How long is she in town for?"

I paused, feeling my throat tighten.

"Um. *He's* flying in tomorrow and leaving on Monday," I responded.

"*He?* Just a friend? Or is he more than a friend?"

"Well, it's— it's complicated," I stammered, unable to hide the truth from my face.

"Wow. You know what, Justine? Have fun. I'm done with this shit," Chad snapped, and before I could attempt to defend myself, he stormed away.

I felt bad things were ending this way, but at the same time, I had no desire to have anything more serious with Chad. I had convinced myself that Josh's willingness to actually come and visit meant he'd surely ask me to be his girlfriend.

Josh's trip came and went in a blur of great live music, sweaty bodies, vodka mixed into Vitamin Water, and his prescription Adderall. We sang and danced and made out to bands like Pearl Jam, Kings of Leon, and Interpol, in thick, sticky crowds of rich kids trying to pull off the hippie-grunge-chic look.

When the weekend was over, I felt a little bummed Josh hadn't asked me to be his girlfriend, but I started thinking maybe we *were* a couple, and it was just unspoken, understood.

Who needs a title, right? We obviously share something special, so who cares? I told myself, even though I did care. A lot.

Josh flew home, and a week passed without hearing from Chad. I went to the gym every day with my mom, but I never saw him there. I assumed he was going at a different time, or working out somewhere else to avoid me.

***

A week before I went back to school, I was spending the night at my dad's condo. I would stay there occasionally when I was home in Wisconsin. Despite the pain caused by the divorce, we had a good relationship.

My dad and I were watching TV after dinner when my phone rang.

"I'm gonna take this upstairs," I said, hurrying up to the guest room where I was staying.

"Hey," I answered, shutting the door behind me.

"I hope you had fun with your '*friend,*' you slut!" Chad snarled.

His voice sounded completely different— ice cold. I froze, feeling my heart climb up into my throat.

I sat down on the bed and listened as he went on.

"I want you to know that you're so ugly I was embarrassed to bring you around my friends. You think you're such hot shit, but you're not. You're *gross*! Every time we hooked up, I was so grossed out. Your boobs are uneven. And you have so much fat on your butt and thighs; it's disgusting!"

His words ripped through me like bullets. He continued to berate me for four or five minutes, which is a *very* long time to have your physical appearance picked apart and roasted.

I sat there paralyzed, speechless, taking it all in. All summer this guy had been building me up and showering me with compliments, and now *this*? He knew exactly where to hurt me, and he went straight for the jugular.

Hell hath no fury like a jilted male ego.

My mind flashed back to that horrible night with my first college boyfriend Anthony, which I still hadn't emotionally recovered from. They say it takes five positive comments to counteract one negative insult, but for someone with a self-image as frail as mine was, I think the ratio is closer to 500 to 1.

I already couldn't get Anthony's hateful words out of my head from that scary night in his dorm suite. Now this was like coarse salt in an open wound. I collected every word as fuel for my fire. I'd even repeat these words to myself over and over again as "motivation" during grueling workouts to come.

Finally, Chad paused. He'd dissected me head to toe, so I guess he was out of ammunition. I heard him take a breath.

"Never talk to me again!" he barked, and hung up.

I sat there with my head spinning for who knows how long.

Finally, I went into the bathroom to splash cold water on my face. I looked up at my reflection in the mirror. I didn't see my real reflection— I saw what Chad told me to see.

Mirrors have always been tricky for me like that. When people praised me, I saw a reflection I liked. When people called me fat, my perception of myself would morph into the chubby girl again. I saw my body as this huge, grotesque thing I hated.

I stepped away from the sink and looked down at my thighs, which I had felt proud of just one hour earlier. I had been working so hard all summer—lunging, squatting, and leg-pressing to tone my thighs—but now all I could see was the cellulite and the excess fat bulging on the sides. I felt disgusted with myself.

I have to try harder, I thought. *I have to get thinner and fitter.*

Like so many other painful, disturbing experiences, I kept this to myself. I went back downstairs, smiled at my dad, and we continued to watch TV together. When people said mean things about me or my body, I believed them, so in some way, I felt I deserved it. I felt too ashamed to tell anyone what happened.

September 2007; 20 years old

I was more determined than ever to get my goal body. I wanted to build a physical appearance that was bulletproof. I wanted to make myself *so* physically perfect that no guy could ever insult me again.

The gym at Hofstra University left much to be desired. It was small and run-down, and the equipment was outdated. It was in desperate need of a makeover. It just would *not* do— my Problem Areas couldn't be fixed there.

Plus, I was eager to get away from campus.

"Let's get some *bitches* over here tonight!" was a phrase frequently overheard in the old, dilapidated house I shared with two of my sorority sisters and four frat guys in a seedy part of town.

The term "bitches" felt offensive, but not for the reason it should have. It stung, because deep down, I couldn't help but wonder what was so wrong with the "bitches" that already resided there.

With a quick Google search, I discovered that ten minutes from campus, there was a massive, state-of-the-art health club, open 24-hours a day, complete with a salon and spa, pool, basketball courts, and countless rows of the best exercise equipment. I *needed* to work out there.

I called my dad and woefully told him about our dingy, old gym on campus, and this Gym-Of-Gods, located so perfectly close to me. I assumed he'd happily agree to pay for it, as both of my parents liked to spoil me extra after the divorce, as a way to ensure my love and loyalty.

"Yeah, I'm not paying for that," he said bluntly, one step ahead. "Why don't you go get a job there?"

Touché, Daddy.

The next day, I put on my cutest fitted track jacket, Hudson jeans, and sneakers, and drove to XSport Fitness. An extravagant display of flat screen TVs greeted me, playing upbeat music videos with a strong baseline bumping in an endless loop. The place even *smelled* new— along with the smell of chlorine from the pool, a smell I'd always loved.

As I approached the front desk, I was enveloped by cases and cases of bottled waters, energy drinks, and protein supplements.

Look at this place! I thought, visualizing myself transforming into a beautifully toned little hardbody between these walls.

The front desk was a giant circular structure, complete with a full-service juice bar that served made-to-order protein shakes and smoothies. A young, pretty brunette working the front desk greeted me.

"I'm wondering if you guys are hiring?" I asked with a smile. She motioned me over to the side of the front desk and approached a man sitting at a desk nearby. He introduced himself as Mike, the front desk manager.

After a short series of questions and some basic paperwork, I walked out with a job as a front desk and juice bar attendant. I was thrilled.

This is even better than the job at Hollister!

Working at the gym opened me up fully to the world of fitness. If the books and magazines I read in my teens had provided my bachelor's degree in nutrition and fitness, *this* place provided my master's. I began to learn so much more about strength training, supplements, and the science of nutrition, pouring over new information daily. I couldn't get enough. I was certifiably *obsessed*.

The gym employed over thirty personal trainers, most of whom were men. These super-hot men had bulging pecs and big, round shoulders pushing the stitching of their tight, XSport Fitness T-shirts to the limit. They were especially friendly to the front-desk staff, partially because we were all attractive young women, and partially so that we'd make them protein shakes for free when the managers weren't looking. Of course, I found myself infatuated with a few of the trainers early on.

Three days a week, when I didn't have classes, I worked the 8am-4pm shift, and worked out afterwards. The other days I came to the gym to get my workouts in after class. I rarely missed a day there.

A couple of the trainers offered to train me for free when they had gaps in their schedules, or last-minute cancellations. I graciously accepted, and attentively absorbed every bit of information I could when they'd train me.

When I didn't have a personal trainer at my disposal, I carried around a copy of *FitnessRX for Women* magazine, with a training program called "Lean, Sexy & Sculpted—From Head to Toe."

My strength and confidence in the male-dominated weight room increased exponentially, week by week. I lived and *breathed* fitness, reading every women's fitness magazine I could get my hands on. I took detailed notes whenever the trainers divulged pro tips and secrets. I bought tubs of protein powders, protein bars, and "fat-incinerating" pills and potions from the pro shop, feeling excited and hopeful that I had *finally* found the right recipe to get the body I so desperately wanted— like the models on the covers of my fitness magazines. Those women had toned, flat abs; round, tight glutes; long, lean legs; and perky, symmetrical breasts. They confidently smiled at the camera, exposing their perfect white teeth. I knew I wanted that for myself. The chubby girl inside of me wanted it more than ever.

Now that I had the right recipe, the right tools and the right environment, I believed I was undoubtedly on my way to becoming one of those women.

November 2007; age 20

I'd just finished my shift at the gym when I ventured out to look for a dress to wear to my sorority's upcoming winter formal. I walked into Nordstrom and a striking, sequined little number immediately caught my eye.

It was *perfection*— dark gray, sparkly, like a flapper dress with fringe at the bottom, but with a more modern fitted silhouette. Sexy, yet sophisticated. I could see myself dancing in this dress already!

I looked through the rack for a size Small, but all I could find was an XL, and an XXS. I sighed and took the XXS into the dressing room with me just in case, along with a few other options I wasn't as enthusiastic about. I unzipped the sequined frock and stepped in. To my astonishment, I could actually pull it up around my body— I just couldn't quite zip it shut on my own.

I quickly did the math in my head: *Twenty days 'til winter formal. Twenty days. I can make this work.*

I paid for the dress and headed home to map out my *get-skinny-fast game plan*. My sorority sister Adriana, one of my housemates, knocked on my door and poked her head in.

"What's all this?" she asked, motioning to the array of notebooks, magazines and cut-out articles I had laid out in front of me, covering my comforter as I sat on my bed.

"I fell in love with this dress today, but the store only had an extra, *extra* small. I'm on a mission to make it fit before formal!" I explained.

"I want in! Tell me what to do and I'll do it too!" she exclaimed, clearing a small space on my bed for her to take a seat among the piles of magazines.

For the next few weeks, she and I were allies in the war against calories and body fat.

"Can I put ketchup on my egg whites?" Adriana texted.

"No. Too much sugar," I wrote back.

"Ugh, fine. So gross tho!"

"It'll be worth it." I responded, with a smiley face.

And it was.

Twenty days of bland meals, no sugar, and hours of cardio and strength training resulted in me shedding six pounds. I felt delighted with myself and my ironclad willpower. Adriana only lost three pounds, but she was happy with that because she admittingly wasn't as disciplined as me. I secretly prided myself on being able to diet harder than her.

The night of the winter formal, Adriana and I did our hair and makeup together in my room. The time came to put our dresses on. I'd bought the tightest Spanx I could find, to give me a little extra help. I pulled on my dress, unzipped.

"Okay, here goes. Can you zip me up?" I asked. Adriana slowly worked the zipper up as I sucked in with all my might, holding my breath. The sequin material had absolutely *no* give.

Please fit. Please fit. Please fit, I silently prayed. I had no Plan B.

"That's it! It's zipped! It fits!" she squealed and we bounced around my room together excitedly.

"Oh my gosh, I'm so relieved! Now let's just hope it doesn't burst open later tonight!"

We erupted into a fit of giggles. By the grace of God, I managed to drink, dance and nibble on exactly *three* bites of food without any wardrobe malfunctions. I adored the way I looked in the pictures I took that night.

But the week after formal, all bets were off. After depriving ourselves for three weeks, Adriana and I made an *event* out of eating ourselves into a comatose state.

"Let's be BAD! Let's get Taco Bell!" she suggested late one night after drinking copious amounts of Franzia boxed wine.

We procured our feast and sat on my bed indulging in burritos, gorditas, and nachos until our bellies ached. I reached over to open the drawer of my nightstand, pulling out a small box.

"What's that?" Adriana asked, stuffing a nacho cheese-drenched tortilla chip into her mouth.

"Laxatives," I told her. "They make you poop a bunch the next day. I take them whenever I eat too much, so I don't feel as guilty."

"Why don't you just throw up?" Adriana proposed, like no big deal.

"I can't make myself throw up. Believe me, I've *tried.* I've just never been able to," I casually explained, judging myself for not being able to do so. I popped two blue laxative pills into my mouth and swallowed them down with a swig of Diet Pepsi.

"Gotcha. Well I want some!" she said, taking the box from my hand and following suit by popping two laxatives.

"You might cramp in the morning," I warned. "And be sure you get to a toilet *fast* when you feel like you have to go!"

We giggled, and turned our attention to a Dane Cook comedy special that we'd watched together many times before. This became our ritual.

It was nice to have an accomplice in my perverse food habits. I binged more in college than any other time in my life, probably because it's when I felt the most awkward and alone. Despite being chosen and accepted into my sorority, I never felt like any of my "sisters" were truly my friends— probably because I didn't have amnesia about the hazing I went through during pledging. Adriana was the first sorority sister who felt like a true friend. She and I formed a special bond through dieting and depriving ourselves, then binging and purging together through the intentional abuse of laxatives, and in her case, trips to the toilet for self-induced vomiting. *Color me jealous!*

We even coined a new word for our chosen lifestyle: "Drunkorexic," meaning we'd diet and purge our food so we could save our calories for alcohol. As a bonus, the thinner we got, the less booze we needed to get drunk. *Score.*

Regardless of what my ill-informed younger self believed, it's a myth that laxatives help you lose weight, or "purge" any food you've consumed. Laxatives work on the large intestine, and by the time food reaches this part of your body, calories have already been absorbed by the small intestine. They temporarily cause the body to shed water, minerals and electrolytes, (things you *don't* want to excrete!) Users might feel lighter, or notice a flatter tummy, but as soon as you drink water again your weight goes back to normal, only now you've disrupted your precious gut microbiome, among other things.

June 2008; age 21

Ten months into working at XSport Fitness, I got the opportunity to take my fitness obsession to the next level. The gym was offering an in-house personal training certification class, and I decided to go for it. The idea of becoming a personal trainer both terrified and excited me. Old thoughts continually crept into my head, and the imposter syndrome I experienced was oh-so-real.

Who am I— a former fat kid— to give people fitness advice?! I'd ask myself repeatedly.

But fitness and nutrition were practically all I ever thought about, outside of doing just enough to get good grades in my classes, which always came naturally to me. Once the opportunity presented itself, to go from enthusiast to professional in the fitness world, I couldn't resist.

Four weeks later, I passed my personal training exam with flying colors. It was official: *I, Justine Moore, former fat kid from Waukesha, Wisconsin, am now a Certified Personal Trainer in New York!*

Since I was friendly with all of the staff at the gym, the management team agreed to let me seamlessly transition from front desk attendant to personal trainer. I'd officially start as a trainer in August— after a trip to L.A. to visit Josh, followed by a trip to Spain for five weeks to study abroad.

Josh had moved to L.A. a few months prior to pursue— well, who knows what, really. Tormenting girls on a different coast? Getting closer to the birthplace of Ed Hardy? One can only guess.

We'd still been texting frequently and talking on the phone, and despite me dating and hooking up with a handful of other random frat guys that year, my heart was always set on Josh. He called me out of the blue one day and invited me to visit him, so I booked a flight right away.

I'd fly to L.A. to visit Josh for five nights before returning to New York to fly to Spain. Naturally, this sent me into a neurotic tizzy of trying to get as thin and toned as possible before my trip.

I did a Google search for *Diets to lose weight fast*, and concluded the Cabbage Soup Diet would be my best course of action. Questionable sources on the internet promised 10 pounds of weight loss in just one week from what they called the "Wonder Soup." *How fun!*

Around this time, blogging was becoming exceedingly popular. Instead of reading fabricated articles like "What J.Lo Eats in a Day," in *US Weekly*, you could get the inside scoop from real women, telling all about their dieting triumphs and defeats.

I landed on a recent post from a blogger whose caption caught my eye:

I'm going to Miami in two weeks and I don't want to take my muffin top with me! I have this sexy form-fitting dress I really want to wear…. WITHOUT SPANX! Whenever I need to lose my gut or 10 pounds fast, I turn to the diet that never lets me down; my latest love affair, the 7-day Cabbage Soup Diet!

This girl gets it! I thought, and printed out all of the instructions.

The diet was uncomplicated— you consume boatloads of this low-calorie cabbage soup— as much as you want! Plus, every day you get to incorporate other random foods, in a very specific order:

DAY 1 – CABBAGE SOUP + ALL THE FRUIT YOU WANT (EXCEPT BANANAS!)

DAY 2 – CABBAGE SOUP + VEGGIES, INCLUDING ONE BAKED POTATO

DAY 3 – CABBAGE SOUP + FRUITS & VEGGIES (BUT NO BANANA OR POTATO!)

DAY 4 – CABBAGE SOUP + UP TO EIGHT BANANAS & AS MUCH SKIMMED MILK AS YOU'D LIKE!

DAY 5 – CABBAGE SOUP + UP TO 20 OUNCES OF BEEF AND UP TO SIX TOMATOES

DAY 6 – CABBAGE SOUP + AS MUCH BEEF AND VEGGIES (EXCLUDING POTATOES) AS YOU'D LIKE

DAY 7 – CABBAGE SOUP + VEGGIES (BUT NO POTATOES) AND UNSWEETENED FRUIT JUICE

Rock solid plan, don't you think? I certainly thought so!

I hit the local Stop & Shop to buy all of the necessary groceries and got to work.

"Oh my god, what is that *smell*?" my housemate Marissa shouted from the couch in our living room.

I was in the kitchen stirring a giant cauldron of cabbage soup on the stove. After wrapping up the semester, I had moved out of my half-sorority, half-frat house and into a nicer, tamer house with four of my sorority sisters.

"It's cabbage soup! I'm doing the Cabbage Soup Diet to lose a few pounds before L.A.," I yelled back from the kitchen.

"Ew, what's in it? It smells like feet and rotten eggs!"

Marissa wandered into the kitchen to get the details.

"Lots of cabbage. Plus, celery, diced tomatoes, and low sodium vegetable broth. And salt and pepper, if you want," I said, listing the "Wonder Soup" ingredients off.

"That is some serious dedication. You're my hero, Justine," Marissa said laughing. She lit up an old joint that was laying on the counter and took a hit of weed. "I'm ordering pizza and wings. Let me know if you change your mind about your nasty soup!"

My other housemates joined Marissa's pizza party. I felt pangs of both hunger and jealousy as I stirred my smelly pot of cabbage water. I distracted myself by imagining Josh catching sight of me looking irresistible at the airport, and running to greet me with a giant hug and kiss.

It'll be worth it! I told myself for the thousandth time. I always told myself that when embarking on a new diet or weight loss program.

My sorority sisters regularly teased me about my workout routines and eating habits. While they were smoking pot and scarfing down bagels and pizza, I was always running around with my gym bag and mixing up protein shakes. And the joke really *was* on me, because they were all still thinner—and happier—than I was.

"You're so *dedicated*!" they'd say.

I wouldn't be if I had your genes, I'd think to myself. *How do they eat like that and stay so thin? How on earth do they not have cellulite, when all they do is lay around and eat junk? It's not fair!*

This was always my perspective on my peers. I believed the majority of women stayed thin naturally, no matter what they ate, and I was some special sort of damaged for having to constantly control my appetite and be vigilant about my weight.

When I look back, I remember sorority sisters frequently ordering their bagels "scooped out," which was a request for the bagel-preparer to tear out the majority of the cooked dough of the bagel— the "meat," if you will— leaving only the outer shell. This defiling of delectable Long Island bagels (truly the best in the world!) was obviously a tactic to reduce carbs and calories.

I can remember another sorority sister would drizzle marinara sauce over iceberg lettuce when everyone else was indulging in pasta. Another girl I lived with would fill up on sauerkraut and pickles, because they're extremely low in calories, but have enough fiber and sodium to make you "feel full."

But these approaches didn't register in my mind as weight control tactics.

My brain was busy doing what brains do best— showing me evidence, or more "proof" that the narrative I believed was true. The narrative I'd been believing for 14 years at this point was that *I* had a weight problem, one that required constant watchfulness and restriction, and other women didn't. So I'd zero in on all the instances I saw my peers indulging, seemingly without a second thought, and without consequence, confirming that I was the only one fighting this unfair battle.

It wasn't until my early 30s, when I was researching statistics about diet culture and body image, that I discovered I was not alone in despising my body and restricting myself to remedy it. I realized my story was *not* unique — but in fact the norm.

I was shocked to read that 91 percent of women surveyed on a college campus had attempted to control their weight through dieting, and 22 percent dieted "often," or "always," according to the National Eating Disorders Association. (Oldenhave, 2002) Over 50 percent of teen girls report using unhealthy weight control behaviors such as skipping meals, fasting, smoking cigarettes, vomiting, and taking laxatives, according to The Eating Disorder Foundation. (NEDA, 2014)

I later learned some of my sorority sisters, who I'd envied for their seemingly "natural" ability to stay thin, fought their own battles behind closed doors. Some of those girls I shared a home with were, in fact, vomiting up those slices of pizza, or taking copious amounts of Adderall to squash their appetites. Many of them even smoked cigarettes to suppress their hunger— after all of the anti-smoking education our generation grew up with. When deciding whether to blacken their lungs or risk having a dreaded muffin top, it was an easy choice.

July 2008; age 21

One week later, it was time for me to pack my bags. After returning from my trip to see Josh, I'd have just one night back in New York before flying to Spain.

I hadn't lost the ten pounds the Cabbage Soup Diet had promised, but that was my fault. I had caved on Day Four—banana and skim milk day— which would have been delicious, except for the fact that I kept getting dizzy spells and could barely stand up.

Though the day started out strong, with a skim-milk-and-banana smoothie, I ended up binging on three bowls of Velveeta macaroni and cheese and a pint of Ben & Jerry's Phish Food ice cream that night. I just lost it. I was literally going mad, and the thought of one more sip of bland, nasty cabbage water made me gag.

Even though I cheated on the diet, I still managed to drop five pounds. I reeled it back in after the macaroni and cheese binge, and I was feeling good about myself, despite not losing the other five pounds I'd been hoping to drop.

Upon landing at LAX, I texted Josh. "Just landed. Can't wait to see you!"

A few minutes later my phone vibrated. It was Josh.

"Running late. Be there soon."

I got my luggage and went to the bathroom, grateful for a few extra minutes to freshen up after the cross-country flight. I touched up my makeup, dabbing on a coat of MAC Lipglass in C-Thru, my favorite shade of nude. I popped in a fresh piece of Extra peppermint gum and sprayed myself with DKNY Apple perfume— my signature scent at the time. My phone buzzed again.

"I'm outside. Hurry up, I can't park here."

I hurried outside to ground transportation and saw Josh standing next to a white Honda Civic. He looked better than ever— sun-kissed, chiseled, and perfectly groomed. He was always *so* particular about his grooming routine. His eyebrows usually looked neater than *mine* did.

He gave me a quick hug before throwing my suitcase into the trunk. I'd been hoping for more than a hug, but I tried to brush it off.

"I hope you're ready to party," Josh said as we drove to his apartment. "I got a hook up to get into Hyde Lounge tonight. Unreal! It's almost impossible to get in! We're meeting a bunch of girls there— plus one of my buddies. Guys can only get into clubs here if you have like, six or seven chicks with you."

My stomach dropped. *Six or seven chicks?* I'd hoped it would be just the two of us. I hadn't seen Josh in months and had imagined us going to a romantic dinner to catch up.

We arrived at Josh's one-bedroom apartment.

"Get changed— my buddy Nick is picking us up in twenty minutes," Josh directed without so much as a glance in my direction. He grabbed himself a bottled water without offering one to me.

I unzipped my suitcase and pulled out a short blue cotton dress. I pulled it over my head and studied myself in the mirror. It was tight, but I felt pleased with how lean I looked, and how toned my legs appeared with a fresh spray tan. I put on flat leather sandals, then plugged in my flat iron to straighten my hair. Josh poked his head into the bedroom.

"You're wearing *that*?" he asked, rolling his eyes at me. "This is a *nice* place we're going."

"Oh," I said, caught off guard, wishing I had packed differently. I hadn't gotten the memo that we'd be hitting exclusive nightclubs. I opened my suitcase up again. "I can put on something else."

"Yeah, I would," he said. Then he noticed the track jacket I had worn on the flight, hanging over his desk chair. He picked it up and handed it to me. "Let's keep your things packed away and out of sight while you're here, okay? You know I like things neat."

I was silent, and felt a little queasy as I tucked the track jacket into my suitcase and pulled out the only designer dress I had brought. I was so thankful I packed at least one. I put on the dress and paired it with nude designer heels I'd borrowed from one of my sorority sisters. I heard a quick knock at the front door and then another man's voice.

"You ready, bro?"

"Yeah, man. Just give us five minutes," Josh replied. He came back into the room and surveyed my outfit.

"Better." He scanned me up and down. "Come on, let's go."

A high-speed, fifteen-minute car ride later we pulled up to the infamous Hyde Lounge. It was my worst nightmare— a sea of skinny, gorgeous, modelesque women in tiny designer bandage dresses forming a giant line out the door. Nick had the valet park his car and the three of us approached the entrance.

"Kim!" Josh called out and a long-legged, sexy blonde girl turned around. She beamed and waved him over. They hugged and he kissed her on the cheek, then held her hand as he stepped back to admire her, looking her up and down. "You look… WOW. I'm speechless."

I couldn't believe the words coming out of his mouth, when he was always so harsh and critical of me.

"Aw, Josh! You're too sweet!" Kim giggled, batting her eyes in his direction. She looked over and noticed me standing awkwardly a few feet away, fidgeting with my cheap Forever 21 clutch. "Is this your friend from college?"

"Ah yeah, my bad," Josh said. "Kim, this is Justine."

"Aw! So nice to meet you! You are just *darling*!" She looked into my eyes with the fakest smile I've ever witnessed, took my hands in hers, and gave them a good squeeze. I smiled back the only way I knew how.

Once inside, Josh vanished, keen to spend the night on his own accord. I wandered outside to the patio and made my way up to the bar alone.

"I'll have a Heineken, please," I told a petite brunette bartender. Normally in diet-mode I exclusively drank vodka seltzer, but the first two hours of my stay in L.A. had me feeling so dismal I didn't even care about empty calories or carbohydrates. Josh had never exactly treated me well, but this felt like a whole new level of disregard for my feelings. I was already wishing I hadn't flown out here.

"Nine dollars," the bartender said, placing the beer in front of me.

For a beer? L.A. sucks, I thought, reaching into my tacky little clutch.

"I got it," a deep voice piped in from behind me. Josh's friend Nick slid up next to me at the bar, placing his credit card on the counter. "And Patron on the rocks."

"Thanks," I told him, taking a big swig of my ice-cold Heineken. The bubbles hit my tongue with their familiar, hoppy taste and immediately calmed my nerves.

"My pleasure," he said, winking at me and pushing his long, wavy hair back. He was a good-looking guy, but something about him skeeved me out. He took a sip of his drink and put his arm around me. I stiffened, not expecting him to touch me. "I think you should stay at my place tonight."

I felt my throat tighten.

"Why would I do that? I'm here to see Josh," I stammered.

"Yeah, well, Josh doesn't have air conditioning— and I do," Nick replied, winking again and grinning at me. *What was up with this dude?* He seemed amused by how confused I looked. "Besides, Josh wants to take Kim home."

OUCH. There it was.

I felt foolish, sick to my stomach, and so out of place. *I shouldn't have come here*, I thought over and over again.

"Thanks, but no thanks. My stuff is at Josh's place. I'm actually going to go look for him," I responded coldly and hurried away from the bar to the bathroom.

In the bathroom I reapplied my lip gloss and stared at myself in the mirror. I noticed nothing but flaws— my face looked so round, my breasts so small and uneven, and my arms too thick and flabby. I chugged the rest of my beer and headed out into the crowded club to search for Josh. Instead, I ran into a familiar face.

"Justine! What are you doing here?" shrieked Amanda, who had been in my sorority before moving to L.A. to pursue a career as an actress.

"I'm visiting Josh," I explained, feeling so grateful to have a friend. "But I don't know where he is right now."

"Well you can hang with me! I'm so happy to see you here! How crazy!" Amanda exclaimed, taking my hand and leading me to the main bar where she introduced me to two of her friends.

We talked, danced, and took shots. Each tequila shooter quieted my heartache a little bit more. As the night wore on, I grew unbearably tired. My body was still on New York time, and after a long day of travel, I was worn out. I hugged Amanda goodbye and thanked her friends for the shots before making my way around the club. I finally found Josh at a big corner booth with Kim, two old dudes who undoubtedly funded the bottle service, and a bevy Victoria's Secret model look-alikes.

"Heyyyy! Where've you been?" Josh yelled over the table once he spotted me. His arm was wrapped around Kim.

"I didn't know where you went," I yelled back. "I'm tired. I'm ready to go."

"One more drink, then we'll go. Here, I'll make you one," Josh said, reaching for the bottle of Grey Goose vodka at the center of the table. He poured a drink for me and slid it across the table. The booth was full, so I stood next to the table, awkwardly drinking and talking to no one until Josh had his fill for the evening.

"Alright, let's go. Nick's waiting out front for us," Josh said, sliding out of the booth.

We made our way toward the entrance where Nick was waiting. Kim tagged right along with us, and when the car arrived, she climbed into the back seat and Josh tumbled in after her. I sat up front in the passenger side, and I knew Nick had been telling the truth.

Why did Josh even invite me out here? I thought over and over again, wishing I had never come. Nick pulled up to Josh's apartment complex and reached across to put his hand on my thigh.

"Last chance for that air conditioning," he said, smirking. I quickly got out of the car and headed toward the apartment, Josh and Kim trailing behind me. Once inside the apartment Josh dragged my suitcase out into the living room.

"You good here?" Josh asked me, motioning to the bare couch. I couldn't find words so I just nodded. Then he pulled me in for a hug. "Thanks for coming to see me. You're such a good friend."

By the grace of alcohol, I managed to get some sleep on the couch while Josh and Kim spent the night in his bedroom with the door shut. I woke up early the next morning once the sun rose.

Upon waking, my stomach sank and my heart ached profusely as I remembered last night's events. I looked at Josh's closed bedroom door and couldn't bear to be in that apartment any longer, knowing I'd been fooling myself all this time thinking one day he'd make me his girlfriend. I reached for my phone and called Mark, a friend I'd worked with at Hollister years ago in Wisconsin. We had stayed in touch over the years and he now lived in L.A.

"Justine! What's up?" he greeted me. It felt so good to hear his voice. I explained I had flown out to stay with a guy and it wasn't going well. I asked if I could stay with him until my flight home, three days later.

"Of course you can stay with me! The only problem is, I have a motorcycle. I won't be able to pick you up with your luggage, so you'll have to get a ride or take a cab," he told me. I thanked him profusely, wrote down his address, and told him I'd text when I was on my way.

Josh woke up and came out from the bedroom, wearing only his boxer briefs. He got himself a bottle of water before coming to sit on the couch with me.

"How'd you sleep, Num Nums?" he asked casually, gulping down water. The weird little pet name for me wasn't funny anymore. For the first time ever, I felt a wave of anger toward him.

How could you do this to me? Why do you treat me like this? I wanted to shout.

"Fine," I responded crisply. I couldn't bring myself to say any of the things I was thinking, or ask how he could do this to his *friend.* "I'm going to stay with my friend Mark for the rest of my trip. It would be nice if you could give me a ride to his place."

Josh didn't flinch. He took another gulp of his water and looked at me nonchalantly. "That's cool. But I'm going to hit the gym and then get some food, so it would be better if you can get a ride. Or I can call you a cab."

"Sure, yeah." My voice faltered as I choked back tears. I felt shocked at his blatant indifference toward me. Josh called a cab as I shoved my possessions back into my suitcase as quickly as possible. He came over and gave me a quick hug as I waited for the cab by the door.

"Good seeing you, Num Nums. The cab should be here any minute," he said, holding the door open for me. I gathered my things and left.

He didn't even offer to help me carry my luggage down.

The tears started to pour. The cab pulled up, and the driver helped me load my things into the trunk. I climbed in and crumbled into the back seat. I sobbed the entire thirty-minute ride to Mark's apartment. The cab driver frequently glanced back at me through the rearview mirror with a sympathetic look, but he never said a word, and for that, I was grateful.

Once at Mark's place, I immediately felt safe again. He carried my things in for me and brought them to his room.

"You can sleep here. All fresh sheets for you. I'll crash on the couch," he said, putting my stuff down. "Now tell me what happened."

I explained the details of Josh and my relationship, and what had happened since I'd arrived. Mark's body stiffened as I recounted the details and he kept shaking his head in disbelief. He listened intently until I finished talking.

"You deleted this guy's number, right?" he asked me. I could tell he was heated.

"What? No…" I responded, caught off guard.

"You deserve better than this, Justine. You should never let anyone treat you like this," Mark said sternly, looking directly at me. No one had ever said anything like that to me— that I deserved better when it came to men. No one ever had a chance, since Mark was the first person I opened up to about the hurtful way someone treated me.

I knew he was right. I knew no one deserved to be treated this way— like I mattered in one moment, then tossed away like rotten leftovers in the next. I felt ashamed having heard the whole story come out of my own mouth.

"I want you to delete this guy's number right now," Mark said. "That way, whenever he gets lonely and texts you, you can respond, 'Who is this? Oh sorry, I deleted your number because you're an asshole.'"

Mark was serious about me deleting that number, so I took out my cell phone and searched for Josh's contact info. I took a deep breath and paused. *Goodbye, Josh*, I thought as I pressed the delete button. It felt better than I had expected, like I had reclaimed the tiniest shred of my dignity, if there was any left at all.

A few months later that song "Gives You Hell" came out, by the All-American Rejects, and I'd play it on repeat during cardio workouts. I'd imagine running into Josh again someday. I even had my outfit picked out in this fantasy: army print cargo pants and a cropped white tube top. I imagined myself looking *so* perfect, *so* fit, *so* alluring that Josh would take one look at me and repent for his cruel ways. I'd blow him off, all cool and casual, and get the last laugh.

Oh, it will be glorious! Victory will be mine!

Spoiler alert: Josh never did text me. But he did write on my Facebook wall for my birthday, four years later, after I'd "made it big" in the fitness industry.

"Looking good, Num Nums! Happy Birthday," he wrote.

I didn't give him the satisfaction of commenting back, but I *liked* it so he'd know I had seen it. *Ha!* So victory *was* mine, I suppose, in an extremely passive aggressive way.

The rest of my time in Los Angeles, Mark and his roommate did their best to entertain me, show me around, and lift my spirits—and they did a damn good job. We saw the iconic Hollywood sign, the Grauman's Chinese Theatre, the designer shops on Rodeo Drive, and went to the beach in Malibu. Still, when the time came to fly back to New York, I felt relieved to distance myself from the whole trip.

I felt even more excited to be leaving the country altogether, to spend five whole weeks in Spain. On the seven-hour flight to Madrid, I read *The Secret*, which I had borrowed from my mom. Some think that book is cheesy and flawed, but it was my first introduction to the power of positive thinking and the Law of Attraction, and it felt like pure magic. The words hit me in a way that made my whole body shout, *YES! TRUTH!*

This was my introduction to the idea that my thoughts and feelings had real power. After feeling like a pile of garbage, it felt gratifying to think that I had some control over the cards life dealt me. I decided I'd put the principles into practice right away, hoping to start to steer my life in the direction I wanted it to go. I realized no one would know me in Spain, so I could be anyone I wanted to be. I could start a fresh new chapter— one where I believed in myself, and *projected* confidence, even if I didn't feel it deep down.

August 2008; age 21

My time in Spain flew by in a beautiful haze of red sangria, seafood straight from the ocean, men with olive skin and accents, dancing, laughter, and *bread*. Oh, the bread! Bread with breakfast, bread with lunch, bread with dinner. There was never a shortage of sangria or bread, and I indulged to my heart's content.

The booze and carbs dulled the pain I felt from finally putting Josh behind me. I could tell I was gaining a few pounds, so I'd occasionally wake up earlier than my classmates to jog around the scenic park near the university where we were staying. But after a few weeks of living the European lifestyle, I just relaxed and told myself I could get back in shape after the trip— this was a once in a lifetime experience.

I got to be someone different in Spain, and part of my European persona included less neurosis around food and my weight. Plus, I didn't have access to a scale over there— or a full-length mirror— so I just let loose and enjoyed myself. Spain rejuvenated my soul, and the endless attention from European guys boosted my confidence.

I arrived back in New York with a little more pep in my step, ready and eager to begin my career as a personal trainer. I was already hired, so the next step was learning the ropes and getting ready for clients. Since I'd be working mostly nights and weekends to accommodate my class schedule, Pierre, the assistant personal training manager, was in charge of training me. I felt excited about this because Pierre had always been nice to me at the gym, and I considered him to be a friend.

The first order of business was learning how to perform a fitness assessment. I proudly marched up to the personal training desk to meet Pierre on my first day of training, wearing black shorts and a tank top with *XSport Fitness* across the chest.

"Look who's back!" he said, grinning ear to ear. Pierre leaned back and quickly looked me up and down. "Damn! You got *thick*!"

My smile vanished and my mind began to race.

Is it that noticeable? How much weight did I gain? Does everyone think I got fat?

Pierre must have realized his comment upset me.

"Relax, you look great! I'm just playing with you! Have a seat," he said, motioning to the seat next to him.

Pierre had dark skin, kind eyes, and big, broad shoulders. He had a high-pitched voice for such a big guy, and a strange but pleasant accent that no one could place. He had grown up in Haiti, and spoke fluent French and Creole. Pierre had a way of making everyone feel comfortable right away— men and women alike. He had a certain charm to him, which contributed to the fact that he had the highest number of sales in the company nationwide, month after month. The general manager loved him for this, and always said, "Pierre could sell a ketchup popsicle to a woman in white gloves!"

"So, young lady," Pierre began, "the first order of business is teaching you how to perform a fitness assessment. I'm going to teach you by putting you through one today. You ready?"

"Ready," I said smiling, still trying to regain my composure after being called thick. He showed me the paperwork to do with a prospective client, and how to get them talking about themselves.

"Once they open up, find their pain points," he advised. "Find their insecurities, and get them to pour their heart out to you. Then, you show them how out of shape they are, and how much they need you, and by the end they'll be *thrilled* to hand over their credit card and sign on the dotted line!"

I nodded, even though it felt gross to get people to buy a service by making them feel bad about themselves. I personally could recall every negative comment anyone had ever made about my body, word for word, (including the one Pierre made just moments ago), so it seemed malicious and unethical to use people's insecurities as a sales tactic.

"So, young lady," Pierre continued, "What are your current fitness goals?"

"Mine? Well," I paused for a moment, looking down at my exposed thighs on the chair, noticing the way the fat spread across the surface. I caught sight of the cellulite I hadn't been aware of earlier that day, when I foolishly chose to wear shorts. "I want to lose body fat. I gained a little weight in Spain— so I'd like to lose that weight and then some. My mom is getting remarried in two months, and I want to get super toned for the wedding."

"I see," he said, jotting some notes down on the assessment paperwork. "It looks like you gained a lot of brown fat, or subcutaneous fat. That's the kind that sits right under your skin. We can help you burn that off. Let's take your measurements and then head to the floor."

Brown fat? What? Ew!

I felt so disgusting, and furious with myself for eating all that bread in Spain.

I followed Pierre over to the scale and he motioned for me to step on. It was a platform scale, and, for a second, my mind flashed back to being seven years old at the doctor's office— the first time someone said I was too heavy. I removed my sneakers and stepped on. Pierre slid the counter weight over, and over some more.

"143 pounds!" he announced way louder than necessary, and recorded it on the paper. It was the heaviest I'd ever been in my life. I was mortified. But it was only the beginning. Next, Pierre took my body fat percentage with a handheld device.

"27 percent body fat!" Pierre exclaimed, oblivious to my anguish. I was appalled by the number. He wrote it down and circled where I was on this "ideal body composition" chart that the gym had probably made up, noting that my body fat percentage was far from ideal.

This is so embarrassing— I'm supposed to be a personal trainer, for god's sake!

Then it was time for measurements, in inches. When Pierre got to my hips, he put the tape measure around the fullest part of my hips and butt.

"*Damn!*" he said again, the same way he had when he greeted me. "Forty-three inches. Like I said, you got *thick*! Very impressive!"

Pierre kept saying this stuff like I'd be flattered to hear it. I understood it was supposed to be some sort of compliment, but to me, it was the equivalent of being called a hippo all over again.

When the humiliation of measurement-taking was over, I wanted to die. But instead, we headed out onto the gym floor for the workout portion of the assessment.

"Okay, I'm going to put you through the most effective exercises for burning fat fast!" Pierre explained.

Terrific.

After being shocked by my own measurements, I was eager to torch the fat off my body as fast as humanly possible. "So first we're going to do one-through-eights. It's an exercise Navy Seals use to get in shape!"

Pierre demonstrated one rep for me. It was like a burpee, with a mountain climber *and* a push up— all stacked into one single REP! Who knew the most hated exercises on the planet could be combined into one hateful, demonizing drill?

Pierre put me through the most grueling workout of my life. And it was only 14 minutes long. I didn't know bodyweight exercises could even *be* that hard. After a few rounds of this psychotic torture, I could do no more. Pierre laughed as I sucked water from my water bottle, like a dying fish.

"Aw, had enough already?" he asked, chuckling. I nodded, feeling defeated and embarrassed. Sweat poured down my face, and I felt myself turning lobster red. The past hour had taken me right back into the headspace of Little Justine, sucking at all things athletic. My cruel inner critic reminded me I'd always, always be running from The Problem.

When we got back to the personal training desk, Pierre presented the package he recommended for my goals and current fitness level. He mapped out a program— three sessions per week for three months, totaling a little over two thousand dollars. Without thinking twice, I dug my credit card out of my wallet and handed it over. Pierre threw his head back and erupted into a fit of laughter.

"I totally had you!" he cried, wiping tears from his eyes from cracking himself up. "You don't need to pay for training! You're one of us now! But I totally had you!"

Apparently, this was a test I had failed. I felt foolish for falling for his prank, and still mortified by how out of shape I had gotten. Pierre continued on by showing me how I would sign someone up and finalize a training agreement if I was the one giving the assessment.

Then he offered to train me himself in his free time. I accepted his offer graciously, and we scheduled my first workout for the very next evening. Those workouts quickly turned into us dating, secretly, because he was my manager. I couldn't help myself. I just *loved* a guy who would put me down and make me feel like a fat piece of shit.

The night after the fitness assessment I went home, stripped down to my bra and thong, and set up my Canon PowerShot digital camera.

I took a series of photos of myself, as my "before" pictures. I studied myself from every angle, looking at how grotesque my body had become. I was unbearably disappointed in myself. I couldn't believe I'd allowed myself to eat the way I did in Spain. In my mind, to succeed as a personal trainer, I needed to be a walking billboard for my services— so I needed to get *serious*.

I spent the rest of the night creating the perfect plan for the next couple of months: Intense workouts six days a week, plus a strict diet with lots of protein shakes and minimal carbs.

This is it. I told myself, always believing my next diet plan would be the last one— a final solution to The Problem and my Problem Areas.

No more messing around.

February 2009; age 21

I was nervous as hell giving my very first fitness assessment as a personal trainer. Miraculously, the guy signed up for training. I had my very first client!

As my client list grew, my confidence grew, too. I loved every minute of my new job, and as it turned out, I was really good at it. Helping my clients get strong and healthy made me feel more fulfilled than anything ever had before— and even though I felt like a total fraud in the beginning, my background of trying to perfect my own Problem Areas had made me way more knowledgeable about fitness than your average bear.

The other personal trainers, who had always been generous with their time when I worked the front desk, were now even more inclined to teach me. I worked out with almost every trainer on staff at some point, just to learn different styles and techniques. In the break room where we ate, I'd inquire about what the trainers were eating and why, taking notes on their nutrition hacks. Some trainers would eat pizza and donuts, or whatever they wanted, but the most fit of the bunch would bring perfectly portioned meals of things like grilled chicken, steamed broccoli, and brown rice.

A handful of trainers competed in bodybuilding shows. Watching them prepare through months and months of meticulous dieting and grueling training fascinated me, and I wanted to learn more. Their bodies changed week after week, right before my eyes. The last few weeks before a show, they'd grow depleted, tired, and cranky, their cheekbones gaunt, and veins bulging out of their forearms. I learned the term for that is "vascular," and it's like a badge of honor in the very peculiar world of bodybuilding. It indicates that you're exceptionally lean.

When someone would snap at work, it was a natural (and accepted) excuse to say they were "one week out," from a show, so they'd have permission to act like a crazed monster. Insanity by carb depletion was a solid get-out-of-jail-free pass at XSport Fitness.

One evening after I finished training my clients, I climbed up onto the StepMill next to Sal, another trainer, who was two weeks out from a competition.

"You look awesome," I told him. He was hunched over, propping his upper body up on the handlebars, slowly climbing this staircase to nowhere, looking all robotic and expressionless. "How are you feeling?"

"I'm shot," he admitted. As exhausted as he appeared, I saw him perk up from my interest and attention in what he was doing. Competitors love nothing more than to tell you about the sacrifices they're making. "Two weeks to go. I'm doing two hours of cardio a day now, on zero carbs."

Since he seemed willing and eager to pass the time discussing the details of his competition prep, I decided to pick his brain on every detail. He got specific, telling me what he was eating, how he was training, how he practiced posing, what those last two weeks entailed, what it felt like to be onstage, and what he couldn't wait to eat when the show was over.

"A whole pepperoni pizza, a regular Pepsi, and a giant bag of Reese's Peanut Butter Cups. I can't *wait!*" he shared with a gleam in his eyes. Then he glanced over at me.

"You know Justine, *you* could compete. It's not just bodybuilding. They have the figure division for women that's not as muscular."

I was speechless for a moment.

Someone thinks I can compete? I could get onstage, in front of hundreds of people, and show off an incredibly fit, awe-inspiring physique?

"Really?" I asked, always thirsty to have my ego stroked by the words of others. "I've never thought about it— but that would be so cool. I'd *love* to be that fit."

"You could totally do it. You have a good frame, and a pretty face. I think you'd do well. It's just dedication, you know? You sacrifice a lot for a period of time— but it's worth it when you get the results," he told me.

I beamed. I imagined myself confidently on stage in a bikini and heels, tanned, toned, abs popping, and smiling a big smile of pride and satisfaction. Just like the fitness models in the magazines I so desperately wanted to be like. The picture of health and fitness!

Right then and there, I tucked that image of myself into my heart to hold close, until the time was right.

October 2009; age 22

After graduating from Hofstra University in the spring, I moved back to Wisconsin to live with my mom and her new husband. I quickly got hired as a personal trainer at a brand-new Gold's Gym nearby. With no real responsibilities or commitments outside of personal training, I decided there was no better time for me to train for a figure competition.

I looked up local shows on the Internet, and two weeks later, I got to witness my very first bodybuilding show. Pierre was supposed to come with me, but a last-minute meeting got in the way, so he moved his trip to the following weekend. I'd expected our relationship to end when I left New York, but he kept booking trips to visit me, sometimes even unannounced.

I drove an hour north and attended the show alone, notebook and pen in hand. Always a student, hungry to learn more. I studied the competitors and marveled at the pliability of the human body. I'd never seen bodies like this— it was like looking at an anatomy chart of the human muscular system. They were magnificent. The women parading around on stage looked like the cover models on my fitness magazines— perfectly polished with tight, perky glutes, chiseled abs, and big smiles.

This is it, I thought. *I'm starting my prep tomorrow.*

And I did, although I had no clue what I was doing at first. Even though I'd absorbed everything I could from the trainers back in New York, I soon realized I had a *lot* to learn. There is a very big difference between "eating healthy" and "eating to compete."

Thankfully I'd befriended a woman at the gym who had competed before. Her name was Jen, and even though she was only five feet tall, she could lift more than most of the guys in the weight room.

"If you're serious about competing, you need to hire a coach," she advised between sets of pull ups. It was back and biceps day. In the world of *serious* weight lifting, you break up muscle groups to hit them separately once or twice a week, enabling you to lift heavier and more frequently, while allowing your other muscles time to recover.

"I know a guy in Pittsburgh who trains hundreds of girls. Dave Michaels," she told me. "I'll text you his information."

I felt excited about hiring a coach and getting one step closer to my dream of being a champion onstage. As soon as Jen sent the information, I emailed the coach to ask how soon I could start.

The next week I received my very first contest prep plan. Dave emailed documents with specific details for my training program, supplement plan, and meal plan. The meal plan consisted of five small meals, plus a protein shake that I was to drink right after training.

- Meal One: 3 egg whites and ⅓ cup plain oatmeal

- Meal Two: 2 plain, unsalted rice cakes with 1 tbsp almond butter

- Meals Three and Four: 3 oz plain grilled chicken, turkey, or white fish, ½ cup steamed brown rice, and 1 cup broccoli or spinach.

- Meal Five: 1 protein shake with water

- Plus 1 protein shake with water after training

"So you eat the same exact stuff every single day?" I asked Jen as we were looking over the plan together.

"Yeah, that's part of competing. Don't worry. It gets easier over time, and eventually you'll just be happy to eat *anything*," she informed me.

Well, that sounds fun.

Contest prep was far more rigid and regimented than I had imagined, but it felt like an adventure. Besides entertaining Pierre when he'd visit, I had no social life to speak of outside of the gym. I hadn't stayed close to anyone from high school, so I didn't feel like I was missing out on anything by not going out and partying. I was far more interested in being crowned a fitness champion than getting drunk at local bars.

My plan also dictated that I drink an entire *gallon* of water every day— which at first seemed straight up impossible.

"I'm peeing every thirty minutes! I can't do this," I complained to Jen.

"You'll get used to it," she promised. And I did. After two weeks I was finally able to drink a whole gallon of water in a day without feeling like a human water balloon, ready to burst. M   y body started changing rapidly. My mom would take pictures of me in my bikini every week to send to my coach, and I could see the changes right away.

After the first month, I was already down six pounds. I loved the results, but I wasn't feeling too hot. After weight training, I often felt nauseous and lightheaded. I reached out to Dave, and after a few days, he emailed me back, telling me to eat an apple right after training to bring my blood sugar back up.

The apple became the tastiest, most enjoyable part of my whole day. When you're eating no other sugar and very low carbs in general, an apple starts to taste like the best candy you've ever had.

Two months into training and dieting for my first competition, I attended a posing workshop, hosted by a woman named Lynette Ray, a local bodybuilding champion.

"Welcome ladies! Thanks for coming," Lynette greeted the group after we had all checked in. She was soft-spoken and petite, but completely ripped. I'd never seen a woman look so muscular yet so feminine at the same time. Lynette had a warm, calming presence about her. She told us a little about her journey, then showed us some posing tricks, inviting us to stand up to practice. She came around to each of us to make adjustments and offer feedback.

"You have a beautiful frame," Lynette remarked when she got to me. I thought back to that moment on the Stepmill, when Sal told me I had a "good frame," and could compete. For so many years I'd been so engrossed with fixing my Problem Areas. It was nice to know my general *structure* was adequate.

As the workshop came to a close, Lynette stuck around to answer questions. I hung out the longest, asking her every question on my mind about dieting and training and supplements and where to order a competition suit (a very bedazzled, overpriced custom bikini.) She answered my questions patiently as I sucked up every detail like a little sponge.

"Are you taking on new clients?" I finally asked. Lynette gave me her card to contact her to get started. She was so knowledgeable, and made me feel seen and safe. I hadn't developed a closeness with my coach in Pittsburgh, and I felt working with a woman would be more aligned for me. I cancelled my program with Dave and started with Lynette the following week.

Her meal plan was a *lot* more flexible. I was able to pick and choose from a long list of foods to total the macronutrient goals she gave me. Macronutrients, or "macros," in the fitness world, are proteins, carbs, and fats. I loved being able to create a more enjoyable eating plan for myself—totaling up my macros like a giant puzzle to create meals that satisfied the goals set for me, *and* my tastebuds.

- Meal One: 2 Blueberry Protein Pancakes
- Meal Two: 2 hard boiled eggs + ⅓ cup oats
- Meal Three: 1 scoop of protein + 1 apple (after training)
- Meal Four: 4 oz turkey breast, 3 oz sweet potato, salad with mixed greens + vinegar and 2 tsp olive oil
- Meal Five: 2 Tuna or Salmon Cakes + ½ cup wild rice and green beans or broccoli
- Meal Six: 1 c. fat free plain Greek yogurt + ¼ cup raw almonds

Her workout routine was a delightful upgrade from my first plan as well. Instead of an hour of cardio every day, Lynette had me doing short bursts of cardio, such as sprint intervals, a few times a week.

My body adjusted quickly, and I felt awesome eating more carbs and fats, doing less cardio, and focusing more on lifting weights. That lightheaded, nauseous feeling disappeared. I was growing stronger every week, setting records of how much weight I could lift. I had never felt stronger, fueled by wholesome, nutrient dense foods, without deprivation.

As the show got closer and my body continued to transform, I *loved* being at the gym. My clients were buzzing with excitement for me, and compliments started rolling in from everyone I knew there—and even strangers.

"You look *fantastic*!" they'd say. "I'm sure you'll win!"

High off validation from others, I began to admire my reflection in the mirror with great pride. I envisioned myself on stage, being awarded first place and overall champion in my division.

Me. A winner. A poster girl for fitness. I can taste it already!

April 2010; 23 years old

I found myself backstage at my first show, wide-eyed and taking it all in. It was crowded and noisy, and the air was thick with sweat, unrefrigerated food, and tanning solution.

Dark orange, greased up bodies were everywhere. You could cut the tension with a knife as everyone tried to stake out a small space for themselves and their belongings. The mood was very serious, and everyone was eyeing one another, sizing up their competition. Bodybuilding is not a social sport— it's actually very isolating. It tends to attract introverts and loners who have something to *prove*. As a result, the environment backstage is usually unfriendly, bordering on hostile.

I found an unclaimed corner to set up shop for the day. I'd been up since the crack of dawn, so I'd already done my hair and makeup. I even put on my competition suit before leaving home, so I didn't have much to do as I waited for prejudging to begin.

I felt like a million bucks that day. Lynette gave me thorough instructions on how to get the perfect tan, using two different products over the course of five days to layer on a dark, even bronze color. I nailed it. My tan was seamless perfection.

My face was glowing from months of eating unprocessed foods and not drinking alcohol. The cellulite I'd always despised on my butt and thighs was nowhere to be found. I looked like the ultimate picture of health—123 pounds, 15 percent body fat— and I couldn't help but smile to myself every time I caught my reflection in a mirror.

But backstage, my self-doubt reared its ugly head as I glanced around the room nervously, eyeing these beautiful, more muscular, and more defined women. My smile quickly faded as I got lost in the trap of comparison. I couldn't fathom how I was going to compete with these other women in the figure division. I looked down at my body and started questioning if I should even get onstage.

The show started promptly at 10 a.m., and before I could talk myself out of competing, a woman with a clipboard came backstage and called for all of the figure competitors to line up according to our numbers. I was number sixty-three, part of the B-Class in the figure division.

Divisions are split up according to height: "A" is the shortest, and each letter afterwards represents a different height range, depending on the number of competitors in the show. This was a very small, local show, so there were only two height classes: A-class, with women under 5'5", and my class, the B-class, 5'5" and up. I watched as the women in the A-class disappeared to go out on stage, knowing I'd be on shortly.

"Okay, Figure B! Figure B, you're up next!" a short, muscular man wearing a tight white polo shirt shouted. I lined up with six other women in my height class, and waited anxiously behind the curtain. I caught a glimpse of the judges and the audience from where I stood, and my heart started racing. The woman in front of me was announced, and I watched her confidently saunter out onto the stage.

I'm next.

"Number sixty-three, Justine Moore from Waukesha, Wisconsin," I heard over the microphone.

Oh God, I thought, my heart pounding out of my chest, palms sweating. *This is IT.*

Somehow, my legs started to walk, as I tried my best not to squint in the bright stage lights. I walked to my designated spot on stage, marked by an "X" with tape on the floor. I hit my front pose and forced a smile. My entire body was shaking.

Calm down, stop shaking! I thought frantically.

I hit my side pose, my back pose, another side pose, shaking uncontrollably the entire time. I finished with a quick wave to the audience before exiting off the other side of the stage. Once backstage, I exhaled deeply, feeling disappointment wash over me due to my body's betrayal. I didn't have much time to process though, as callouts were upon us.

Callouts in a fitness competition are when all the competitors in a class come back on stage and line up, and the judges call you out by number, according to how well you're going to place. Typically, the first five competitors called out will place as the top five. Judges will ask competitors to switch places with one another to compare physiques until they have their final line up. After the callouts are over, you usually have a pretty clear idea of how you're going to place.

Once lined up, the backstage expeditor motioned for us to go back onstage.

Please, please, please don't shake this time, I silently prayed.

The head judge asked us to do quarter turns, as the panel of predominantly male judges assessed our physiques from every angle. I pulled my abs in tight and forced a big, fake smile, hoping the audience couldn't tell how nervous I was. The judges scribbled notes and whispered to one another.

"Numbers sixty-five, sixty-one, sixty-six, sixty, and sixty-four, please step out," the head judge called out over the microphone.

Five of the other women in my class stepped forward and began posing their hearts out. Only myself and one other woman remained on the backline. The other competitor who wasn't called forward was clearly out of shape. I heard her story backstage—

she'd lost nearly fifty pounds over the past year and just wanted to get on stage to celebrate how far she's come.

So, it was just her and I who wouldn't place in the top five. Since the show was small, many classes only had four or five competitors, so nearly every single competitor would be leaving with a trophy except for her and I.

I felt my heart drop, along with the smile on my face. I felt so foolish to have thought I could win— and here I was, leaving empty-handed, not even able to place top five in a tiny Wisconsin show. I started thinking of all the people at my gym who had wished me luck and cheered me on throughout my prep.

I can't believe I thought I could actually do well in this. What will everyone at the gym think? Will they laugh at me behind my back?

The head judge dismissed the women in the top three spots. I inched closer to the front of the line and quickly regained my focus next to the fourth and fifth place competitors. This is how judges attempt to ease the low-scoring competitors' humiliation. The judges quickly scribbled their scores as the head judge bellowed, "Thank you. Please exit stage right."

I choked back hot tears as my clear plastic heels clicked off stage. My body somehow kept moving fervently toward my belongings, as my mind wandered aimlessly.

That night as I drove home from the show, empty-handed and defeated, I concluded Lynette's plan for me hadn't been aggressive enough. After seeing the winning competitors up close, I realized the desired look at these shows isn't fit and healthy. It's extreme. I'd been so proud to reach 15 percent body fat, but I estimated the women who placed well were much leaner than that. And if I wanted to be a winner, I needed to be much leaner too.

The next morning, I woke up at 6 a.m. sharp to do fasted cardio— which is cardio in a fasted state, not eating or drinking anything before hand, other than water. Lynette didn't believe in this method, but her loving, gentle approach to getting fit obviously wasn't cutting it for me.

I was desperate for any help I could get to drastically improve before my second show in just thirteen days, so as I torched body fat on the elliptical, I sent a text message to the one person I knew could help— Pierre. He'd stopped visiting me three months prior, after he went through my text messages when I was asleep, and discovered I'd been hanging out with a guy from the gym. Despite me breaking his heart, we had kept in touch through occasional texts, and I knew he had recently started training with a big-name bodybuilder professional.

Pierre immediately agreed to help and told me he'd get advice from his coach on what I could do to up the ante for this next show. Later that day he reported back with suggestions:

- 60 minutes of fasted cardio every morning

- Cut all carbs

- Meal one: 6 egg whites and asparagus

- Meals two through four: vary between 4 oz grilled chicken, extra lean ground turkey, salmon or tuna, and 1 cup of broccoli or spinach

- Meal five: 2/3 cup low fat cottage cheese

- Whey isolate protein shake with water after training

I dove right in. But within two days, I began having nasty hypoglycemic spells. If you've never tortured yourself with a carb-free diet, kudos to you. Here's what you're missing out on—nausea, dizziness, blurry vision, inability to think clearly, and extreme crankiness. Think hangry meets mentally unstable. I was a real treat to be around.

Later that week, my family was thoughtful enough to prepare a meal I could actually eat with them— grilled salmon and asparagus, plus a big spinach salad. Only my dad's fiancé made the mistake of putting sliced strawberries on the salad and serving it to me.

"I can't eat *strawberries*!" I ranted as I whipped about thirty calories worth of berries off my salad like they were poison. Everyone else at the table rolled their eyes. Even if I had eaten those strawberries, I don't believe I would've placed better than I did in my second competition—eighth out of thirteen.

"I can't wait for this to be over," my dad said under his breath. Who knew my obsessive new lifestyle wouldn't be "over" for another four years?

May 2010; age 23

Despite the feelings of failure and defeat from my first competitions, getting into peak shape wasn't a total loss for me. I did a photo shoot with a local photographer the week of my second show, and when the pictures came back, I was awestruck by how good I looked. The professional studio lighting beautifully accentuated the lines of my abs, the curve of my tiny waist, and my toned backside, all of which I had worked *so* hard to perfect.

Eager to post them on Facebook, I uploaded ten of my favorite images, along with photos taken at my competitions. Within two days, I had over a hundred likes and dozens of comments and messages— from relatives, friends, co-workers, and even from people I went to high school with, who I hadn't spoken to in years. Guys who wouldn't give me the time of day back in school started coming out of the woodwork, flirtatiously complimenting my looks, and saying things like "I wish we'd spent more time together." I'd sit in front of my mom's desktop computer and re-read the messages over and over again, savoring every speck of the attention like a gourmet feast.

Sal, my old pal from XSport Fitness who planted the initial seed about competing, reached out to say how proud he was. He suggested I build a profile on a website called Model Mayhem to get some exposure with fitness photographers.

Within a day of being on the site, I had an inbox full of messages from photographers who wanted to work with me. Most were offering "TFP" shoots— which, in the modeling world, stands for Time For Photos, or giving your time as a model in exchange for the images, with no money exchanged between either party.

I felt a giddy thrill over all the attention, and the possibility of actually becoming a fitness model. But in my mind, if I was *really* going to achieve success in the fitness world, I needed a breast augmentation. The compliments boosted my ego, yet I knew I needed to do more. The majority of the women I'd competed with had implants, along with most of the fitness models in the magazines I studied daily.

I despised my natural breasts. They were small, tragically asymmetrical, and sort of cone shaped. Unfortunately, it was a Problem Area that couldn't be corrected with crunches, sidekicks, or a diet, or else I sure as hell would have done something about it by then.

Since I couldn't fix it, I hid it. I'd wear padded bras, even *underneath* my sports bras at the gym. When I hooked up with guys, I'd do whatever I could to keep my bra on.

Two years prior, I had begged my mom to let me get implants.

"You're still so young," she argued. "Your breasts will change as you get older."

And now they *had* changed— they were even smaller after losing so much body fat. I'd lost all faith that my boobs would eventually "come in."

Although my mom still wasn't keen on the idea of me going under the knife, she came with me to the consultation.

In the waiting room of the plastic surgeon's office, I felt dizzy with excitement as I leafed through glossy pamphlets with Before & After images, imagining my future body. About 90 percent of my daydreaming revolved around my future body. All day I'd obsess over how to make my body better, fantasizing about how amazing I'd look, which surely would translate to *feeling* amazing too. Once my Problem Areas were fixed, I would *finally* feel better about my outward appearance, I reasoned.

"Justine?" an attractive blonde nurse called out. She led my mom and me to an exam room.

"Dr. Keller will be with you shortly," she said, leaving us alone. A few minutes later, the door opened and Dr. Keller stepped into the room.

He dove into questions about my ideal breast size and shape, as well as the various methods for inserting the implants. After discussing all of the details, we moved on to the physical exam portion of the consultation.

"Hmm, yeah. So, you've got a *lot* of asymmetry. Over a half cup size variation between the left and the right, which is really significant," Dr. Keller mused, peering over his rimless glasses as he slid a cold magic marker across my naked breasts. I would realize five years later that more than half of all women actually have asymmetry in their breasts, but facts like that don't sell expensive surgeries. "Your breasts are very cone-shaped, so the surgery will give you a much rounder, more aesthetically pleasing shape."

Silence echoed across the room as my mom purposefully looked away, as she hadn't seen me topless in at least ten years. Dr. Keller nonchalantly drew all over my uneven cone-shaped mutant boobs like a football coach mapping out a game plan. I felt exposed and embarrassed, but it was just another day at the office for him.

He must think I'm a freak of nature, I thought.

"How soon can I have the surgery?" I asked, impatient to fix the train wreck on my chest so I could look like a *real* fitness model.

"We can probably squeeze you in sometime next month," Dr. Keller responded. "After taking a closer look I know you're going to be extremely happy with your results."

I took the first available appointment.

The total cost was $8500—$5500 for the breast augmentation, and an additional $3000 for a lift, which I hadn't been expecting. I figured it was kind of like a mutant tax, for having such uneven boobs. I had $7500 saved in the bank, which I had expected to cover the entire surgery. I was determined to pay in full to avoid interest charges, so now I needed to come up with an extra $1000.

"I'll help you pay for it," my mom offered the second we were back in her car.

"You're in favor of this now?" I asked, surprised by her drastic change of heart.

"I didn't realize they were so uneven. I want you to feel good about your body," she replied. "You need to tell your dad before you have the surgery, though. He'd be upset if he found out afterward."

"Yeah, I know," I said, already dreading that awkward conversation.

Before my surgery date, I took a trip to Las Vegas to meet up with Adriana. It was our first time seeing each other in ten months, since I had moved from New York after graduation.

Post-competition I was super into eating everything I wasn't permitted to eat during the six months of contest prep, so indulging at Vegas restaurants—particularly the buffets— was high up on my wish list of activities.

Sadly, Adriana wasn't on the same page. When she arrived at The Palms, I immediately noticed she had lost a lot of weight. She'd always had a beautiful, athletic, fit body, but now she looked noticeably underweight. After sitting down for a couple of meals together, I saw why.

She had taken our old "drunkorexic" lifestyle to a whole new level. Every time we'd go to order she'd glance over the menu anxiously and say, "I'm not really hungry— but *you* should eat!"

So I would. I'd feast my heart out and she'd just sit there and sip a glass of wine. I didn't see her eat more than a bite or two the entire three-day trip. Years later I would reconnect with her on social media after we had lost touch, and I was relieved to hear she had worked through her issues with food.

Our last day in Vegas, I was tapped out with the party scene. Adriana left me in bed and went down to the raging 10 a.m. pool party. Thirty minutes later I got a text from her, insisting I come join the party because she met some "fitness people."

I chugged a bottle of water, threw on a shimmery gold string bikini, cut-off denim shorts and five-inch heels. My body was still super fit from competing the previous month, so I was feeling more confident than usual. I put sunglasses over my tired eyes and headed to the pool.

Across a sea of gorgeous people, I spotted Adriana flirting with the most muscular dude I'd ever seen. I made my way over to them.

"You're here!" Adriana shrieked, reaching for my hand and pulling me up to the elevated cabana. She introduced me to her new Hulk-like friend, Derek. As impressed as I was with Derek's eight-pack and bulging biceps, I was even more impressed when he introduced me to Ken, the brand manager of MET-Rx, one of the largest supplement companies in the world.

I pounced on the opportunity to tell them I'd just competed, showing them pictures on my phone from my professional photoshoot. Ken was impressed. He gave me his card and told me to email him when I got back home.

"We're always looking for brand ambassadors to work expos and stuff like that. Your look is exactly what we want," Ken told me, then excused himself to go to a meeting. I wanted to pinch myself.

It's really happening! How lucky am I?! I thought, marveling over this random encounter with a renewed sense of hope I could achieve my dreams in the fitness industry after all.

I tucked that business card away for safekeeping.

When the plane landed in Wisconsin, I typed up an email to Ken. After proofreading it a dozen times, I took a deep breath and clicked "send."

Then I waited. And waited. And waited.

Ten painfully slow days later, I got an email back. Ken told me there wasn't really work for me in Wisconsin, but he'd do his best to have me work the Arnold Sports Festival next spring in Ohio. I was over the moon. What a thrill, imagining myself working the world's largest fitness expo!

Ironically, Ken lived in Long Island, where the MET-Rx headquarters were. The wheels began to turn. I knew if I really wanted to give this fitness thing a go, I needed to move again. It wasn't going to happen for me in Wisconsin. New York made the most sense, since I already knew the area and had connections there. I quietly began arranging a move back to New York later that year, after healing from surgery and saving up some cash.

***

The week before my breast augmentation, I went to my dad's house for dinner.

"Hey Dad," I said as I joined him on the deck where he was enjoying a beer after work. "I have to talk to you about something."

"What's up, sweetie?" he asked.

"Next week I'm getting surgery. I decided to get breast implants. I've been thinking about it for a long time, and I decided I really want them."

"I knew it," he responded with a sigh. "I knew this was coming after I went to your show and saw all those other women. But you know I always support you. Whatever makes you happy."

My parents always let me make my own decisions, for better or for worse. Some of those decisions have been pretty rotten, but I've always been grateful they let me figure things out on my own. I'm a passionate little creature— a true Aries, if you're into astrology like me— so I don't think I would have learned any other way.

June 2010; age 23

The day came for my breast augmentation. The surgery was scheduled early in the morning—so I woke up at the crack of dawn, drank some water (since nothing else was permitted) and tried to stay calm as the nerves of being put under for surgery crept in.

My mom drove me to the hospital where I checked in and they set me up in a private room and started my IV. Everything moved so quickly. Before I knew it, the anesthesiologist was having me count back from ten.

"Ten, nine, eight, seven..." and I was out like a light. I remember waking up groggily, feeling like a semi-truck hit my chest. My mom saw my eyes open and rushed to my side.

"Hi baby! Everything went great! How do you feel?" she asked.

"Sore," I mumbled. "And nauseous."

The next three days were a blur of falling in and out of sleep, waking up only to take more prescription painkillers. The worst part was the pain from the stitches around my nipples. My breasts were enormous and swollen from the implants and massive inflammation post-surgery, so my nipples were being stretched to the max. The stitches tugged at my skin, feeling like they were going to explode right off of my body at any moment.

Swelling and painful stitches aside, I was beyond delighted with my results. My breasts were round, full, big, and beautiful—and perfectly symmetrical. They looked like the flawless breasts of Victoria's Secret models, or like my childhood Barbie dolls. They were fantastic.

I hadn't realized that changing the size of my breasts would make me feel different about my entire body. Suddenly the rest of my Problem Areas seemed less problematic. Large breasts made my lower half, which had always been fuller or "pear shaped" according to magazines, feel more proportionate. My new D-cups made my waist look smaller, and my tummy flatter.

As a woman, you're supposed to have curves in "all the right places," or in other words, have body fat in your boobs and ass only, while being skinny everywhere else. It's a scientific impossibility for almost all womankind, but through dieting, exercise, and now surgery, I did it. *Mission accomplished!* Every time I'd look down at my body or look in the mirror, I'd smile. I felt sexy naked for the first time in my life, and now, nothing could stand in my way of having the perfect body.

September 2010; age 23

With my body more "perfect" than ever, I set my sights on giving fitness modeling and competing my all. My bank account was drained from the surgery, but practicality never stopped me. Even if I failed miserably— I had to try.

I packed up my Saturn Vue and drove back out to Long Island. My parents told me they would always support me and my dreams— but financially, I was on my own.

Pierre ended up being a lifesaver, helping me find a place and paying my first month's rent. I knew his underlying motive was trying to get back together, but I wasn't in a place to refuse any sort of financial aid in making my dreams a reality.

My first six months back in New York, I had nothing more than a mattress on the floor, a small kitchen table with two chairs that I'd bought used, and my personal belongings in a dreary basement apartment. Rent was dirt cheap, because basement apartments were illegal in New York, but that's what I could afford.

It was the ugliest place you can imagine— wood paneling on the walls, dark brown carpeting, and next to zero natural lighting, since it was underground. Aesthetically it was a hideous place to live, but I loved it. It was *mine. All* mine— the first place I had to myself. No one could tell me what to do, or verbally accost me over cracking countless eggs on the countertops, discarding the yolks in the trash and stinking up the kitchen baking salmon. I was free to live my weird little lifestyle in peace.

I got my job back at XSport Fitness with a generous raise from Pierre, and even got to reunite with some of my old clients. With school behind me and bills to pay, I was working more than ever— sometimes training up to ten clients a day. It felt great to be back at that gym, surrounded by the personal training team I'd grown so close to over the years.

I reached out to Ken, the brand manager of MET-Rx, to share the news of my move.

"This is wonderful!" he told me when I called. "Now that you're in New York we can hire you to do demos in your area!"

Ken put me in touch with the regional manager for the northeast, and a week later, they began booking me to go to gyms to represent MET-Rx. I'd set up a table and hand out samples of pre-workout drinks and protein bars while telling gym go-ers why they should use our products. My fitness modeling career was up and running!

The other benefit of being in New York was a higher level of competition. In Wisconsin, I had competed at small, natural shows— natural meaning they drug test the competitors. But if I *really* wanted to be somebody in the fitness community, the NPC and IFBB organizations were the way to go.

The NPC, or National Physique Committee, is the largest amateur bodybuilding organization in the United States. The competition is stiff, partially because their shows are the most popular, and partially because drug use is rampant.

NPC shows are open to anyone who thinks they are ready to compete, whereas you must *earn* your way into the IFBB Pro League, or International Federation of Bodybuilders. To become an IFBB Pro, you have to place top five at a state level NPC show, then place first at an NPC National Pro-Qualifier, a.k.a. "Nationals."

It was my dream to become an IFBB pro, or "get my Pro Card."

I selected my next show: the NPC Metropolitan in April of 2011, one year after my first two competitions.

It was at this very time that the NPC and IFBB created a brand-new division for women: Bikini Division. It was the look of a toned fitness model— the kind of girl you'd see on the beach and think, "My gosh, what a body!"

These ideal bikini competitor bodies were not only thin, but chiseled and toned in all the right places. I thought they were so beautiful, like sculptures, painstakingly crafted through months and months of discipline. You'd take one look and think, "*A lot* of work went into that!"

The desired look was less muscular than the Figure Division. The official guidelines for the NPC Bikini Division state:

Bikini athletes should display:

1. A foundation of muscle which gives shape to the female body

2. Full round glutes with a slight separation between the hamstring and glute area

3. Small amount of roundness in the delts

4. Conditioned core

5. Overall look- hair, makeup, suit, and tan

Hearing about the new Bikini Division was music to my ears. My genetics make building muscle extremely challenging. To this day, I've never been able to do a real pull-up. It would have taken *years* of intense training, meticulous dieting, and steroid use for me to measure up to the women who were winning shows in the NPC Figure Division.

When it came time to select a new coach, I asked Sal, the trainer who first suggested I compete nearly two years prior. He agreed to help me train and diet for the show, and together we crafted a game plan.

Once again, I dove in and contest prep consumed my entire life. This time I wasn't alone though— five of the other personal trainers decided to compete in the same upcoming show, including Pierre.

I loved having people around me who actually *got it*. Instead of explaining why I couldn't eat egg yolks to my family, I was surrounded by a new sort of family, who spoke my language using terms like "two-a-days," (where you do two bouts of cardio, broken up throughout the day), and "water loading," (doubling your intake of water the week before a show to get your body to expel extra water, before drastically decreasing it to get your physique as "dry" and tight as possible.)

Since Pierre and I worked together and were now preparing for the same show, we began spending a lot of time together. Almost unconsciously, I found myself in a relationship with him again. I didn't love him the way he loved me, but he offered the support and stability I felt I needed to achieve my dreams. He understood exactly what I wanted to achieve, and believed in me enough to help me make it happen, and I loved *that*.

I never bothered to ask myself, *What's best for me and my wellbeing? What does my heart and soul want?*

Instead, it was only, *what will advance my fitness career? What will help me make it to the top in this industry?*

I trained and dieted my butt off, quite literally, losing the fifteen pounds I'd gained after surgery the summer before. As my next show got closer, my physique looked better than ever. Random people would stop me in the gym to applaud my hard work.

Men would say things like, "You look awesome! Good luck!"

Women would say things like, "You look amazing! Are you taking new clients? What are you eating? Can you teach me how to look like you?"

I held an image in my head of myself onstage, a vision of perfection and grace, having my hand held up high as the crowned first-place winner, a bouquet of flowers in my arm, a shiny gold trophy at my feet, while the crowd cheered loudly. In this vision I felt euphoric and victorious. I imagined this scene countless times as I was training through physical exhaustion, or saying "no" to pizza in the breakroom while choking down slimy pre-cooked chicken breasts.

April 2011; age 24

I found myself backstage at the Metropolitan in New York City, surrounded by the XSport Fitness crew of myself, Pierre, and four other personal trainers competing that day. My attention was fixed upon the other bikini competitors. There were over a hundred.

At the shows in Wisconsin, there were just two height classes, with less than fifteen women in each of them. But here in New York City, there were *six* height classes for the bikini division, with at least twenty in each class.

I began to study the other women and realized again I didn't measure up. I was the leanest I'd ever been, and this was my first competition post-breast augmentation. But my spray tan was blotchy, my hair looked greasy from spraying too much oil over my tan, and the suit I ordered online was ill-fitting and unflattering. Little aesthetic details can make or break you when you're onstage.

I'm still not as good as them, I thought to myself.

A year had passed since my first competitions— another year of training and dieting, not to mention undergoing surgery and moving back to New York, and still I couldn't measure up to these women I was competing against. It felt so defeating to work so hard, to be at my *third* competition, and to still feel so far from where I wanted to be.

I noticed a large group of women wearing matching black cover ups with "Knockout Squad," emblazoned across the back. They huddled together in their own private section, as if they were royalty, keeping their distance from the peasants.

Each woman was more stunning than the next. They were like the most pristine box of crayons— all uniform, except in different colored jewel-toned bikinis. They were living, breathing Barbie dolls, flawless from head to toe, with perfect hair, perfect tans, perfect suits, and impossibly tiny waistlines. I marveled at them from afar, and wanted to do whatever it took to be in that circle.

What are these girls doing? I wondered. *I need to learn their secrets.*

I was not surprised when all of the top five trophies were awarded to Knockout Squad competitors.

I placed eleventh out of twenty, which wasn't bad considering I was a "nobody" in the NPC. In other organizations you can be unknown, show up, and place well in a show if you look better than everyone else, but not in the NPC.

The NPC is extremely political— you not only have to look the part, but you also need to know the right people, hire the right coaches, and kiss the right asses. I learned this quickly, and accepted the challenge. I wanted to learn the rules of this game and play it better than anyone else.

After the show, Sal came up to congratulate me.

"So, what do I eat now?" I asked him.

"Whatever you want! You're in the off-season now. Go nuts."

For someone who had been surviving off of plain broiled chicken breast and green vegetables for months, this was lethal advice.

I *did* go nuts, and then some. I began binge eating right after the finals and didn't stop for two days, except to sleep. I scarfed down bags of Easter candy, cupcakes, brownies, McDonald's chicken nuggets and French fries, pancakes, chips and pizza.

Before the show, I was so preoccupied with what I couldn't eat that I would actually journal extensive lists with all the yummy foods I was going to consume afterwards. This kind of behavior isn't at all uncommon in the industry. I even knew competitors who would make their phone background some sort of delicious "food porn," to gawk at while doing endless hours of cardio.

Aside from the way restriction messes with your head, it messes with your hormones, too. When you reintroduce sugary, fatty, or high-carb foods to your body after a period of deprivation, a hormone called ghrelin is released in excess, making it nearly impossible to stop eating.

And if that wasn't enough, your body becomes inflamed from all of this binging, and you retain massive amounts of water, because your body isn't used to high sodium and carbohydrate intake.

I gained fifteen pounds within five days after my show that April.

Fifteen pounds in five days!

My entire abdomen felt painful to the touch, because my poor internal organs were so swollen from the abuse I had put my body through.

After that I tried to clean up my diet and find some sort of balance, but I just had no idea how. During the week I'd return to my ways of over-restricting until I couldn't take it anymore, then on the weekends I'd binge on pasta, cake, and whole pints of ice cream from Cold Stone Creamery. Once I even ate a whole quart!

Just like in college, the whole binge, repent, restrict, repeat cycle was highly detrimental, and within a month, twenty pounds of body fat took up residence on my body. Yet again I was out of shape and feeling defeated.

I couldn't stomach it anymore. If I was serious, I needed professional help from the best in the business. I recalled what I'd observed at the last show, and knew the next step. The Knockout Squad was the answer I was looking for to achieve my ultimate goals and to win.

24-year-old me, in an image that went viral in the fitness industry.

Part III: The Plan

"If you live fat in your head, then you are. If you believe you are unattractive, you will experience the world as an unattractive woman. If you hound yourself about everything you put in your mouth, you won't enjoy eating.

Regardless of the number on the scale, if the number inside your head is large, insurmountable, and loaded with meaning, then you will feel weighted down by its implications."

~Courtney E. Martin; Perfect Girls, Starving Daughters

July 2011; age 24

What are they going to think of me? I wondered incessantly on the flight to Jacksonville. *Am I going to be the most of-out-shape girl at camp?*

I tried to brush my fears aside telling myself that was *why* I was going to camp: To get the professional help I so clearly needed to get back on track and to *stay* on track, for once.

The Knockout Squad was run by the highly-esteemed Tammy Roy and her business partner, Rick Campbell. Together they'd created a notorious fitness empire, working with thousands of women worldwide. Their brand was disguised as something that empowered women, using terms like "sister," and "sisterhood," and the color pink to disarm prospective clients and hide the immense amount of psychological, emotional, and physical harm they inflicted upon so many women.

Three months had passed since I spent the day ogling the Knockout Squad competitors backstage. I'd officially joined the team and pledged my allegiance to Tammy and Rick for the low, low price of $10,000, my soul, my long-term health, and my dignity.

I was required to kick off my membership by attending a boot camp at their headquarters in Jacksonville, Florida, along with paying yearly and monthly member dues, plus additional mandatory fees for products and services I'd learn about along the way.

It cost me a pretty penny— nearly $2,000 just that first month, and what I was making as a personal trainer wasn't cutting it. Pierre generously paid for my first camp, as I picked up a second job bartending at a nightclub to supplement my income. He had recently moved in with me, after we officially became a couple again.

As my plane touched down in Jacksonville, I felt anxiety coursing through my veins. I knew joining the team was my best bet to succeed in getting my IFBB Pro Card, but I didn't know anyone on the team, and had no idea what I was getting myself into. I felt especially self-conscious and vulnerable because of the twenty pounds I'd packed on after my last competition. Extra weight on my body always felt like a massive chink in my armor.

My first Knockout Squad camp was my personal hell on earth. It was like all the demons of my childhood and adolescence were in cahoots to orchestrate the most soul-sucking, humiliating weekend imaginable.

For starters, Florida in July is no treat, especially for a Midwest girl. The mid-summer sun was blazing hot, and the humidity was so thick you could barely catch your breath just sitting around.

And there was running. Lots and *lots* of running. I came face-to-face with my old nemesis: Attempting to run alongside a herd of my peers. And by "alongside" I mean bringing up the rear, panting, utterly determined to keep up. This time my peers weren't fifth graders— they were a flock of real-life Barbie dolls, each one more impossibly perfect-looking than the last.

Veronica, one of the assistant Knockout coaches yelled to the herd of gorgeous, sweaty women, "Run to the end of the bridge and back three times! Then come inside and get ready for posing with Tammy!"

Somehow, I managed to do what I was told, choking down sticky, hot blood in the back of my throat while gasping at the muggy air. Sweat and humidity drenched my clothing right down to my lacy Victoria's Secret thong.

Once back at camp headquarters, twenty or so Knockouts grappled for personal space and a turn in one of the two tiny bathrooms. The smell lingering in the air will forever haunt me—a vile combination of sweat, rubber, asparagus pee, and self-loathing. The scent of rubber made sense when I discovered the Knockout Squad Secret for their signature inhumanly small waist: the infamous "Squeem."

"What's that thing you're wearing?" I asked a girl changing next to me. She had on this tight, rubber, corset thing around her waist.

"It's a Squeem. A waist cincher. You must be new, huh?" she replied.

"Yeah, this is my first camp. I'm not on a plan yet."

"Well, buckle up, sister! You'll be wearing one of these suckers by the end of the weekend," she told me as she picked up her plastic posing heels and went out to the main studio. I followed her out to join the other Knockouts for posing practice.

I stopped dead in my tracks. A quick scan of the room confirmed my deepest fear: I was the chubbiest girl there.

And the pastiest! I thought, berating myself. *Why the hell didn't I get a spray tan before this trip?*

I stood there completely exposed, still dripping sweat, clad in a shiny leopard-print string bikini, and clear, plastic posing heels, bedazzled with rhinestones. I desperately wished I could just evaporate into the humid air, or at the very least, have some sort of cover-up to hide my blubbery, bloated belly and cellulite-ridden butt and thighs.

The other girls pranced around, showing off their posing routines while admiring their fit, toned bodies in the full-length mirrors that encircled the room. I envied their tight, chiseled abs, flawless bronze skin and buns of steel. Almost every woman there had breast implants, and the few that didn't had padded bikini tops tied up so tight that their modest breasts were practically grazing their chins.

A hush fell over the room as Tammy Roy appeared, and everyone stood up a little straighter. Tammy sauntered over to the center of the room and sat down on the floor with her notebook, leaning back against the mirror in the front of the studio.

"Alright, Knockouts, show me what you've got! Pros are up first!" she commanded. Her voice was low and raspy from years of steroid abuse.

All of the girls sat down on the floor around her, except for the six IFBB Pros in attendance. They knew the drill. One by one, the pros came out to display their posing routines and get critiqued by Tammy.

"Yes, mama. Very nice," she said. "Arch your back harder. Arch more— *really* arch that back— think doggy style! There you go. Hold that tummy in tight, sister! And s-low *dowwwn!*"

After the pro girls wowed us with their magnificence, the remainder of us, just over a dozen "amateurs," formed a line. One by one, we were to show Tammy our posing routine for feedback.

I stood at the back of the line, dead last. I kept sweating profusely, both from the humidity and the uneasiness of knowing I had to pose in front of all of these stunning women, and have them look upon my fat, bloated, and pale body.

"Very nice, mama. You've come a long way. Keep practicing every day and you'll kick some ass at Nationals," Tammy told the girl in front of me as she finished posing. "Next!"

That was my cue.

I took a deep breath and walked to the center of the room. My plastic heels click-clacked on the hardwood floor beneath me. I stopped and hit a front pose.

All eyes were on me. Judging. I thought the girls must be holding back laughter looking at this awkward tub-of-lard posing like a complete novice.

I did some sad little quarter turns with the biggest fake smile I could muster up and then stopped when I was facing forward again. Tammy was silent the entire time, looking at me like I was a disgusting cockroach that had crawled into her pristine home. She set her notebook down and stood up.

Oh God, this can't be good. She didn't get up for anyone else.

My mind raced as she made her way over and stopped directly in front of me. Face-to-face, we were the same height. I studied her as she studied me. Her eyes were icy blue, unflinching as they pierced my soul. Her lips and cheeks were overly plump with fillers, and her straight, bleached blonde hair cascaded over her muscular shoulders. She wore a tight tank top that said, "Move Your Ass!" (one of her signature slogans) revealing the largest breast implants I'd ever seen on a human in person.

Finally, Tammy Roy spoke to me.

"How old are you?"

"Twenty-four," I replied, shifting nervously in my five-inch heels. She narrowed her eyes and leaned in closer before she spoke again.

"You are too young, too pretty, and have something too special about you to be this fat."

She might as well have just throat-punched me. I choked back hot tears and tried to swallow the lump in my throat. Everyone's eyes stayed glued to me as I did everything in my power to not fall apart in front of them. Tammy returned to her spot on the floor to give the room of Knockouts some general posing tips as I shuffled my hefty body off to the side and took a seat on the floor as well, still awkwardly hanging out in a string bikini and plastic heels.

Later that night, back at the Knockout Palace where I was staying, the humiliation continued. Knockout Palace was a big Floridian house less than a mile from headquarters, where team members were encouraged to stay while attending boot camps (another fee to be part of the team.) It slept up to ten, and was at full capacity the weekend I was there. Two of the girls staying with us were IFBB pros.

Everyone was lounging around in the living room in their pajamas, recovering after a long day of intense workouts and stifling humidity.

"Oh my god, who brought *BREAD* to camp?" a voice shouted from the kitchen.

Sam, one of the pro girls emerged, dramatically carrying the loaf of whole grain bread I'd brought with me.

My face turned as red as a cherry tomato. We were instructed to bring our own food for the weekend, and since I was just joining the team, I wasn't on a meal plan yet. I tried to bring sensible food that would hold up in the heat— including whole grain bread and peanut butter, to make peanut butter sandwiches, I mean, come on, it was *whole grain*!

"Um, that's mine. I brought it," I said sheepishly. Internally I began to reprimand myself.

They must be thinking, of course you did! Of course, the fat girl brought bread!

Sam looked at me and laughed. "Live it up, sister! Once you get your plan you won't see bread for a loooong time."

The other girls around me erupted into a fit of giggles like a pack of hyenas. Laughing *at* me. There I was again, in the familiar position I constantly tried to avoid. Even though I had breast implants, a job with MET-Rx, and three competitions under my belt, I was still just the fat girl getting laughed at.

That night I struggled to fall asleep. I kept reliving the day's events, hearing Tammy's voice, over and over again: *You are too young, too pretty, and have something too special about you to be this fat.* Then replaying the scene of the other girls laughing at me and my bread, like I was a fat-ass loser.

I will redeem myself, I thought. *I'm here for a reason. I'll diet and train harder than ever, and show Tammy and these girls, and everyone else! I'll show them all what I'm really made of. I'll win.*

The next day at camp, I kept my head down and did as I was told, hoping I could just keep up enough to blend it and not get called out again. Thankfully, I made it through Day Two unscathed, and even made a new friend.

"I hear you're from Long Island!" a woman with big, fluffy blonde hair said to me. She looked to be in her early forties. "I'm Cheryl. I live in Massapequa. What gym do you train at?"

"Oh awesome! I'm Justine. I train at XSport Fitness!" I responded, excited to find *some* common ground with a member of the Knockout Squad. "How long have you been on the team?"

"Over a year now! I joined last May. So glad I did— they really are the best in the biz," Cheryl told me. "We'll have to train together back home! We Knockouts have to stick together!"

For the first time that weekend, I felt a sense of reassurance that I was in the right place, and this was the right decision. *It'll be worth it*, I kept telling myself.

The third and final day of camp, we each got a private meeting with Tammy and Rick. This was the time to discuss a game plan of what shows I would do next.

I nervously entered the office as they called me in, and closed the door behind me. Shiny trophies and awards packed the walls and shelves. I sat down in an empty armchair facing Tammy and Rick.

"Okay sister, let's get to it," Tammy's raspy voice broke the silence in the room. "We'll get you on your plan tomorrow and then I'm thinking you can get onstage next spring."

"I was actually thinking I'd do the Easterns this November," I told them.

"That's four months away," Rick spoke up. "I don't know that we can have you ready by then. You have a lot of weight to lose."

My heart sank. I hated myself for gaining so much weight after working *so* hard to get in shape earlier that year.

"Can I at least *try* to get ready in time?" I pleaded. "My body responds quickly. I really think I can do it."

"We can try," Tammy said. "But the real question is, can you diet?"

"Yes! I swear I can. Once I start it's like a switch gets flipped in my head, and I don't stray from my diet at *all*," I insisted.

They stared at me with skeptical looks, as if I had told them I had a pet unicorn back home.

"We'll see about that. Now what's this I hear about *you* working with MET-Rx?" Tammy asked incredulously.

"Oh yes, I do demos for them! I even worked their booth at the Arnold Expo this past spring!" I replied proudly.

Tammy raised one eyebrow, staring me down. Then she looked over at Rick, who cleared his throat.

"Listen, Justine, you're a pretty girl. With your blue eyes and dark hair, you're a photographer's dream. And being connected with MET-Rx is a big opportunity. But you've gotta get your weight down and keep yourself in check. You could have a bright future in this industry, but we don't know if you have the willpower it takes. Our girls who succeed stay on their plans 12 months out of the year. There is no 'off-season.' Only improvement season. So we want you to do every single thing on your plan and trust us, and I promise, we can help you go far," Rick told me.

"It's really that simple. We know what we're doing. We've turned hundreds of girls pro. Just STICK TO THE *PLAN*," Tammy added, emphasizing every word. "Don't question it. Just follow it, word for word. That's all you've gotta do."

I took a deep breath, feeling a fire in my belly as I imagined myself turning pro, and becoming a real sponsored athlete with MET-Rx.

"I can do it! I know I can! I'm going to make you both so proud," I promised, ready to put my health in their hands without asking any questions. Tammy nodded skeptically and waved me out of the office to give the next girl her turn.

"Oh, I almost forgot. I live close to the Old School Iron Gym. Do you think I should start working out there, to get to know judges and people in the industry?" I asked.

Tammy and Rick looked at one another. The Old School Iron Gym was owned by one of the head judges of the NPC/ IFBB, who had been a world-champion bodybuilder back in the eighties. Everyone who was anyone in the fitness industry worked out there when they were in New York, and many of the local pros trained there regularly.

"No. Do *not* go in there. Not yet," Tammy replied sternly. "Let's get your weight down first, mama. *Then* you can go there."

I nodded in agreement, and left the office.

My final step of initiation that weekend was purchasing my very own Squeem from the Knockout Squad boutique.

"We'll start you with a Size Small. There are three rows of hooks, and you'll want to wear it on the tightest setting possible," explained Veronica, the assistant coach. "Week by week the constant pressure will make your waist smaller. Plus, you'll be losing weight with your diet and training plan. As your waist gets smaller, you'll want to order an Extra Small. That should happen within a month or two, if you're following your plan. Then if you get really, *really* tiny, you'll graduate to our smallest size: Extra *Extra* Small! That's what I'm wearing!"

I forked over seventy dollars and became the proud owner of my very own waist-cinching torture device. I was told to wear it at least eight hours every day, ideally ten to twelve hours.

I spent fifteen minutes wrestling my fat into my new Squeem. It was made of rubber, with over a dozen hook-and-eye clasps at the front, and thick metal boning all around it to hold its shape. It came all the way up to the bottom of my breasts and stopped at my hip bones, squeezing every inch of my body in-between with the death grip of an anaconda. After wrangling my way into the Squeem, I admired myself in the mirror.

My internal organs cried out, *Please, no!* but the reflection in the mirror screamed, *Girl, yes!*

Aside from the fat on my hips bulging out at the bottom, I looked significantly slimmer already, with a striking hourglass shape that begged the question, *Are those dimensions even humanly possible?*

After being physically and mentally beaten down all weekend, I finally felt armed with the tools and motivation to climb to the very top of the fitness industry. *Top five, here I come!*

At the airport the next morning I saw a familiar face.

"You must be on my flight!" Cheryl exclaimed, waving me over to where she was seated at the gate. I wheeled my luggage over and took a seat next to her. She was funneling pre-cooked, room temperature asparagus into her mouth. I smelled its very familiar scent.

Does every meal have to include asparagus? I wondered.

Minutes later I had my answer, when I checked my email and discovered I'd received my very first Knockout Squad Plan.

Ahhhh, The PLAN! Excitement bubbled up in my body. It contained all the secrets I needed to be a champion.

"I got my first plan!" I squealed to Cheryl, opening the email as quickly as my thumbs would let me.

"Let me see! Let me see!" Cheryl cried out, almost as excited as me. I read through my meal plan out loud:

Meal One: 3 egg whites, ⅓ cup of uncooked oats, 1 tsp flax oil, 8 blueberries, 6 spears of asparagus

Meal Two: 3 oz ground turkey breast, 12 spears of asparagus, ⅓ cup of green beans

Meal Three: 3 oz cod or tilapia, 2 cups of fresh
spinach, 1 tsp olive oil, 1 Tbsp balsamic vinegar, 2
cherry tomatoes

I paused. "*Two* cherry tomatoes? *Eight* blueberries? This is very specific!"

"Oh yeah, girl!" Cheryl responded. "Be sure to read *every* detail on how to prepare your food too! They are extremely precise. Workouts too! Read it all carefully, print it out, and follow every step *exactly* as they say."

It was intense, but I felt thrilled. Elation poured through me as I realized I had the secrets of the Knockout Squad in my own two hands. The diet was rigid, but the extraordinarily detailed workout plan intimidated me even more.

Reading through the workouts, I saw I was to perform *two* strenuous cardio sessions, plus one vigorous strength training workout, six days per week. My only "rest day" still included an hour of cardio. The strength workouts had more sets and reps than I'd *ever* seen in a single workout, with three years of experience as a personal trainer.

"This leg day will take me six hours!" I lamented.

"You gotta move FAST! That's what's special about Knockout training," Cheryl told me.

The cardio workouts were downright insane— the instructions didn't even seem *possible*, let alone safe.

Lunge on a moving treadmill? Run on an incline while holding weights? Seriously?!

"I don't think I'm coordinated enough to pull these off without falling on my face!" I told Cheryl. She just laughed. I read on.

"Before all cardio, apply cellulite gel to the waist, lower back, upper thighs, hamstrings and glutes, then put on your neoprene waist wrap and neoprene shorts. Contact the Knockout Squad store to order cellulite gel and neoprene wraps," I read aloud. "What's all that?"

"It's this gel that tightens the skin— and the neoprene helps you sweat more to tighten you up too," Cheryl informed me.

Tighten. That's a word I'd hear about 1,312,987 times during my experience with the Knockout Squad.

The excitement in my stomach was now swirling with heaps of anxiety, unsure if I'd be able to follow through with all of these instructions. My first cardio workout with the Team looked like this:

2 minutes running on an incline of 3.0 while holding 3-pound dumbbells

1 minute of lunges on an incline of 3.0

2 minutes running on an incline of 3.0

1 minute jogging backwards on an incline of 3.0

2 minutes running on an incline of 3.0 while holding 3-pound dumbbells

1 minute jogging backwards on an incline of 3.0

2 minutes running on an incline of 3.0

Hop off treadmill

1 minute of narrow squat jumps

1 minute of wide squat jumps

1 minute of mountain climbers

Get back on treadmill

Repeat for 4 rounds.

And this was just *my first* cardio program! I was instructed to do this or something equally challenging (and death-defying) followed by an insane strength training program *and* another cardio program— all in *one* day. Then get up the next morning and do it again.

Even the supplement plan was complicated— I was to take "fat burners" two days on, one day off, along with a ton of other powders, pills, and potions.

It was overwhelming— basically a full-time job to follow every detail of The Plan. And all of it cost a small fortune too. *Beauty is pain*, but beauty is also really freaking expensive!

I wanted to succeed with the team so badly, but even after years of obsessing over fitness magazines, picking personal trainers' brains, and competing three times, this Knockout Squad Plan was some crazy shit. It had elements of fitness advice from the Stone Age that most bodybuilding coaches still doled out, coupled with wildly random details, like they collaborated with Quentin Tarantino while tripping on acid.

I took a deep breath. *You can do this,* I told myself again and again. *You* will *do this. And you'll show everyone what you're really made of!*

September 2011; age 24

After the flight back to New York, I printed out multiple copies of The Plan and got down to business. Every Sunday I was to email progress photos to Tammy, wearing a bikini and heels, along with my weight. Tammy expected my weight to go down at least 2 pounds on a weekly basis in order to prep for the November shows.

I designated Pierre as my photographer. I'd have him take the photos in the morning, when I felt the leanest. We had been living together for a few months at this point, and even though I still wasn't sure how I felt about the relationship, I truly enjoyed having him support my fitness journey. He'd snap photos of me in my front pose, back pose, from both sides, plus close ups of my midsection and backside.

"I followed the plan 100% this week!" I typed.

I was elated in my first weekly email to Tammy with my progress report. I couldn't wait to share how diligent I'd been, to prove I had what it took to be a front-runner.

"I just need to work my way up to the intensity of the cardio workouts. OMG they're so hard! I'm about ready to collapse, but I already lost 6 pounds!"

Two days later, Tammy emailed back.

"VERY nice! So proud of you for jumping right in and making it GO!!! Do NOT get cocky and slow down!! We are obviously going in the right direction!"

My thirst for approval was quenched by her positive feedback, but I still felt her judgement and lack of faith in me, as I read between the lines of "Do NOT get cocky and slow down."

To me it implied I was nothing without The Plan, and I shouldn't dare to start feeling good about myself.

I sent weekly updates to Tammy without fail, as the pounds continued to drop off. In addition to getting a direct 2-4 sentence response from her each week, we'd receive mass emails sent to every member of the team, labeled as "Public Service Announcements." This is one treasured email I'll never forget:

CAUTION! LONG-BUTT DISORDER IS RAMPANT!!!

ANY type of Ellypitical machine is NOT a ProForm Trainer!!!

Do NOT swap a random ellyptical for a ProForm Trainer!!!

An Ellypitcal is a WASTE of your time and devleops a NICE LONG ASS!! YIIIIIIKES!!

If you do not have an ProForm Trainer at your gym my first choice is for you to JOIN A NEW GYM! Second choice is to swap for the incline treadmill program each time. But be advised - the ProForm WILL make a difference in your butt!!!

This has been a Public Service Anouncement from Knockout Headquarters

I immediately bashed myself when I received this email, as I had been replacing a ProForm Trainer with a regular elliptical machine for some of my cardio workouts. XSport Fitness didn't have the ProForm Trainers, and I figured it didn't make a difference. Now I knew I was wrong about that. I joined an additional gym that had ProForm Trainer machines, determined to prove myself to Tammy and the Knockout Squad.

The next week, I received another Public Service Announcement. I took a deep breath as I opened the email, afraid of what I'd done wrong now.

So, you have lost some pounds and changed your shape a little?

GOOD FOR YOU!

Think you can relax, skip a cardio session or have some extra nibbles here and there since you are doing so great?

THINK AGAIN, SISTER!!

NOW is the time that you need to push even **HARDER**!! If you ease up you WILL move backward!

The girls being chosen at the National level are extra TINY and extra TIGHT!

Tinier than we've EVER seen before.

EVERY nibble, EVERY extra bite will keep you from achieving your goal.

Be DEDICATED to your goals and STOP the nibbles and little cheats.

Trust us, it makes a HUGE difference.

Do NOT slow down, do NOT give in- those who stay true to the plan will look INCREDIBLE come showtime!!

This has been a Public Service Announcement from Knockout Headquarters

I took every word sent by the Knockout Squad very seriously.

Long-butt syndrome? Oh no, not me! Extra tiny and tight? Comin' right up!!

This went far beyond the reverence I'd had for fitness magazines over the years. I clung so tightly to the top-secret advice of the most esteemed coaches in my chosen industry, it basically became my religion. And much like my actual religion growing up, it left me feeling fearful and less-than. Even though Tammy was 1,000 miles away, I always felt like she was watching my every move. Judging. Expecting me to fail.

As summer faded into fall, I soldiered on every day as a faithful Knockout.

I applied my cellulite gel, wrapped my body in a neoprene waist wrap and shorts, daringly risked my life lunging and jogging backwards on the treadmill, took my fat burning pills without bothering to read the label, did squat jumps 'til the cows came home, and ate my *eight* blueberries— no more, no less! I even sized down from a Size Small Squeem, to the Extra Small, which felt like a monumental accomplishment. This accomplishment I was so proud of was, in actuality, muscle atrophy at its finest. The dictionary states atrophy is:

1.   *Decrease in size of wasting away of a body part or tissue*

2.   *Gradual decline in effectiveness or vigor due to underuse or neglect*

Those impossibly small waistlines on the Knockout Squad competitors? They were the result of a purposeful intent to weaken the core muscles to the point of wasting away. This intent was made even clearer in the "Additional Instructions" portion of the emails we'd receive containing The Plan:

Core Training— Don't even THINK about it, sister!

- In addition to your Squeem, be sure to wear a weight belt any time you pick up a weight.

- Training without a belt will engage your core— we do NOT want this!

- **Do NOT** do any oblique exercises. **NO** side to side movements!

- **Absolutely NO core training, core classes or Pilates**! This includes yoga too— be sure that you do NOT work your core!

P.S. Do NOT tell **ANYONE** about your Squeem! **Let's keep this a KNOCKOUT SQUAD SECRET!**

At the time, I thought these were totally acceptable instructions. Who needs core muscles anyway? They're only central to stabilizing all movements of the human body, and protecting your spine. No big deal.

I was wearing my Squeem for 12 hours a day, at minimum. I was working day and night to finance my dreams, and felt thankful my jobs as a personal trainer and bartender kept me on my feet, because those Squeems were brutal to wear sitting down! When I sat, the metal rods would often bend and break, poking through the rubber and digging into my sides, stabbing me.

Wearing that tight rubber corset for so many hours (and sweating in it, too) started giving my skin a rash, so I began cutting the tops off basic white Hanes tank tops to serve as a thin cotton barrier between the rubber and my skin. *How resourceful of me!*

I did every last thing the Knockout Plan told me to do, and I did it all with a smile on my face. I trusted I was working with the best of the best, and trophies to acknowledge my diligence were in my very near future.

Six weeks into being a member of the Knockout Squad, my body rejected The Plan, for the first of many times. My calf muscle started throbbing with pain during a Monday morning cardio session. By Wednesday, it was so painful and swollen I could barely walk, let alone run, jump, lunge, and jog backwards.

I went to see my chiropractor, who specialized in sports injuries and was a long-time member of XSport Fitness. He understood my demanding training schedule and my urgency to get better so I could compete that fall. He had been around enough hellbent fitness competitors to understand the mindset— that nothing can get in the way of succeeding onstage. The general sentiment is, *push through at all costs!*

Dr. B told me my calf was "shearing off the bone," which is precisely as atrocious as it sounds. It was something he'd seen before— an injury from overtraining. He told me to rest it completely for a few days, ice as much as possible, and come back the following week. He promised to get me up and running as soon as possible.

With a bag of frozen peas on my injured leg, I tearfully wrote an email to Tammy:

"I know you are busy with shows this weekend," I began, always apologetic for things I didn't yet understand I shouldn't be sorry for.

I reported the details, and then expressed my frustration toward my body. There was no sense of, *maybe I shouldn't be training this way in the first place?* I only placed judgement on my body, for not being able to hold up to The Plan, when clearly so many other women were able to follow it without a hitch.

"I am SO upset and discouraged by this because I felt like I was on a roll, making such awesome progress. I went from feeling unstoppable to this. I do NOT want to fall behind or backtrack in any way. Today is 9 weeks out from my next show. I'm wondering if I should adjust my diet to account for these missed workouts?"

Three days later I got a response:

"Hey girl, do as much as you can and stick to your diet 110%. It's more important than EVER."

At this point I started to sense that unless you were a favored member of the Knockout Squad, Tammy and Rick would never adjust your plan. It wasn't worth their time unless you had a solid chance at turning pro in the near future, and unfortunately that wasn't me; at least, not *yet*.

The Knockout Squad had a social network with an online forum for members to connect. This wasn't their best move, because as we connected one-on-one, we'd eventually compare plans, and realize we all had the same one. The flavor of the month. They'd send the exact same plans to thousands of girls, based on the general goal— fat loss or muscle maintenance. It didn't matter if you were 5'10" and worked all day on your feet, or 5'0" sitting at a desk all day— if you needed to lose body fat, you were getting the exact same prescription for cardio and calories.

And if something went wrong it was *your* fault. "The Plan never fails!" Tammy would insist. Over and over again, I agreed. If only my body would cooperate, I believed this was the surefire path to getting my Pro Card and, of course, fixing all of my Problem Areas for good.

October 2011; age 24

My calf muscle healed quickly, and within two weeks, I was able to resume my normal training. The resilience of the human body is truly miraculous— especially when you're 24. I certainly didn't see it that way at the time, though. Instead of appreciation for my body, I just felt irked by the health flare ups I was experiencing, which I viewed as "setbacks."

Along with the calf injury, I got two colds and a sinus infection in the three months I was in competition prep, along with ongoing dizziness and nausea from low blood sugar. I shared all of this in emails to Tammy, hoping she'd give me sound advice, or at the very least, commend me for being such a trooper, refusing to be stopped by injuries or sickness.

But that didn't happen. Instead, most emails just said things like "Do NOT slow down!! You gotta be STRONG! You're doing great- but we gotta get you TIGHTER!!"

Tighter, tighter, tighter. I thought about this all the time while forcing my exhausted, calorie-depleted body to keep up with three workouts a day.

My workouts were grueling, but I had the right fuel. A buildup of seething anger, frustration, and the pain of rejection from verbal attacks of my past made for a powerful propellent.

When I wanted to quit, I'd replay painful memories of people who had called me fat, or told me I wasn't good enough. I'd hear their voices echo through my head with every single repetition. Like a collector, I'd saved every insult, every cruel word— from childhood, to guys I'd dated, to Tammy— and I'd pull from it like a backup reserve of extra motivation. I wanted to show them all how wrong they were about me. I wanted them to eat those words. I wanted the entire world to validate me and tell me *YES, your body is perfect! You are not fat— you are thin and perfect and desirable in every way!*

This obsessive, deeply-rooted longing to be seen as worthy paid off. After following The Plan for three months, I had lost twenty-five pounds. I was now in the smallest Squeem available, the XXS, with my waist measuring a shockingly teensy twenty-two inches. Every square inch of my body was the most toned it had ever been.

With Tammy and Rick's seal of approval, I entered two shows that November, one week apart. The first was a small show in New Jersey. The second was The Eastern USA Championships, the most prestigious local show on the east coast.

Unlike my first few experiences competing, I had no delusions of placing first. But in my heart of hearts, I hoped to place within the top three in New Jersey, and top six at the Easterns.

The week before New Jersey, I became privy to more Knockout Squad secrets, with the Competition Week Prep regimen. I gladly forked over the extra $100 for these top-secret instructions. They were as meticulous as the rest of my plan, including specific directions for diet, workouts, hair, makeup, nails, pedicures, exfoliating, body hair removal, tanning, every last detail, and more. It was a very tall order to execute.

No wonder their girls look so good, I thought as I re-read the details on Skin Prep:

- Monday, Wednesday and Friday morning SHAVE EVERYTHING, neck down!

- We mean everything! Legs, feet, tummy, back, butt, chest, shoulders, arms, hands, ALL BODY HAIR below your neck. This applies to

EVERYONE- even if you're blonde!! ANY tiny hairs or "peach fuzz" will screw up your tan!

- Do NOT get waxed! It will mess up your tan
- Use a tanning bed on Sunday & Tuesday. NO tanning after Tuesday!

This regimen also included instructions on how to drop water before a show. There are many tricks to get the human body to excrete water, which leaves you dehydrated as hell (obviously) but also as crisp as a paper cut, in terms of muscle definition. Dropping water weight feels like dying a slow death but it looks like your body has been wrapped up in shrink wrap— very, very, very *tight*!

The Knockout Squad protocol included water manipulation and dandelion pills, which act as an herbal diuretic. Oh and of course, loads of asparagus. If you haven't picked up on it, asparagus and bikini competitors go together like peanut butter and jelly. The green veggie is a natural diuretic, a.k.a. anything that makes you pee.

The Competition Week Prep instructions laid out every detail for me to bring the most "perfect, polished package to the stage."

That's what everyone calls competitors' bodies in the industry— a *package*. As in, *I'm bringing my best package yet to the stage this season.*

And what a hot little package I was!

I was overjoyed when I got first callouts in New Jersey. I felt way more confident on stage this time, feeling so victorious knowing I was finally being *seen* for all of my hard work.

At finals, I stood onstage proudly in my glittery, royal blue bikini and sparkly plastic heels, arching my back and twisting my waist in unnatural poses to display my "package" at the very best angles. Contorted, unnatural angles are just *so* flattering.

The emcee called out the names of the fifth, then fourth place competitors in my class.

I made the top three!!!! I screamed in my head with glee.

"The third-place trophy goes to Amanda Martinez."

I'm top TWO!!!! I tried to keep my composure, steadying my body as I smiled so hard my cheeks hurt.

"Second place goes to… Justine Moore!"

I felt like I was in a trance as the show expeditor placed the second-place trophy at my feet and shook my hand. For the first time, instead of *watching* the winners pose for pictures onstage with their trophies, I *was* one of those winners!

As I left the stage and entered the backstage area, Pierre and Cheryl rushed to meet me.

"You were robbed!" Pierre insisted, shaking his head. My dreamlike bliss came to an abrupt halt.

"You look *so* much better than that first-place girl. Her butt was *jiggling,* for crying out loud!" Cheryl protested in a hushed voice.

My heart sank. I had wanted top three, and there I was, top *TWO*. But my posse's initial responses told me I should be disappointed, and suddenly my shiny new trophy felt tarnished. I brushed it off and tried to soak in the victory of finally not walking away from a show empty-handed.

It was my fourth show. Two years after embarking on this punishing, expensive, and time-consuming quest, I was now the proud owner of a cheap, plastic trophy that told me my "package" looked good enough that day.

November 2011; age 24

Tammy and Rick hadn't attended my smaller show in New Jersey, but they would be at my next show— the Easterns— the following Saturday. After hearing that I'd placed second in Jersey, it was clear they began to see me differently.

Now they'll take me seriously, I thought, and I was right.

Overnight I had special changes to my plan— which had never happened before. Tammy also emailed me instructions on where to meet them the night before the Easterns, so they could take a look at me in person.

My mom and her husband flew into New York City for the weekend to attend the show and celebrate with me afterwards.

When they arrived on Friday afternoon, I went to greet them in the lobby of the W Hotel in lower Manhattan, where we were all staying. I had on a skintight, long-sleeved gray dress with a black belt that could fit an infant's waist. I spotted my mom across the lobby. She turned and our eyes met.

"Baby!" she exclaimed, rushing to give me a big hug. "Oh my gosh, look at you! My beautiful daughter is so *TINY*!"

I soaked in the praise, like a little kitten soaking up a patch of sunlight.

There's a slogan in fitness, "Nothing tastes as good as being fit feels." It's a spin-off of Kate Moss's infamous quote, "Nothing tastes as good as skinny feels."

For me, nothing tasted as good, or satisfied me more than praise for my body from other people. It made it all feel worth it— all the hard work and sacrifice.

I had become a validation junkie, addicted to the high I'd get off of comments about how "tiny," or "fit" I was, both in person and on social media. When I didn't get my drug of choice, I felt empty, agitated, and uneasy.

At 8 p.m. that night, I stood before Tammy and Rick, hoping they would provide me with my next hit. I'd cabbed it across Manhattan to get about 90 seconds of their undivided attention. It was the first time they'd seen me in person since that tragic boot camp experience in Jacksonville.

We met in their hotel room, along with a handful of other Knockout Squad competitors who were also competing the next day.

Again, I found myself standing exposed, in a bikini and heels with Tammy's eyes fastened on me, sizing up every detail. Only this time, I was twenty-five pounds smaller, with a second-place trophy sitting on my dresser at home.

"Turn," she said. I went through my posing routine. When I was facing forward again, Tammy and Rick looked at one another, emotionless. Tammy raised her one eyebrow, seemingly giving Rick the floor to give me my final instructions before the show.

"Three more dandelion capsules tonight. Only drink water when you *need* to. Stick to the plan tomorrow morning," he told me in his soft, raspy voice. "Nice work, honey."

"Yes, good work, mama. I knew you could do it," Tammy added, before indifferently waving the next girl over.

Did she though? Did she really believe in me? I thought to myself as I walked away with a satisfied smile. There's no way in hell you could convince me she did, but I didn't care one bit. I had proven myself, and I had gotten my fix for the night.

The next morning, I awoke before the sun came up and got into the lucky blue bikini I had placed second in one week before. I went into the bathroom and stepped on the scale that I had brought with me to the hotel. 111.2 lbs.

YES! I thought.

This was the smallest I'd ever been for a show— more than ten pounds leaner than my first shows back in Wisconsin.

Extra tiny and tight? Double check!

A smile spread across my face and I began practicing my poses in the mirror, snapping selfies on my phone. I chose the best photo of myself, out of thirty or so, and posted it on my Facebook Fan Page with the caption: *Ready for prejudging! Let's DO this!*

A flood of likes and comments started gushing in immediately, but I had to put my phone away and focus on the show.

Backstage was a zoo as always, but this time I got to hang out in prime real estate. There was a small loft area up a flight of stairs, and Tammy and Rick had staked it out for the forty-something members of the Knockout Squad competing that day. It was No Boys Allowed— Knockouts Only, and I savored being one of the cool, elite girls.

Once prejudging was underway, all of the Knockout girls went up to Tammy one by one, for her to make final adjustments. We formed an assembly line to receive hair and makeup tips, get our bikini tops tied, and have our bikini bottoms glued onto our toned, perky behinds.

Yes, *glued.* Good old Elmer's Spray Adhesive, to be specific. Glue was imperative to make sure you were showing the exact right amount of butt cheek— not too little, not too much! Think borderline scandalous, but not overtly obscene.

"Come here, sister, I need to tie up your top!" Tammy said as I approached her, displaying the "package" I brought that day.

I thought my bikini top already *was* tied, but I was wrong. Tammy's fingers quickly untied the strings around my neck and then yanked them back up *hard*, re-tying it.

"Ouch! This is too tight!" I protested.

"No, trust me. You want it tied that tight. Look how good your boobs look!" Tammy motioned to a full-length mirror propped up nearby. I examined my breasts perched impossibly high on my chest. I looked like a living, breathing brunette Barbie doll.

Beauty is pain! I reminded myself as the ties burrowed into the skin on the back of my neck.

"Lemme see your makeup," Tammy commanded, grabbing my shoulders and whirling me back around to face her. "Bright pink lipstick before you go onstage. More eyeliner on the bottom. And more blush. Bright pink, right on the apples of your cheeks."

I walked back to my belongings and dug into my makeup kit to follow orders.

Over the years, I lovingly named this look "Stripper Clown Makeup." I also sort of felt like one of those voiceless little pageant girls on that TV show *Toddlers and Tiaras*. I tried making both of these jokes repeatedly backstage, but no one ever appreciated my comedy material. The ladies of the Knockout Squad, including myself, were an interesting combination of high strung from adrenaline and nerves, and zombie-like, from overtraining and carb depletion. This made passing time backstage pretty bleak.

A show this big meant five or six hours of prejudging, and the bikini division always went last, because it drew in the largest percentage of the audience. There was lots of time backstage to wait, and wait, and *wait*. During this waiting period, I'd always start to psych myself out. I'd look around, and those familiar feelings of not-enoughness would start creeping in.

"What's wrong with you?" Cheryl asked, noticing my mood had shifted. She was also competing that day, but in the Figure Division.

"These other girls have more abs showing than me," I confessed.

"So what? It's just Bikini! They don't *want* ripped abs in Bikini. You look great— even better than Jersey! Stop comparing yourself. Let the judges do that," Cheryl insisted.

Her pep talk (with a dash of backhanded compliment about the Bikini Division) brought a little of my confidence back. I spent the rest of my time backstage with headphones on, bouncing my hips around to Pitbull and Rihanna, distracting myself from obsessing over the women I was competing against.

I carried the confidence I'd mustered up with me as I lined up to go onstage for prejudging. If I let my guard down for even one second, I'd start to think anxiety-provoking thoughts like, *THIS IS THE MOST IMPORTANT MOMENT OF MY ENTIRE LIFE!!!!* and other wildly delusional things I wholeheartedly believed at the time.

When my turn was up, I boldly sauntered across the stage like never before, making full eye contact with the judges and flashing a cheeky smile. After hitting my poses, I found my place amongst the herd of bikini competitors on the side of the stage, waiting for callouts.

The expeditors did their best to keep us all spaced out evenly, but bikini girls can be ferocious, elbowing one another in an attempt to be front and center for the judges to see. We'd angle our bony hips to beam our numbers in the direction of the head judge, our body language desperately screaming out, *"Pick me! Pick me! Oh, please, pick me!"*

"Numbers 143, 145, 151, 154, 156 and 158," the head judge boomed over the microphone.

154!!!! That's ME!

The rush of making first call outs flooded every cell of my body. I felt giddy as I posed alongside the other top contenders in my class.

"Number 154 switch places with number 158," the judge called out, bringing me closer to the center. My heart wanted to burst right out of my chest and onto the judges' table. "Thank you, ladies. We'll see you back here tonight."

Backstage I quickly gathered my things and rushed to meet my family and Pierre.

"Congrats, superstar!" Pierre exclaimed, picking me up in a hug and swinging me around.

"I think I'm in the top four!" I told my mom and her husband. "I was hoping for top six, so this is amazing!"

"That's great, baby!" my mom replied. She never really knew how to react at my shows. Previously I'd emerged from backstage heartbroken and distraught, so she'd learned to wait and gauge my mood before saying a word.

Later that night, I was awarded the third-place trophy in front of a sold-out audience. I'd never been happier. Onstage I posed for pictures with the other women who placed in the top five, our arms raised up high in victory. I beamed with overflowing pride, having beat out such tough competition. My smile was one of genuine glee. It felt like I'd truly made it. I had arrived. I'd vindicated the little girl of my past who felt ugly, chubby, and not as good as other girls.

Before reuniting with my family and Pierre to go out for a celebratory feast, I stopped to snap a picture with Tammy, Rick, and my new trophy.

"You looked great out there, mama! We just need to polish up your posing next season," Tammy told me.

"You've got potential, kiddo. Let's keep things *tight* over the holidays and we'll get you that Pro Card next season," Rick said with a wink.

My mom, her husband, Pierre, and I went to a swanky restaurant in SoHo to toast to my victory. I placed my tacky plastic trophy on the table to marvel at, like it was an Olympic gold medal.

The waitress must have wondered what award I'd received— for being so tan and so gaunt? For nailing my "Stripper Clown Makeup"?

She kept eying me curiously, along with other patrons in the restaurant, but in my mind, they were all just admiring my achievement of physical perfection.

I ordered champagne, a cheeseburger, and waffle fries, but I held myself back from going overboard this time. Even though I wouldn't get back onstage for four months, I kept replaying what Rick had said, *keep things tight and we'll get you that Pro Card.*

The following week I felt equally victorious. The photos I'd posted online sparked a frenzy of likes and comments, praising me for my tiny, chiseled body. I began receiving messages from acquaintances and strangers alike, asking me if I'd coach them or share what my meal plan looked like.

The praise translated in real life, too. I had started working out at the Old School Iron Gym after losing my first ten pounds on the Knockout plan. When I returned to the gym the week after placing third at the Easterns, I was blown away by how many of the gym regulars knew who I was.

Men and women in passing would say things like, "Nice job at the Easterns!" or "You looked great onstage, Justine. Congratulations!"

They know my NAME! They know who I am!

I couldn't believe it. I was becoming a star, just as I had envisioned in my mind so many times.

Having placed top five at the local level, I was now qualified to compete in National Pro Qualifiers the following year. Placing first or second in one of *those* shows would earn me the title of IFBB Pro, which would enable me to compete at Pro level shows, where you can win money for placing well. But mostly, it just gets you a lifetime of bragging rights to the miniscule part of the population who knows what IFBB Pro even means. That status was what I *really* wanted, more than anything at the time. In my warped little mind, turning Pro meant my life would be perfect, and I'd live happily ever after.

My fitness goals were all I cared about. I craved validation so much that I said "yes" to Pierre when he asked me to marry him two weeks later. I wasn't in love—I hadn't been in love with him for years—yet I said "yes" to the support he gave to my fitness industry dreams. I posted pictures of my gorgeous, 2.6 carat diamond ring all over social media, but none of Pierre, or us as a betrothed couple. Looking back, I realize I liked the *idea* of being engaged, and I guess it didn't matter who I was engaged to. That big rock on my left hand signaled to the outside world that I was chosen, desired, and wanted as a woman, so I accepted it and wore it proudly.

March 2012; age 24

I gazed out the window on the flight to Columbus, Ohio. This was my second trip to the legendary Arnold Sports Festival with MET-Rx, and I was determined to make a splash.

I thought about my experience the previous year. I hadn't known anyone other than Derek and Ken from MET-Rx, who I'd initially met in Vegas, and Jim, who was my boss while I did demos in gyms throughout New York.

I'd served up samples of protein bars and energy drinks quietly, with a smile on my face. I'd diligently worked the booth, showing up early and leaving late. I felt grateful and happy just to *be* there, having my flight, food, and hotel accommodations covered. On the third and final day of the festival, someone had mentioned the daily pay, and I was dumbfounded.

"We get *paid* for this?" I asked, having thought it was already a sweet enough deal to get to represent the brand *and* have expenses covered.

"Ah, yeah, duh! Of course we get paid for this. You thought you were doing this for free?" another brand ambassador responded, laughing hysterically, before alerting the entire team to the misunderstanding. "You guys, she didn't know we were getting paid for this!"

Everyone found this amusing, but I also think they took note. I didn't feel embarrassed about my misunderstanding of our compensation. I was willing to work hard to get what I wanted, and I wanted others to know that. So this was the perfect introduction to many of the managers and team members of the company— I was the "girl who didn't know we were getting paid."

I went far with MET-Rx, and when I did, plenty of people diminished my success with salacious, sexist comments like, "Who did she sleep with to get *that* deal?"

Though I was no saint during my years in the industry, I never used my body or sexuality to advance my position with MET-Rx. I worked my ass off for the company, traveling far and wide around the New York state area. I did it all with pride and immense appreciation, simply for the opportunities. I practiced the manifestation technique of "Act As If," from Day One.

"Act As If" is a Law of Attraction method popularized by the movie *Boiler Room*. The idea is to pretend as though something you want is already yours. You must walk, talk, dress, and think as if you already *have* what you are dreaming of, and eventually it will be yours. Basically, it's a step beyond the concept of "dress for the job you want."

I believed with my whole heart if I acted as if I already *was* a sponsored athlete for the company, someday it would surely be my reality.

As the plane began its descent, I focused on how I wanted the weekend at the Arnold to be. How I wanted to present myself.

I was now on the radar within the industry— an up-and-coming star, someone to watch. I was part of the Knockout Squad; I'd placed in the top three at my most recent shows; and I had a loyal and rapidly growing following on Facebook, of over 10,000 fans at that point.

In addition to handing out product samples, the company had printed 8x10 photos of me, at my request, for me to sign for fans throughout the weekend. I knew there was a buzz of energy around my name and a photo that had recently gone viral, and I wanted to capitalize on my growing popularity. If I could show MET-Rx how beloved I was, and the attention I could draw to their brand, they'd surely want me on board as an official endorsed athlete.

Time to shine! I thought as I picked up my suitcase from baggage claim and made my way to the hotel.

The next morning, I woke early, took my fat burners and ate my first meal. I had cooked, measured, and packed almost all of my meals for the weekend, so that I could adhere to The Plan as closely as possible. I froze anything perishable (which was most of it) and called the hotel in advance to make sure I had a mini-fridge and microwave in my room.

Meal One was my favorite of the day: three egg whites and 1/3 cup of oats. When you eat bird-like portions and minimal carbs, oatmeal is a real treat. It's like a plate of brownies for a hungry bikini competitor.

I did my hair and makeup before getting dressed. I had three identical outfits to wear, which had been mailed to me by the company: a skin tight red and white tank top with "MET-Rx" embroidered on the chest, and tiny black shorts

I took the clothing out of the plastic packaging and put it on, over my Squeem. I completed the look with my brand-new Nike Dunk low-top sneakers, which I had bought with the $100 Jason had tucked into my pocket earlier that week at the gym.

"Treat yourself to something new for the Arnold," he had whispered in my ear.

Jason was one of the "superstars" who worked out at the Old School Iron Gym regularly. The month prior he came up to me while I was between sets of shoulder presses. Many guys made the mistake of giving girls "pointers" in the weight room as a way to flirt with them, which I always found to be very insulting. Jason knew better.

"I've seen you around here and you look great. When did you turn pro?" he asked.

"Oh, thank you! But I'm not a pro yet," I replied, feeling flattered and instantly drawn to him.

"You should be. You certainly look like a pro. I'll see you around, gorgeous," he said and walked away. Later that night I wrote about the exchange in my journal, to reflect back on if I ever forgot what hot stuff I was.

Jason was a very big deal in the industry. He was 15 years older than me. Charming. Confident. Successful. Very muscular. And very married.

The day after we first spoke, I gave him my number. In our first conversation via text, he told me things weren't working out with his wife. He said they would be getting a divorce soon, and all those other classic lines married guys use on girls to keep them interested. And I *was* interested, despite the engagement ring on my own finger. I was always a sucker for male attention, especially from men who had power.

The texts turned into calls, which turned into Jason and I hanging out when both of us could create an excuse to get away. He'd take me to Whole Foods, aka Whole Paycheck, and buy all of my groceries for the week. At first it seemed harmless, but I certainly wasn't encouraging him to go away, and I hid the relationship from Pierre.

Before walking to the convention center for Day One of the Arnold Sports Festival, I admired myself in the mirror. I felt pleased with what I saw. I had gotten a spray tan before the trip, and at five weeks out from a competition, I was already close to my target stage weight. I looked every bit the part of the hot, new fitness girl I longed to be. I couldn't wait for the day to unfold.

Working the expo matched all of my wildest dreams about what it would be like to actually be *that girl*. I quickly realized, *I am* that girl!

I barely handed out a single sample, because lines kept forming with fans from all over the world who wanted *my* autograph, and pictures with *me*! I went through close to a thousand 8x10 photos, signing them all, "Never give up! XOXO, Justine Moore," before posing for a photo. My jaw hurt from smiling by the time the day was over.

It all felt a little surreal, like I was getting what I had wanted *so* badly. But deep down, I felt a little empty inside. The year before, no one knew me, *literally.* This year, it felt like everyone knew who I *was*, in terms of my name and my image, but still, no one at that entire expo of over 175,000 attendees really *knew* me, apart from my image. I was just a soulless little doll, a plaything, something to look at and approve of and photograph.

"I'm glad we printed extras of these!" one of the MET-Rx booth managers said, bringing out a new stack of my photos from storage.

Everyone observed what was happening— the managers, the executives, the athletes, and other brand ambassadors. They couldn't help but notice the stir I was causing.

Aside from publicly causing a stir, there was no shortage of sparks flying for me behind-closed-doors that weekend. The male attention I was receiving extended beyond my Internet fans.

Having left my fiancé at home, I had a bevy of suitors to choose from to stroke my insatiable ego. There was Jason, of course, who checked up on me nonstop and frequently stopped by the booth to see me, despite the fact that his wife had come along on the trip. There was Derek, who I played arm-candy to while attending the evening shows and hottest after parties. He had all the best hook ups. And there was Xander, a friend who I'd recently done a steamy photo shoot with back in New York. Xander was quite possibly the best-looking male specimen I'd ever laid eyes on, with his godlike body and chiseled jawline.

When he invited me to his room the second night of the festival I accepted, telling myself it was innocent, he was a friend and training partner, but knowing what I was getting myself into. In truth I think I wanted to confirm that I had become the kind of girl a guy like Xander would want. I heard Josh's words echo in my mind from long ago, and I needed Xander to want me. Alone in his room, we talked about the weekend, and soon we were kissing. I let it go as far as him taking off his clothes before I cried out, "I'm sorry— I can't. I can't do this. I need to go."

He was fuming as I left the room.

I convinced myself I was doing nothing wrong in order to justify my behavior, and my incessant hunger for men to validate me.

I stopped it, didn't I? Kissing isn't really cheating.

It felt like I was getting everything I ever wanted—fame, validation, attention from attractive and powerful men—and I became intoxicated from it all. After so many years of feeling like I wasn't good enough, and feeling rejected, insulted, and disrespected by men, I now had all of these guys flocking to me. And not just any guys—attractive guys, with connections in the industry, ripped abs, and broad, muscular shoulders. I felt powerful being wanted by them. It felt like a game to me, to see how much I could get away with and how long I could keep their attention and affection. It was as if my addiction to validation had escalated, and I was employing riskier, messier means to get the fix I so desperately needed.

Despite my personal affairs clouding my judgment over the weekend, at the booth, I was focused and professional. The third and final day of the expo I looked up from signing a photo and noticed John Lisbon was standing nearby.

This is your chance! Introduce yourself!

John was a legend in the industry— a well-known fitness model, former champion bodybuilder, and the editor-in-chief of multiple fitness publications. He was someone to know, and now he was standing just a few feet away from me. I worked up the courage to introduce myself.

John told me he had a position back in New York that might be perfect for me. He took my card and promised to call with details the following week.

He did call, and four days later I was hired to run a three-month fitness program for a group of employees at the corporate headquarters that housed MET-Rx and dozens of other brands. I was promised it would be an ongoing program, and I'd get paid a whopping $200 per session, all in advance. I promptly quit my other jobs, where I earned $20/ session at XSport Fitness and roughly $30/ hour bartending at a local nightclub.

Besides the massive pay raise, the position gave me the opportunity to get to know high-up executives at MET-Rx, seeing them on a daily basis at the office. This was where I'd prove myself, and build the connections that would eventually lead me to realizing my dream of becoming a sponsored athlete.

June 2012; age 25

Three days had passed since I'd placed third in my most recent competition. I sent an email to John Lisbon for feedback. He'd become a mentor to me, taking me under his wing since I'd accepted the corporate training position with MET-Rx. He had been on the judging panel at the show, so it made sense to go to him for advice on how I could improve before my first National Pro-Qualifier, Team Universe, in four weeks.

Tammy and Rick always advised us to ask judges for feedback no matter how we placed, to show our respect for their opinions and our dedication to excelling in the "sport." Basically, we were supposed to kiss the right asses.

John's email response was "call me this afternoon," so at 1 p.m., I dialed his number, feeling excited to have this kind of access to someone I admired so much.

"I have to be honest with you, Justine, because I only want what's best for you," John began.

Oh God, this doesn't sound good.

"Saturday, you did not look your best," he stated, as if he were talking about a steak that wasn't cooked properly. "I don't know what's going on with you, but something isn't working. All the judges thought you looked much better back in March, at the Metropolitan."

"Okay," I said, feeling a bit wounded. I agreed, I didn't look my best. My last cheat meal two weeks prior to the show escalated into an all-out binge, but I didn't think the damage was *that* noticeable.

Pierre and I had been out in the West Village of Manhattan at my favorite sushi restaurant, and I had gotten tipsy off the cucumber martinis I had with dinner. After a hearty sushi dinner complete with sugary cocktails, my drunk and never-not-hungry alter-ego took over, insisting upon *DESSERTS*! Emphasis on the plural.

When Pierre brought me a king-sized Butterfinger and a pint of Double Chocolate Chip Haagen Dazs, I ate it *all*. The next day, I felt ashamed and disgusted with myself, but thankfully my weight came right back down after one day back on The Plan. Tammy and Rick had looked at my pictures leading all the way up to the show, and they kept telling me I looked great, so I didn't have any reason to believe otherwise. But now I was filled with regret.

"It was like you had this filmy quality underneath your skin," John continued. "Maybe you were holding water or something, I don't know. It was like you were *jiggling* onstage. One of the other judges even leaned over to me and said, 'She got fat!' You still placed third, because I was on the panel, but I'm letting you know if you come into Team Universe next month looking like that, you won't even crack the top 15."

Silence. I felt like I'd been punched in the gut.

John's brutal honesty burned itself into my psyche. I was paralyzed by the painful sting of his words, feeling embarrassed I had gotten onstage looking so repugnant.

Looking back on that show I remember my waistline measured just under 22 inches, which is almost unheard of for someone of my stature. I weighed 115 pounds— only 3 pounds up from my best show to date. But I internalized what John passed on to me— that I looked disgustingly fat, despite these numbers proving I was tiny. After nine blissful months of actually feeling *good* about my body, John's "constructive criticism" hit me hard.

I started to unravel. Self-doubt and self-hatred climbed back into the driver's seat, taking the wheel. The confidence I'd gained from my wins in the industry was replaced by an internal voice constantly screaming at me:

You're gonna blow it! They are going to see who you are! You are the chubby girl, remember?! You have to work harder than everyone else! And you're getting sloppy! Maybe other competitors can get away with extra cheat meals, but not you! Have some self-control!

I thought about what Tammy always said: *Do not get cocky!*

Here I'd thought I was such hot shit for a second— this was my brutal wake up call. I'd come so far in the industry, and my dreams felt closer than ever, but my weaknesses seemed to be nipping at my heels.

The things I'd been doing to my body for the sake of competing were already pretty rough, but this is where it got downright ugly. There was no longer any trace of a playful, enthusiastic, ambitious quality to my journey. All that remained was a demented, desperate quest to prove myself.

What else do you have to offer if you're not physically perfect? You'd better get it together! My inner mean girl warned mercilessly.

I thought about all those people who had stood in line at the Arnold Sports Festival to see me— and here, I was blowing my shot at becoming an IFBB Pro for some ice cream and candy bars. What a fraud I was!

I gave myself zero grace, and didn't consider the fact that I had been meticulously following The Plan for a whole year now, without as much as a week off. Through holidays, my birthday, and travel, I had stayed adamant about not giving into my appetite, eventually turning me into a ticking time bomb. That kind of discipline with food is enough to drive anyone insane, but I viewed myself as weak, and that last binge eating episode as a breakdown of self-control.

Taking a break was not an option— it wasn't even on my radar. I had to improve my physique fast, and I was willing to do whatever it took.

The next four weeks I doubled down on The Plan, adding in extra bits of cardio and tightening up my meal plan to be more extreme than ever before. I was determined to redeem myself at Team Universe.

At the gym I confided in Jason about John's feedback, and he had another solution for me.

"Don't sweat it. I'll get you some gear and you'll look better than ever," he promised.

The next day we met up near the gym. I climbed into the passenger seat of his brand-new white Range Rover and he handed me a brown paper bag. Inside there were three boxes containing pills, with names I could barely pronounce.

Clenbuterol. Anastrozole. Liothyronine. I examined the labels which gave me no additional information. Two of them weren't even printed in English, aside from the name.

"The Clen is your fat burner. The blue pills are an estrogen blocker. And the little white pills are to speed up your thyroid. Sometimes I even take an extra one if I cheat on my diet," Jason explained to me, grinning.

"Are you sure these are safe for me? I've heard they can really mess you up," I asked warily.

"Justine, trust me. I've been taking ten times that amount for years and I'm fine. Everyone uses this stuff. It's a wonder you've gotten as far as you have naturally," Jason responded coolly. "You just have to cycle on and off so your body doesn't get dependent. I'll help you with all of that. Trust me, I've got you. You're gonna look unreal in a few weeks and get that Pro Card!"

The next day I started using my new performance enhancing drugs, or "gear," as those in the bodybuilding world call it. Again, I didn't question what was given to me. I didn't bat an eyelash. I was willing to do *anything* to win. People use the term "on steroids" to describe taking something to the extreme, and that's what this was, in the most literal sense— my disordered eating and poor body image, *on steroids*. I'd officially gone to the dark side, and there was no turning back.

The same week, I received the most exciting news of my entire fitness career: MET-Rx was signing me as an endorsed athlete! I would actually get *paid* to compete, along with having travel expenses covered for competitions, and a substantial cash bonus for placing within the top three at any show. I had dreamt of this every single day for the past two years, but when the moment came, I couldn't even feel joy or gratification.

I had the awareness that this was a huge moment in my life, and a massive achievement. I even had a colleague record a video of me signing the contract in the MET-Rx corporate office, so I could look back on it forever. But I couldn't let myself actually *receive* this honor. I was incapable of feeling good about it. I was still too bruised from what John had told me, and too obsessed with the *next* milestone: trying to get my Pro Card at Team Universe

That's the problem with external goals— it's never enough. It never feels as good as you think it will. I'd become so addicted to constantly striving that I couldn't stop and smell the roses, and appreciate that the very thing I'd been fighting for was now mine.

Most amateurs dream of turning pro so they will hopefully be signed by a company. Here I'd already done that. I had achieved the prize, yet I couldn't just be happy.

Instead of celebrating the victory, I used it as a way to put *more* pressure on myself, which would eventually be my downfall. After signing that contract, I started saying things like, "I'm getting *paid* to do this."

Punishing my body relentlessly with dieting, overtraining, and drugs was my version of "just another day at the office." The passion and fun I once felt for fitness was replaced by impossibly high standards. Now the reward seemed substantial enough to rationalize the risks I was taking. My paycheck became my permission slip to abuse myself. It was the perfect way to justify how exceedingly fucked up my life was becoming.

October 2012; age 25

I was back at the cattiest place on earth: Knockout Squad camp in Jacksonville. This time though, I was in the best shape of my life. After that mortifying phone conversation with John Lisbon, I hadn't been messing around!

I was very thin— already at the weight I competed at (and placed at) earlier in the year. I was running every morning 3-4 miles on an empty stomach, then eating no more than 1100 calories a day of mostly white fish—tilapia or flounder—a bit of sweet potato and, of course, asparagus.

When I say "mostly white fish," I'm not kidding. Truly I wish I was joking. The Plan I received from the Knockout Squad called for fish at *every* meal of the day. I was eating fish for breakfast. Fish for lunch. Fish for an afternoon snack. Fish for dinner. I am gagging uncontrollably just *thinking* about it. While flounder is way tastier, it's very flaky and falls apart, making it hard to pack. Since Knockout Squad competitors were always on the go, many of our meals were eaten straight out of a plastic bag. Cold. For months, I ate cold, slimy, gross-tasting, unseasoned tilapia for *breakfast*. It was next level self-inflicted torture.

"If your food tastes good, you're probably doing something wrong! It's fuel! Got it? Not every bite needs to taste like a gourmet meal!" Tammy would say.

In the world of bodybuilding and "bro-science," there is a firmly held belief that white fish makes your skin thinner, and therefore makes your conditioning that much crisper. And by conditioning, I mean muscle definition, those lean lines everyone wants. Those lines say, *I've made tremendous sacrifices for this body!*

I showed up to camp that fall with that kind of conditioning on my skinny, starving little body. I felt incredibly proud of how far I'd come since my first Knockout Squad camp, just over a year ago. Yet I knew more work was necessary to get my Pro Card.

The last time I'd been there, I was accosted by Tammy for being fat and made fun of by a teammate for eating wheat bread. At that time, I knew no one, and was a nobody in the industry. I had zero trophies to my name.

Now, I was a seasoned Knockout. I'd been following The Plan for fifteen months, and it showed through my incredible endurance and my impossibly tiny waistline. Everyone knew who I was, because I was a signed MET-Rx athlete, getting *paid* to compete, something no other amateur girls on the team had.

I could tell the other girls were envious of me by the way they'd ask, "How did *you* get *that*?"

I now had four trophies proudly displayed on my dresser at home— two for second place and two for third place. I hadn't gotten my Pro Card at Team Universe, but I'd placed eighth, which wasn't terrible for my first National Pro-Qualifier.

I knew everyone at camp except for the new girls. It was clear who was new from their wide eyes, their lack of a Squeem, their inability to keep up with the fast pace of Knockout workouts, and the general look of terror on their faces. They'd learn quickly, though.

Most of the other women on the team still weren't nice to me, by any means, but at least I felt like they *respected* me.

I'd traveled to camp from New York with Cheryl. We lived just fifteen minutes apart, so we'd gotten close as workout buddies over the past year. On our last day of camp, we had a 6 p.m. flight booked to fly back to JFK airport.

"I just got off the phone with Doug and we might not be flying out tonight," Cheryl said with a worried look on her face.

"What? Why?" I asked, confused and alarmed.

"Hurricane Sandy. It's supposed to be really bad tonight and tomorrow. They're starting to cancel all the flights on the east coast," she explained. Her phone vibrated and she looked down to read a text. "Shit. Our flight is canceled. Let me call Doug back."

I was silent as I tried to process the thought of not getting back that night as planned. I was competing in less than a week, and I only had my meals packed through that night. I became more and more frantic by the minute.

What am I going to do? It's Sunday and my show is on SATURDAY! This is the Eastern USAs— I have to win!

Before I had time to completely unravel, Cheryl returned from calling her husband.

"I have good news. Our friend Paul lives thirty minutes from here. He said we can stay at his place until we can get a flight back."

"Okay," I said slowly, still feeling very distressed about my meals and workouts, and all of the Competition Week Prep instructions before my next show.

"Don't worry," Cheryl said with a reassuring tone. "Paul knows about competition prep. He said we're free to use the kitchen for everything we need. He's working overtime so he'll hardly even be around. And we can find a gym nearby to get day passes from!"

I felt relieved that at least I wasn't stranded alone. At least I was here with a friend who was also competing, to help me stay on track.

That evening, we left Knockout Camp and took over Paul's house. Thankfully he wasn't around, as Cheryl promised, but I can only imagine what this poor guy thought when he returned to his pristine bachelor pad and found the kitchen bursting with the potent stench of fish and asparagus.

The next day, we still couldn't book a flight out. We cooked, trained, and made the most of our situation. I tried to see the bright side of things and be grateful I was safe in sunny Florida, with electricity. Back in Long Island, almost everyone had lost power. Pierre confirmed our apartment was now without power, and things were a mess of chaos and panic there as the storm raged on.

I think the extra adrenaline from stressing about the hurricane made my metabolism go into overdrive. I was so freaking *hungry*! I'd gotten used to feeling hungry and unsatisfied every waking hour of the day, but this was next level. It felt like my stomach was devouring my insides.

That evening after dinner, my last meal of the day, I went to the kitchen to figure out what I could eat to quiet the hunger pains without doing any damage. I sliced up a medium sized cucumber and put the slices in a bowl with ground pepper, a little red wine vinegar and one packet of calorie-free stevia to sweeten it a bit. It reminded me of a cucumber salad my mom used to make in the summertime.

I took my 15-calorie cucumber delight back to the living room where Cheryl and I were watching *Real Housewives of New Jersey* on Bravo.

"What are you eating?" Cheryl asked immediately as I sat down.

"A sliced cucumber with vinegar," I replied, staring at her blanky.

"I thought your meals were done for the day. Is that on your plan?"

Mind your own damn business! I wanted to scream. I was not in the mood for this.

I'd had it with Cheryl giving me the third degree about my plan, incessantly asking if I was following it. It was bad enough how insanely jealous I was of *her* plan. She was one of the lucky ones, who was always ripped and got the "muscle maintenance" plan. She stayed insanely lean no matter how much she ate, so Tammy and Rick prescribed minimal cardio and extra meals. She got *seven* meals when I got *five*! And her meals included things like steak, white potatoes, and rice cakes with peanut butter. *PEANUT BUTTER!*

Don't even get me started on her pre-show meal of pancakes and syrup. You read that right. While I was choking down slimy tilapia, Tammy and Rick would tell her to eat *pancakes* and *syrup* the night before a show, to "fill out" her muscles. And it would *work*! She'd look even more ripped the next day after having freaking pancakes with Mrs. Butterworths! Her body stayed so lean they actually had to fight to keep weight *on* her.

Are you kidding me? Why can't I have that problem? I'd think, driving myself mad.

So there I sat, out of my element, stranded in a stranger's home in another state, trying to quell my hunger pains with a cucumber, and now having to defend myself to this pancake-eating persecutor.

"It's not on my plan, but I'm *hungry*," I replied, gritting my teeth and trying not to lose it. I hoped that would be the end of it.

"I really don't think you should be having extras right now," Cheryl continued to harp on me and my goddamn *cucumber*.

"It's just a cucumber, Cheryl," I said curtly.

Back OFF, bitch.

"Every bite counts. Tammy always says that. Every little bite adds up," she lectured me.

"I'm starving, okay? My stomach is growling and I can't take it. Not all of us get to scarf down rice cakes and peanut butter and pancakes, Cheryl," I snapped. "I am so hungry all the fucking time, which is something *you* wouldn't get! So just leave it alone!"

Cheryl really wasn't the type to take things lying down.

"Fine! I'm only trying to help. It's not *my* fault you're not as lean as me! You don't have to be a bitch about it," she fired back.

I'm the one being a bitch about it? I thought. *WOW*.

My heart was racing, as it always does when I'm in conflict with someone. I didn't want to fight with her though. I was at *her* friend's place, stranded with her until we could get home, so I had to keep the peace. I bit my tongue and stared at the TV screen as I ate the rest of my stupid cucumber with smoke practically fuming out of my nostrils.

We finally got a flight back to New York that Wednesday—three days later than expected. We took *three* flights to be exact. Where normally a nonstop flight from Orlando to New York is easy to book, things were so backed up from Hurricane Sandy we couldn't find anything until the following week. Cheryl's husband Doug managed to pull some strings to find us a roundabout way to get home.

I arrived home to find Long Island in a state of pandemonium. Gas stations were selling out of gasoline and many homes were still without power— including mine. I had to cook my meals over at Cheryl's house, shower at my gym, and wrap myself in every blanket I owned to sleep at night without heat. Still, I clung to The Plan, priding myself on "soldiering through" these trying times.

The real kicker came when the Easterns was postponed by two weeks— a last minute call because New York was in such a state of disaster. I had envisioned myself winning the Easterns, then riding that wave of hype and momentum to Nationals in Atlanta, where I'd surely be repaid for my gallant efforts with a Pro Card. Now the order was backwards, and I'd be doing Nationals first.

I was convinced more than ever that this was my time. It had to be. I was the tiniest I'd ever been— physically I'd been stage-ready for weeks. I'd paid my dues to the NPC by now— and then some. And I bemoaned the hell I'd been through and the obstacles I'd overcome, making myself the #1 victim of the hurricane because *I* was in contest prep, people! While everyone else got to stress-eat during this time of crisis, I was still choking down cold tilapia for breakfast. I viewed myself as a victim, though thousands of people didn't have power for weeks, and families weren't able to work to feed their families.

I imagined myself onstage in Atlanta, being crowned the winner and an IFBB Pro, tears glistening in my eyes and being asked how I overcame it all to get here. I'd say something profoundly inspiring like, "Never give up!" and the crowd would go bananas.

I was so convinced that a glorious victory would be my reward for all I'd been through that I booked a flight for my mom to attend the show in Atlanta.

"You have to be there. I just have this feeling this is *it* for me!" I told her over the phone. "I mean, there's no way God would put me through all this for me to walk away empty-handed."

Competitors' brains get wacky like that. After a bajillion minutes on the treadmill and not enough nutrients to support proper brain function, you truly believe you're doing something really noble. You forget you willingly signed up for the self-inflicted torture, and start believing everyone around you should accommodate your needs and praise your endeavors.

Unfortunately, God, the judging panel and I were *not* on the same page at the show in Atlanta, and I did in fact walk away empty-handed and inconsolable.

November 2012; age 25

I woke up on the day of the Eastern USA's feeling uncharacteristically rebellious. For years I'd been compliant, doing exactly as I was told by judges and coaches. But not today.

I put on the shiny black bikini I'd recently ordered. When I'd told Tammy I wanted to try a black suit at one of my shows, she was clear on her stance.

"Absolutely not. Your color is blue," she told me, in her matter-of-fact way. She used that same matter-of-fact tone when I experimented with red lipstick backstage at one show. "No, no, NO! Your lip color is hot pink. Go change it now."

Tammy provided way more than meal plans and workout instructions. She'd tell you who to be, and what to show the world.

"You're the *sexy* girl. You're not the cutesy girl, okay? You are not the girl-next-door. But you're doing this cutesy stuff in your posing routine, and it confuses people. It doesn't work for you. Less bouncy, more slinky and sexy," I recalled her saying earlier that year after I placed second at the Metropolitan. This was her reasoning for why I didn't take first— my posing wasn't sexy enough.

She even weighed in after my engagement, advising, "Don't ever talk about your relationship status. No one wants to hear you have a boyfriend, or a fiancé. They want to *fantasize* about you— like they have a chance, so always let them think you're single.

Tammy always had an answer for why you didn't place as well as you wanted to. Your hair was too flat, or your tan was too light, or you were holding water in your thighs. In the rare event she couldn't come up with anything, she'd simply say, "You were overlooked."

This is what she'd said the week before, when I didn't place at the National Pro-Qualifier in Atlanta, despite coming in very tiny and tight, and looking flawless, head to toe.

"You were overlooked" stung the most, because here you got everything *right* for once— after preparing for months, or in my case, *years*— and it just wasn't your day. Like, thanks for playing and better luck next time!

"Overlooked" felt like an understatement. Despite my grandiose expectations, I didn't even make the Top 15 at Nationals in Atlanta. I took a bath afterwards at the hotel, and I can remember feeling so distraught, angry, confused, embarrassed and heartbroken that I didn't want to be alive anymore. I wanted to just float away from this existence that felt more hollow every passing day. Since my teens, I'd struggled with depression and anxiety, but my punishing daily habits and impossibly high expectations of myself exasperated my struggles. Both my physical and mental health were deteriorating a little more each day.

A week later I was no longer feeling hopeless, but after being "overlooked" like that, I didn't even want to do this show. The Eastern USA was a prestigious show, but it wasn't a National Pro-Qualifier, so my dreams of becoming an IFBB Pro in 2012 had been extinguished in Atlanta. It felt pointless to get onstage again, but I'd already registered and I was getting paid for it, so I decided to just show up and do my thing, not caring about what everyone else wanted of me for once in my life.

My detachment made all the difference. I got onstage in that shiny black bikini, cool and confident, feeling indifferent to the judges and what they thought of me.

Usually my energy screamed, "Please, please, *please* like me! I *need* you to like me and I'm *dying* to place first!" but today it was more like, "I'm fierce and skinny and sexy and I know it! And for the record, I don't even want to be here."

It worked for me. I won.

That day I took first place in my class, and then my head almost exploded when I was also crowned Overall Champion for all of the Bikini Division. I couldn't believe it— the *one* show I didn't really care about, I won.

After winning the Easterns I had a six-month break before I'd be back on stage. This was unusually long, but I decided having taken the Overall First Place Title home, I was no longer competing in shows that weren't National Pro-Qualifiers, and the first of the season wasn't until the following May.

So, I began to let myself eat. And eat. And eat. Tammy's words, "There is no off season!" became a faint echo in my head, and soon, I neglected The Plan altogether.

After surviving on five meals a day that consisted of tilapia, asparagus, and a couple chunks of unsalted sweet potato, my hunger was a bottomless pit. Aside from that one sushi-and-desserts episode, I'd stuck to my diet religiously for over 16 months.

My cravings and appetite became uncontrollable, and all hell broke loose. I felt as though I couldn't stop myself from eating. Throughout the week, I'd do my best to "eat clean," and maintain some structure in my diet, but when the weekend came, all bets were off. I'd allow myself to eat with reckless abandon.

Much like my freshman year of college, it was an extended binge after such a long period of restriction, often fueled by alcohol. I'd go out for dinner and order a cheeseburger with sweet potato fries, along with a couple of beers or martinis, and then on the way home I'd stop at the 7-Eleven across the street and buy a pint of Ben and Jerry's ice cream. I'd eat it all in one sitting, tipsy on my couch. When I'd wake up in the morning the guilt was unbearable. I'd shove the empty Ben and Jerry's carton way down into the trash, so I wouldn't have to see it and be reminded of my lack of self-control. As if hiding the evidence meant it didn't happen, although my inner critic reminded me every 0.2 seconds.

You're such a fat ass, why can't you ever control yourself? You're disgusting and you're going to gain weight again if you're not careful.

But I wasn't careful. I went home to Wisconsin for Christmas and the entire week I ate anything and everything I wanted. And of course, plenty of drinking. Once again, booze silenced my inner critic so I could devour my fried chicken tenders, pasta, pizza, mashed potatoes and gravy, cookies and custard in peace. But in the morning, when the booze had worn off and my belly was grotesquely bloated, a sense of peace was nowhere to be found. I'd be haunted by my actions of the previous night, totaling up the calories in my head of everything I'd eaten.

That must've been over 3000 calories, I'd think to myself with immense shame and disgust.

Within three months of this behavior, I gained thirty pounds.

It was uncanny how reminiscent it was of my freshman year of college, when I had also put on a substantial thirty pounds of weight. It left me feeling revolted by my lack of discipline, when, in fact, I was fighting my body's own physiological urges to survive.

Knowing what I know now, I refer to deprivation as "a binge in the bank," because it chemically sets you up for a backlash. The longer and more intense the period of deprivation is, the more you can bet on the backlash matching that intensity.

Deprivation only makes us want something more, psychologically. If I tell you *not* to think about the color red, I have a pretty good idea of what color you're thinking of. And if someone tells me I can eat anything except for brownies, I suddenly find myself longing for a brownie... or six!

Our biology fights deprivation, too. To our bodies, restriction is dangerous. Our bodies perceive diets as a famine, so naturally, they go to work doing what bodies are designed to do— keeping us alive.

When our bodies sense the danger of restriction, a series of biological changes occur, including reduced production of the "fullness hormone" leptin, and an increased production of the "hunger hormone" ghrelin. Food-seeking signals go up during periods of deprivation, as well as the reward value of food to our brain, making you a loose cannon around food— *not* an epic failure. This is why an astonishing 95 percent of dieters regain the weight they lost (and often even *more* weight) within one to five years. (Bijlefeld, 2003)

Again, your body is trying to be of *service* to you by helping you get the nutrients you need so that you don't starve to death. Our caveman bodies and brains haven't caught up with our societal desires to look like Kate Moss. Unfortunately, I didn't get the memo on this until years later, so instead of appreciating my body for doing its dutiful job, I hated myself more with every bite I swallowed, and, come springtime, found myself struggling to lose the "rebound" weight once again.

October 2013; age 26

I was ten days out from the Fort Lauderdale Cup when I started feeling sick. At first, I figured I was just fighting off a cold or something, but my symptoms were strange. I felt tired, and I had this terrible throbbing pain up and down my legs. It was like an aching deep in my bones, but there was also this dull burning sensation all over my skin— like a million little pins and needles were poking into my flesh. I'd never felt anything like it before, and even though it wasn't super intense, it was constantly present.

I kept Tammy updated through emails as it continued to get worse. I'd spent the year proving myself to her again, as I diligently followed The Plan to drop all the weight I'd gained.

"I'm so sorry you're sick— but you LOOK GOOD!" she wrote, so I continued to push through each day, following The Plan to the best of my ability.

Training my legs was the hardest part, because they hurt so much and felt weak. For cardio, I'd plop myself on one of those old-school Stairmasters with the pedals and just force my legs to push, hoping the circulation would help the pain, but it never did. But by this point I knew very well that the final days before a show it's all about the diet and the little details— so I kept reassuring myself it would be okay. I could still do the show.

Tammy said I look good, so it's fine, I'd tell myself a hundred times each day. *Beauty is pain.*

The Tuesday morning before the show, as I was weighing myself naked, (to be sure my clothes weren't adding any weight) I discovered a cluster of red blisters on my right butt cheek.

"*AAAAAHHHHHHHHHHHHHHHH*!" I screamed. *What the hell is this?*

I called my doctor immediately, losing my mind.

"I HAVE A RASH! AND I'M FLYING TO FLORIDA ON FRIDAY! I'M COMPETING ON SATURDAY!" was the gist of what I shrieked at him in my panicky state.

"Calm down, Justine. It'll be okay," Dr. Russo said soothingly. "Come in as soon as you can. I'm pretty sure I know what it is, but I need you to come in to be sure."

Dr. Russo was a lifesaver. I'd been introduced to him through other competitors. He used to compete in bodybuilding so he understood the drastic and sometimes hazardous measures one must take to be a champion. Apparently, some of the guys even got their estrogen blockers prescribed by him. I'd started seeing him that summer, and felt relieved I could be honest with a doctor about my behavior, without judgement or a lecture.

I was in and out of Dr. Russo's office within ten minutes.

"Yep. Just what I thought. You have shingles," he said, examining my bare butt. My eyes widened.

"Shingles? Isn't that something old people get?" I asked, stunned.

"Normally, yes. But anyone with a weakened immune system can get it, and from the year you've had I'd say you fit that criteria very well," he explained. "I'll write you a prescription for generic Valtrex. It's an antiviral medication that should clear it up and help you feel better."

Valtrex? I recognized the name and now I was even more confused. "Isn't Valtrex for—"

"Herpes," Dr. Russo finished the question for me. "Yes. Shingles is in the same family as herpes. It's actually called Herpes Zoster."

Neat. I'm 4 days out from a show and have "herpes zoster" on my ass cheek!

I didn't tell Tammy about the shingles, or the medication. I felt embarrassed and remorseful, like this was all my fault for not being able to stay in shape year-round. It was my fault I had to take such extreme measures all year, because I got so out of shape during the off-season. I made my life so much harder by constantly ruining the progress I'd made, and having to start all over from scratch.

THREE times now I'd been in competition shape and then I blew it all by eating my face off 'til I was twenty or thirty pounds above my stage weight. Tammy always told us to stay within five pounds of our stage weight, and the other women on the Knockout Squad seemed to have no trouble doing that. But not me.

Why couldn't I just stay disciplined? I finally have everything I've worked so hard for and I'm blowing it.

I believed it was my burden to bear to always be on the strictest of plans. Tammy and Rick kept me on a super low-calorie diet and two cardio sessions a day without a break, because that's what was required for me to succeed. When they'd dropped my food intake from 6 to 5 meals a day the year prior, I questioned why. They simply told me, "You weren't getting lean enough on that amount of food." That amount of food being 1300 calories max.

Plus, I'd been pumping my body full of fat burning pills and hormone-altering substances for six months straight, even though I knew this was harmful to do long-term. Lots of things people do to prepare for shows aren't good for your health, but you tell yourself it's just for a short period of time to get a desired result. The problem was, it wasn't a short period of time. It was a constant pattern for me. I'd started training for my first show four years prior at this point, and rarely took breaks. When I did take breaks, I was binge eating and gaining weight rapidly, which was also no picnic for my physical body.

The past two years, I'd been killing myself to compete in six shows a year for the paychecks, which was already a tall order. In between shows, I kept getting booked for photo shoots. The opportunities coming my way were straight out of my *dreams*— but when they manifested in my life, the timing was never right. I *would* have given my body a break after my last show in early July, but MET-Rx had booked me for huge shoots in August and September. The corporate executives who booked them didn't have a clue as to what my regimen was like, so they didn't think twice about consulting me for ideal dates. They expected me to be in shape 365 days a year. I was signed as a fitness model, so I was supposed to be *fit* at all times. That's the deal if you want to succeed in the industry.

My extreme lifestyle compounded over time, though. The overtraining and over-dieting, the chemicals I was putting in my body—month after month, year after year—was about to take a disastrous turn. Going off the deep end to binge-city sporadically never helped either.

That Friday, I flew down to Fort Lauderdale alone, because Pierre couldn't take extra time off work. It was actually a good thing I was traveling alone, as Pierre's doting on me often exasperated my fits of anxiety. I never even stopped to consider backing out of the show. I was so disempowered by my thoughts of "I *have to*." I *have to* do this show. I *have to* do this shoot. I *have to* look this way, and I *have to* weigh this amount.

Beauty is pain.

It was never about what I *wanted* to do, or what felt right, or what was actually in my best interest for being a healthy, functioning human being. I simply accepted that this was my life, the life I had chosen, and I had to see my choices through. My existence was joyless, but I had convinced myself that if only I could get that Pro Card, *then* I would be happy.

By the time I got to my hotel room, my body looked so puffy and bloated from the gigantic antiviral pills, the virus my body was fighting, and water retention from the flight. I phoned Dr. Russo.

"You have to help me. I'm so puffy! I'm retaining water like crazy. Can you prescribe me Triamterene?"

I asked for prescription water pills by name, like I was ordering a side of avocado with my salad. Dr. Russo called it in, and I got a girl from the Knockout Squad to drive me to a CVS to pick it up. I took my pills that night and hoped for a miracle.

The next day I looked better, but not my best.

I noticed every bite I ate and every drop of water I consumed seemed to make my body expand and get puffier, so I tried to abstain from eating and drinking all day.

All day I tried to keep it together, going through the motions. The blisters from the shingles were still just as prominent as the day I'd found them, but thankfully I was able to discreetly cover them up by gluing my suit bottoms right over them.

It wasn't lost on me that with all of the skin I was exposing on stage, somehow the patch of shingles happened to be in an area covered by the minimal fabric of my teeny tiny Swarovski crystal-studded bikini. I delusionally interpreted this as a sign from God that I was supposed to be onstage that day, as if I was carrying out some incredibly commendable plan for my life.

I'm quite sure that wasn't the message the Universe was trying to send me— but this was a positive turning point for mc. The shingles incident forced me to start caring about my health.

You'd think a personal trainer turned fitness model would care deeply about her health, but being *healthy* had nothing to do with my pursuit. I wanted to be fit, sexy, and validated, and if my health went down the drain doing so, sadly, I didn't really care.

But since I was hellbent on turning pro, winning shows, and being a world-renowned fitness model, I had to come to terms with the fact that I couldn't do those things if I kept getting sick, or having health flare-ups.

Deep down, I knew many of the things I was doing in the name of succeeding in the fitness industry weren't good for my body, but I was so out of touch with what really mattered that I couldn't be bothered to care. Fixing my Problem Areas and being praised for my tiny, "perfect" body was more important than anything happening on the inside of my body.

I surrounded myself with people who validated the poor decisions I was making. There was this sentiment of "everybody's doing this stuff to win," along with "nothing is more important than winning," so I pushed my better judgment aside and hoped my poor choices wouldn't catch up to me. Now they had. Unfortunately, I didn't respect my body and myself enough to take care of my health sooner, but now I had no choice.

I placed fourth in Fort Lauderdale, which stung. It should've been an easy win for me, since it wasn't a National Pro-Qualifier.

Tammy was surprisingly cool about it.

"You looked great, but you weren't at your best from being sick. It's okay. Let's focus on Nationals in November," she emailed.

When I got back to New York, I started researching anything and everything that could strengthen my immune system and boost my health so I could keep competing successfully. I started drinking a gallon of alkaline water a day from a special shop in

Long Island. I bought a green superfood powder that tasted like grass and dirt. I started taking Lysine supplements to combat the shingles virus from flaring up in my body again. I began buying organic produce and hormone-free meat, instead of whatever was cheapest. I began getting colonics.

These were my first steps down a path toward taking care of my health solely for the sake of my health, but it was still quite twisted. I was doing anything and everything to boost my health so I could continue to get away with abusing my body for the sake of my ego-driven goals of getting that Pro Card.

March 2014; age 26

I was with Adriana in an Irish pub in the West Village of Manhattan, singing out loud with the band as they played a cover of "Yellow," my favorite Coldplay song. A night out for me was highly unusual, as I normally stuck to my routine of working out, eating, feeding my ego via Facebook, and sleeping.

As the band went into their next song, I compulsively refreshed my Facebook Fan Page, despite having checked it about eighty-two times already that day.

"Look!" I yelled to Adriana, thrusting my iPhone in front of her. "Sixty thousand followers! My page just hit *sixty thousand*!"

"Oh my God! You're famous, Justine!" she yelled back. "We have to celebrate! Let me get you one more drink!"

I'd promised myself I'd only have two drinks that evening, but the thrill of Internet stardom had me feeling invincible, and I thought, *one more vodka soda won't hurt!*

"Fine, *one* more!" I shouted over the band. Adriana went to the bar to order as I typed up a new post for my page to commemorate the special moment.

60K following this page— I can't believe it! I feel so blessed! So thankful for all of you!

I posted the caption along with a professional photo of me wearing lace panties and a loose, sheer gray T-shirt. In the photo I'm seductively pulling my t-shirt up to expose my ripped abdominal muscles, my long black hair cascading down my shoulders, my eyes looking away from the camera in that indifferent, stuck-up-model sort of way.

As soon as I posted the picture the likes and comments started rolling in. I read comments from strangers from all parts of the world:

"So sexy baby."

"You look yummy."

"Hermosa."

"Call me. I wud show you a good time."

"I wanna look like her!"

"So fit and beautiful. Perfect body."

"Bangin' body!"

"Now this doll is flawless perfection. You are a masterpiece."

"OMG! Goals!"

"So damn hot I can't focus."

Adriana returned with our drinks and we raised them up for a toast.

"To Justine's superstardom! Don't forget me now that you're famous!" Adriana shouted and we toasted. I already felt intoxicated from the comments praising me. Validation continued to be my drug of choice and social media was the quickest way to get my fix. Men saying they wanted me. Women saying they wanted to look like me. It was everything I'd been chasing for years, and I told myself *this* is what I've worked so hard for. All those hours logged in the gym, all those times I ate nasty fish and asparagus instead of pizza and cookies. *This* was why.

Just one week later, that page reached 70K, continuing to grow like a wildfire in a dry field. Six months after that night out with Adriana, my page reached 600K, and that number snowballed every day. Although she was supportive that night in the pub, Adriana later showed her true colors by making cutting remarks about my "fan base," driving a wedge between us.

Social media stardom was undoubtedly the most insidious thing that could have happened to me at the time. Along with that elusive blue checkmark officially verifying my page, my Internet fame verified all the Unspoken Rules I'd been playing by for nearly twenty years. The overflow of attention served as concrete evidence that I had come out on top with Unspoken Rule #7: *Your value is directly correlated with how desirable you are to men.* And it confirmed the way I was treating my body was worth it— as stated in Unspoken Rule #5: *THIN is more important than healthy.*

Though I certainly had established myself as a winner, I held on firmly to Unspoken Rule #10: *There is a limited supply of attention, success, and resources available for women. You will constantly have to strive to come out on top.* At that point, my following had surpassed every other member of the Knockout Squad, and even the Knockout Squad Facebook Page *itself.*

I truly believed every other woman envied me, especially my Knockout Squad "sisters," and now I felt like I needed to strive to *stay* on top. I needed to constantly defend my place on the throne, which was built on shaky ground. I'd somehow fooled everyone into believing the fat girl could be a fitness model, and now I'd have to be relentless in keeping up the act.

This "prize" of a massive following didn't always feel rewarding. More followers meant more eyes on my page, eyes on my pictures, and eyes on my body. This also meant more comments and messages, and not all of them were complimentary. I put myself out there as an object to look at, so people treated me as such.

While so many people shared kind words telling me how I'd inspired them to make healthy changes, other people took their pain out on me. Behind the safety of their keyboards, humans can be quite brutal. According to an online survey by YouGov, a market research company, 28 percent of Americans admit to participating in "malicious online activity directed at somebody they didn't know."

Unfortunately, I've seen it all. Comments on my body ranging from "You're so skinny it's gross. Eat a burger!" to "Ew you look fat. Less cheat meals, more time in the gym!"

I've been called a "butterface," which, according to UrbanDictionary.com is "a woman regarded as having an attractive figure but ugly facial features." I've been called a slut, a skank, and a whore.

One time, someone commented on a close-up selfie of my face, writing, "This is the stuff nightmares are made of." After reading the comment, I stared at that photo for so long, dissecting it and analyzing all of my flaws until I agreed I was ugly.

One of the worst messages I ever opened read, "Kill yourself, [c-word]." And yes, I'm censoring myself, in my own book, because that's not a word I use, even to quote someone.

You get over the negative comments, eventually. You understand that they come from a sad place, and tell yourself there's a strong chance that the guy who wrote it is 42 years old and living in his mother's basement. You try to send them love, and hope you'll never be in such a sorrowful state that you would hurt another human like this.

But all of that reasoning, and even time, doesn't take away the hurt and sting of vicious words directed at you. I personally never forget a cruel comment, whether it's said in person or written on the internet. I wish I could, but they just never leave me.

They say you've made it when you have haters, especially on the Internet, but these comments wounded me deeply.

Oh, and let's talk "dick pics," shall we? Thousands of them. I've seen so many unsolicited penises that no amount of therapy can ever help me unsee. Many things about the male psyche remain a great mystery to me, but the notion that introducing yourself penis-first is a good way to pique a lady's interest surely takes the cake.

There I was in the middle of it all— utterly consumed by the opinions of others via likes, comments, and messages. Truly believing it was all about me. When someone praised my body, I internalized it, applauding all of my sacrifice. When someone took out their anger on me through a scathing comment, I internalized that, too. How I felt about myself could be influenced by a random comment on my appearance from some stranger living in Moldova. That carrot still dangled in front of me, fooling me into thinking if only I could be perfect enough, the whole world would be pleased with me and only positive comments would come in.

My fragile sense of self rested in the hands of significant others, judges and now, 600K strangers on Facebook. I continued to fall down, down, down, deeper and deeper into the rabbit hole of my narrow little world, completely losing touch with my true value. Eventually, I wouldn't be able to fall any further. Eventually, I'd have to hit the bottom.

June 2014; age 27

That morning started like any other. I woke up in bed alone. Earlier that year, Pierre and I had tied the knot in Las Vegas, despite the fact that he'd been sleeping on the couch for a year at that point. I thought reciting vows in an expensive white dress and actually remaining loyal for a change would be enough to make our relationship better, but it went in the opposite direction. Being legally bound to one another sent us further down the downward spiral we'd been trapped in for years. The resentment, anger, shame, and hurt between us was suffocating us both.

I got out of bed and went to the bathroom. I weighed myself and wrote it down, the way I did every morning. 124.2 pounds.

While this is on the low end of a healthy weight for a female of my height, it was a solid ten pounds up from where I expected myself to be, considering the strict regimen I'd been following.

Very heavy.

I kept repeating these exact words that one of the judges had used to describe my "package" onstage the week before at the National Pro-Qualifier in Chicago.

Ugh! How embarrassing.

I berated myself, cursing my uncooperative body.

What is wrong *with me?*

Later that day, I would, in fact, find out what was wrong with me.

A few minutes before 7 p.m., I walked out of the massive corporate building that housed MET-Rx and other nutrition brands. Two years later I was still training employees there three nights a week (a job I loved.) I looked at my phone as I crossed the sprawling parking lot to get to my car.

One missed voicemail from Dr. Russo.

I climbed into my Jeep Liberty and played the message.

"Justine, it's Dr. Russo. I got your blood work back," he said in a tone that made my stomach drop. "Call me as soon as you can. I'll be available tonight so just call whenever you get this."

I took a deep breath and noticed my reflection in the rearview mirror. So often the way I perceived my own reflection was distorted by other people's opinions, but in that moment, I saw myself so clearly, and it caught me off guard. I pulled the driver's side sun visor down and flipped the mirror open to get a closer look.

Staring back at me I saw two weary eyes, pleading for change. I saw the corners of my mouth downturned to form a frown, which was the general expression my face took anytime I wasn't faking it for a camera, a conversation, or with Pierre. I noticed my skin looked dull and dry, grayish in color. Flakes of skins were scattered throughout my hairline.

OMG you're SO gross! My inner critic continued to punish me.

After hearing the urgency in Dr. Russo's voice, I considered for the first time the possibility that there might actually be an underlying health issue. Maybe it wasn't a matter of me needing more willpower, more cardio, or fewer calories. For months now I'd been disappointed and downright *angry* with my body for not doing what I needed it to do. For not obeying me.

Since I was thirteen years old, I'd been able to manipulate my body through restriction and exercise, but over the past few months, all of my tricks stopped working. I had cut my carbs. I had cut my fats. I had added more intensity to my cardio sessions. None of it worked, and I was mortified with how I'd looked onstage this year.

After not even placing Top 15 in my past two competitions, I had decided I was just a fat loser who wasn't trying hard enough. I'd accepted that my greatest fear of being overweight had finally caught up to me. But after hearing the concern in Dr. Russo's voice, I intuitively sensed that maybe that wasn't the case.

I dialed Dr. Russo and after two rings he picked up.

"Dr. Russo, it's Justine. I just got your message."

"Hey kiddo, glad you called back. I've got some bad news," he said gently. I braced myself. "Your blood work shows your thyroid has shut down, and your hormones are completely out of whack. I'm sorry kiddo, but you need to take a break."

His words hit me like a massive ocean wave, and I immediately felt like I was drowning in fear and uncertainty. Life as I knew it, and everything I'd worked so hard for, was being washed away in an instant.

Take a break?! I wanted to scream. *Team Universe is nine days away— that's* my *show! I'm supposed to turn Pro this year! And this is my* living*! Doesn't he get that?*

"I— I don't know what to say. Isn't there anything we can do?" I pleaded. I figured there had to be *some* pill, *some* diet, *some* workaround to coax my body to do what I needed it to do. I wished it could be as simple as him calling in a magical prescription to CVS, the way he had the year before when I had shingles and needed to shed water weight fast.

"Unfortunately no, sweetie. Your body is worn out," Dr. Russo told me. "You need to take some time off to let your hormones balance out. I think with some rest your thyroid could bounce back without medication. I can't say for sure, but you're young. Right now you need to give your body some rest, and stop dieting for a while. You know, just eat normally so your body can balance itself out."

Eat normally?!

Taking a break seemed ludicrous enough— now he was telling me to eat normally?!

What the hell does that even mean? Doesn't he know I've been dieting for 15 years?!

My thoughts raced. I felt like I might scream, cry, or implode into smithereens, so I decided to end the call as quickly as possible with some dignity.

"Thank you, Dr. Russo. I appreciate you taking my call so late," I said, trying to steady my voice to disguise the fact that I was about to have a complete meltdown.

"You bet, that's what I'm here for. We can test your levels again in a couple months and go from there. Take care of yourself, kiddo! You're going to be just fine," he promised.

That night I couldn't sleep. As I laid in bed alone, my thoughts spiraled out of control. I didn't know where to begin with breaking the news to everyone—my coaches, my sponsors, everyone at the gym, and all of my fans and followers. I imagined everyone would be so disappointed in me.

What's going to happen to me? Will I lose my sponsors? Will I lose followers? Will I gain a ton of weight? Will I ever be able to compete again? Will I never turn pro? Will I end up a failure, a nobody, a loser? What am I going to do?

All the uncertainty made me sick to my stomach. I had become a one-trick pony, and my one trick was looking fit, lean, and perfectly toned.

But at the same time, a little tiny voice— a voice I'd never heard before kept saying, *this is for the best. This is for the best.*

Some part of me actually felt relieved, which terrified me more than anything.

How could I feel relief over this? Am I crazy? After all I've sacrificed to get the attention and opportunities in the industry, how could I possibly be okay with letting it all go?

For years, I had solely focused on winning, and being what I thought everyone else wanted me to be. I tried to do all the things I thought would make me loved, valued, and successful in this world.

Now I *had* it all— the Internet verified this for me daily. I'd constructed a body and an image so impressive that people wanted to *pay* me for it. Companies everywhere were dying to work with me. I'd paid my dues and knew I was next in line to get my IFBB Pro Card, if only I could show up looking perfect onstage *one* more time.

Yet I was lying to myself, pretending the relief came out of nowhere. On the inside, behind the carefully crafted physical appearance, I didn't feel loved, valued, or successful. I felt unfulfilled, fearful, exhausted, and alone. I felt like a fraud every time I saw those comments saying "GOALS!" from women, knowing damn well my life was anything *but*.

My anxiety was so excruciating I had to recite Bible verses every time I had to leave my apartment. After reading "The Power of Positive Thinking," I'd recited Philippians 4:13, "I can do all things through Christ who strengthens me," so many times that I got it tattooed onto my wrist. But it didn't help. I never felt at peace. I was a slave to whatever plan, whatever coach assigned to me at any given time. A slave to the number on the scale each day. A slave to the number of likes I had on my newest post. A slave to the place I took in my most recent show, decided haphazardly by judges who were as crooked as corrupt politicians.

After five years of this alienating, self-centered quest, I had no close relationships, and no one I could really talk to, or open up to. My then-husband made my blood boil just from the way he breathed. Cheryl and I had a falling out earlier that year, and I never made another close friend through the Knockout Squad. I wasn't speaking to Adriana after her snide remarks about my fan base, and I hadn't stayed in touch with anyone else from high school or college. My parents continued to be supportive, but I kept them at a safe distance knowing that if they had the full picture of what my life had become, they'd surely try to intervene. And I'd savagely manipulated my physical body in every way imaginable for *two decades*— and now it was refusing to cooperate any longer. Even my own body had turned against me, sending me a big fat message of, *Screw you, Justine*!

During those two decades, I'd viewed my body as something to battle against. Something I could hate into being perfect. I'd developed a bitter resentment toward my body at such a young age, and learned to use any means necessary to overpower it, forcing it to be as thin as possible. I had disrespected my body so many times it was as if she was finally putting her foot down and insisting, *NO MORE.*

All of my obsessive, controlling ways had led me *here*. All of the constant striving to win, striving to be on top, and here I was, at an all-time low. I felt as though I couldn't possibly sink any lower.

By 3:30 in the morning, I was going mad. My thoughts were racing, and I could no longer bear the tightness of anxiety in my chest. My feelings and fear were suffocating me.

With nowhere else to turn, I crawled out of bed, got down on my knees, and started to pray. As soon as I did, I broke down sobbing. Like that hysterical, ugly-cry kind of sobbing. I sobbed and heaved, letting all of the pent-up pain, frustration, and loneliness pour out of me.

Please God, if you can hear me, I need you right now. I don't know what to do. I feel so alone, and I can't do this anymore. I can't live like this. But I don't know what to do. I've come so far. I've worked so hard for all of this. Please show me what to do. What do I do, what do I do, what do I do?

That tiny, unfamiliar voice spoke up again.

What do you want, Justine? What's going to make you happy?

I was bewildered. I couldn't even begin to answer those questions. I had turned down the volume on my true desires for so long that they were muted. I couldn't hear them anymore.

Out of nowhere, I felt a wave of calm wash over me. My body relaxed, my teeth unclenched, and my neck and shoulders released the tension I'd been holding onto for the past 20 years of trying to prove myself worthy. I felt myself physically and mentally surrender, which was really the only card I had left to play.

That tiny, unfamiliar voice spoke up again, repeating those questions I didn't have answers to.

What do you want, Justine? What's going to make you happy?

July 2014; age 27

My mom had booked a flight to New York to support me at my next National Pro-Qualifier, which took place over the Fourth of July weekend. But with my doctor's orders to take a break, we were free to make other plans. I knew my mom was secretly thrilled about this, but she kept it under wraps since I was still grieving the Pro Card I believed was meant to be mine at that show.

We embarked on a little mother-daughter getaway, wine tasting at scenic vineyards and indulging in fresh-caught seafood and homemade ice cream from old-fashioned parlors.

The North Fork of Long Island has this wonderfully nostalgic vibe, making you feel as though you've been transported back into a simpler, slower-paced time. The atmosphere is so beautiful and tranquil that it makes you forget your cell phone even exists. It was the perfect place for me to forget all my woes over not being able to compete, and just be present with my mom like a real human being. You know, eating, drinking, and *living,* without weighing myself or obsessing over everything that crossed my lips. I didn't even bring my scale to the hotel for the first time in five years.

On the last day of our getaway, I had a call scheduled with my coach, Jay Harris, who I had started working with only two months prior. I'd finally gathered enough self-respect to say goodbye (and good riddance) to Tammy and the Knockout Squad at the end of the previous season. I hoped the grass would be greener with another top coach in the industry — and it was, but it was too late for me. My body was already a wreck when I began working with Jay.

I was terrified to call him and report that I hadn't eaten a single thing on the meal plan he'd sent me, nor had I worked out *at all,* aside from walking around wineries and chocolate shops the past four days. I knew what Tammy would say about this— "Get it together, sister! No more nibbles! No more cheating!"

I imagined Jay would be equally disappointed in me, and would think I wasn't taking him seriously, although I had emailed him regarding my health after speaking with Dr. Russo.

"Hi Justine! How's it going?" he asked. Always a terrible liar, I blurted out the truth.

"I haven't worked out since last Wednesday, and I haven't been sticking to my plan at all," I confessed like I was confessing my sins to a priest. "My mom is visiting from out of state, so we've been dining out and I've been eating whatever I want. I'm *so* sorry. I promise I'll get back on track tomorrow."

Jay was silent at first.

"Shame on you, Justine," he finally said, followed by a long pause. My heart stopped beating for a moment as I, a grown woman, waited to be scolded by this grown man for indulging my hunger on a weekend vacation. Instead, Jay burst out laughing.

"I'm *kidding,* Justine! I'm messing with you!" he said, still cracking himself up. Then his voice softened and he said something that blew my mind. "Listen, you're just living your *life*, and that's *okay*! That's what you *should* be doing! Have fun with your mom and stop beating yourself up for enjoying your life!"

I was stunned. *Enjoy my life? Without a meal plan? What a concept!*

I thanked him and hung up the phone, a different person. Here was this man I respected in the fitness industry giving me advice and *permission* to enjoy myself for once.

After dropping my mom off at the airport, I returned home and immediately weighed myself to see the damage I had done. Despite Jay telling me not to beat myself up, it was a habit to shame myself anytime I ate something "bad."

It was early afternoon and I was a few meals in, so I was shocked to step on the scale and see I'd actually *lost* three pounds.

How is this possible? I wondered.

Over the next few weeks, as stress melted away without the immense pressure of an upcoming competition, the pounds I'd been desperately trying to lose melted away too, effortlessly. I was working out less, and actually honoring my cravings and hunger to let me know what to eat. As I navigated life without a rigid diet plan, I noticed I didn't have the strong desire to binge on cookies and ice cream. I was surprised by what my body was craving— whole eggs, fresh salads with avocado and chicken, nuts and nut butters, and fresh fruit. It was mind boggling for me that I could exercise less, not be so strict with my eating, and somehow *lose* weight.

This turned everything I believed about my body, dieting and weight loss upside down, and I began to wonder what else I'd been wrong about. I started to question my methods of punishing my body for the very first time.

August 2014; age 27

I thought I couldn't sink any lower on the night I got the news from Dr. Russo, but I was wrong. For the first time in my life, I couldn't even think about how my body *looked*, because the way my body *felt* was all-consuming.

Even after sleeping a full eight or nine hours, I'd crawl out of bed as though I hadn't slept in *weeks*. I'd down giant cups of coffee, or take the caffeine laden fat-burning pills and pre-workout powders I'd been dependent on for years, and they'd only make me feel *worse*. A thick cloud of brain fog enveloped me, rendering me useless.

By early afternoon, I couldn't function. I couldn't think clearly. I couldn't return emails, or write back to fans' comments and messages. The exhaustion was debilitating. Day after day, no matter how much I'd sleep, I was in a constant state of excruciating tiredness.

I called Dr. Russo who assured me I just needed more time to rest, and my hormones would rebalance themselves.

But I can't live like this! I thought, and started looking for additional support.

My longtime chiropractor, Dr. B referred me to Dr. Grant, a local naturopath who met with me promptly and sent me for more comprehensive blood work.

"Medical doctors only run tests for certain hormonal markers, but it's way deeper than that. We're going to run a complete hormone panel to get the full picture of what's going on," he explained.

As soon as my lab results came back, we met again.

"Good news and bad news," Dr. Grant said, laying out sheets of paper with lab results in front of me. "The good news is what's going on with you isn't chronic, so we should be able to get you healthy again without any long-term complications."

"Okay," I replied, bracing myself for the bad news, wishing he'd started with that part.

I feel like shit, just tell me what's wrong already! I thought, agitated. I've always been impatient, but the permanent state of unbearable exhaustion made it next-level.

"The bad news is, you have severe adrenal fatigue." Thankfully he continued on, because I'd never heard of adrenal fatigue. "In plain terms, your adrenal glands are completely shot from stress. This is likely the cause of your thyroid dysfunction, because the two go hand-in-hand."

He continued on, explaining my lab results in detail.

"So what do we do next?" I asked, eager for a quick fix to feel normal again as soon as humanly possible.

"I'm afraid recovery will take some time, because your case is so severe. I've printed out a treatment protocol for you here."

He handed me a blue folder with papers inside.

"You'll need to cut all caffeine to give your adrenals a break. You'll be taking natural supplements to nourish and heal your adrenals. And you'll need to give your body a serious break from working out. No strength training or intense cardio for at least five or six months."

"Seriously?" I blurted out. No caffeine sounded bad enough. *Stop training for five or six months? Is he crazy? This is my job!*

"I'm afraid so. Exercise puts stress on the body, and when the body is healthy, it responds positively to the stress, by getting stronger. But with how depleted your adrenals are, they can't handle any added stress," he explained. The look on my face must have displayed my shock and horror, because he added, "You can go for short, slow walks though, if you're itching to get some activity in."

Great. I'll take short, slow walks *to get in peak condition,* I thought. *First I have to take a break from competing and now I have to take a break from training altogether?*

I was too tired and foggy-headed to appreciate the fact that this diagnosis was temporary, and still too caught up in my obsession with winning to acknowledge it could've been so much worse, given the strain I'd put on my body for so many years.

That soft voice within me spoke up again, saying, *oh thank God.*

A deeper, wiser part of me was sick and tired of being ignored. Ironically, it took getting literally sick and tired to start the process of my awakening. That wiser part of me felt tremendously relieved by these doctor-facilitated, life-altering interventions. My ego brain was throwing an all-out tantrum, but every other part of my body, heart and soul wanted kindness, love, respect—and *rest* for heaven's sake, after years of relentless abuse.

I'd never once stopped to consider the risks versus the rewards—the rewards being plastic trophies, Facebook "likes," and some bragging rights; and the risks being my overall health and well-being. I wagered my *health*, which I would later realize is the most important thing in the whole world, in an attempt to be seen as "perfect." Now I was paying the price.

I drove home after meeting with Dr. Grant and went straight to my bedroom. I stood in front of the full-length mirror and stared at the reflection of someone I no longer knew. Someone I didn't even recognize. Someone whose choices landed me *here*: in a vengeful body and a life that felt like absolute shit.

How did I get here? I wondered.

I had worked so damn hard to be lovable and valuable. I'd tried my very hardest to win. Yet here I was, in an apartment I hated, in a town I hated, in a marriage I hated, and in a body that hated *me*, for good reason. I was physically and mentally unwell, with no real, healthy relationships in my life, and I had no one to blame but myself.

I was still wearing my Squeem underneath my tank top, the rubber and metal forcefully digging into my skin. One tiny metal clasp at a time, I unshackled myself from the archaic contraption.

I can't do this anymore. I can't do this anymore. I can't do this anymore, I repeated in my head as I undid each clasp. My tiny little midsection breathed a sigh of relief as I freed her.

I laid down in my bed. Again, I felt like I had no one to talk to and nowhere else to turn, so I prayed.

Please God, I need you. I'm so sorry I've gotten myself here. I'm so sorry for taking my health for granted. I promise I'll do better. I promise to start respecting my body. Please help me heal. Please just let me feel good again. Please show me the way, because I have made such a horrible mess of my life.

I knew it was all over. I'd go on to tell my sponsors and followers that this was just a break, and I'd be back onstage very soon, but I knew in my heart this was the end of the road. I thought my life was over, but really, it was just beginning. Out of my darkest moment, the life I was meant to lead, and the person I was always meant to become, was birthed.

Unspoken Rules of Being A Woman

1. ~~Unspoken Rule #1: Lose weight to feel great.~~

2. ~~Unspoken Rule #2: Be the right size, as determined by society.~~

3. ~~Unspoken Rule #3: Do whatever you need to do to eradicate your "problem areas."~~

4. ~~Unspoken Rule #4: Do not trust your hunger. Magazines and diets will tell you how much to eat.~~

5. ~~Unspoken Rule #5: THIN is more important than healthy.~~

6. ~~Unspoken Rule #6: The purpose of exercise is to be thin. Exercise as much as possible, and as hard as possible.~~

7. ~~Unspoken Rule #7: Your value is directly correlated with how desirable you are to men.~~

8. ~~Unspoken Rule #8: Other women are not your friends. They are your competition and your enemies.~~

9. ~~Unspoken Rule #9: Pretty girls are "taken." It is better to be in a toxic relationship than to be single.~~

10. ~~Unspoken Rule #10: There is a limited supply of attention, success, and resources available for women. You will constantly have to strive to come out on top.~~

11. ~~Unspoken Rule #11: Keep your feelings to yourself to keep others comfortable. The uncomfortable things that happen to you are yours to carry. Alone. In silence.~~

31-year-old me at "The Bliss Project"— happy, healthy, whole, and enjoying life.

Part IV: The Phoenix (Healing)

*"and i said to my body. softly. 'i want to be your friend.'
it took a long breath. and replied 'i have been waiting my
whole life for this."*

— *Nayyirah Waheed*

September 2014; 27

Beautiful things happen when your life falls apart. When it all crumbles to the ground, you have no choice but to build it back up— but this time, you are armed with the wisdom of your own life experience. You get to choose what you build this time around. You are given an opportunity to start fresh, with intention.

Most of us end up in lives we didn't intentionally choose. In childhood, we're asked, "What do you want to be when you grow up?" As if we're supposed to pick one singular thing to be for the rest of our time on earth.

As teenagers, we're encouraged to go to college—choose a college, choose a major. Choose your friends, choose your lovers, choose a spouse. Choose a career, choose your home.

Before long, we wake up in a life we chose for ourselves at a very young age—an age where perhaps we weren't fully equipped to make such monumental choices. In our late teens and early twenties, we may be operating from a place of, *how can I be loved, admired, affirmed and accepted? How can I get everyone to like me? How can I succeed in meeting the world's expectations of me?*

Often our answers to those questions are shaped by cultural programming, what our caregivers modeled to us, and even our own trauma. When these things are in the driver's seat, it typically doesn't lead to the best life choices.

By the age of thirteen, my brain had adopted and solidified the belief of, "Fat is bad. Don't be fat. People don't like you when you're fat. Be thin. Thin is good. People praise you when you're thin."

With this belief gnawing at me day and night, I went on to attract people and experiences to mirror it back to me. Our brains don't want to make us liars, so they fight to *prove* our beliefs, regardless of whether those beliefs are helpful or harmful.

My life became a game of constantly striving to stay two steps ahead of my deepest fears. I did everything I'd believed I was supposed to. I played the game. I followed the rules. I had proven my value as a woman to the world— hadn't I?

But no matter how low my body fat percentage went, or however many comments on the internet praised me for my physique, it was never enough. I thought all the achievements and validation would make me happy—but I found myself in a place where I couldn't have been further from happiness.

In trying to be everything I thought the world wanted me to be, I had abandoned myself. In manipulating and controlling my body, I had silenced my spirit. My true desires. My own intuition. My inner guidance system. And I didn't have the slightest clue how to make it right.

I was willing to admit defeat, and to admit I'd created an awful mess of a life for myself, but I felt terrified to move forward. Clearly, I had been so wrong before. How could I trust myself to choose better now?

So, I asked for help. Day after day, I humbled myself in prayer and really sincerely *begged* for help.

I truly believe if you ask for help—if you pray for guidance from a power beyond yourself—you'll get it. But you have to accept the guidance when it comes. That's the tricky part. Faith means trusting in the unseen. Faith means moving forward on the path even though you don't know where the path leads. Faith requires an exchange of power, a surrender of control, humbly admitting we don't have all the answers, and our way isn't always the best way.

If you find yourself struggling to row upstream, it's a surefire sign there's a better way for you—but you need to be willing to let the new way in. The start of the healing process is like pulling the thread of a sweater. As you say "yes" to change, everything starts to unravel before the real healing can begin.

My first step toward healing was accepting that the greater plan for me looked very different from the course I was on. I had to accept that I'd taken some wrong turns, and that maybe the things I thought I wanted so badly weren't ever meant for me at all. I had to accept that I was in a failing marriage. I had to accept that I had no healthy female friendships. I had to accept that no amount of validation and praise for my body was ever going to make me happy. I had to accept that it was time to course correct.

Healing our hearts and minds is like healing a physical wound— often it gets worse and hurts like hell before it gets better. But I accepted the pain. Every fiber of my being wanted out from the life I found myself in. I let everything burn to the ground around me and allowed myself to feel every emotion that came up while doing so. And little by little, I started getting nudged in the right direction.

November 2014; age 27

I needed to get out of New York. Reducing my stress was imperative to getting my health back, so I needed to make some drastic changes. They say you can't heal in the same environment that made you sick, and I recognized this. But I found myself paralyzed with uncertainty.

I prayed for guidance on where to move, while researching different cities as options. When the answer came to me with such clarity and certainty, it was the very last place I expected: *home*.

On November 1st, I woke up back in Wisconsin— for good. I drove from New York to Milwaukee with all of my belongings and I never looked back. I ran away from the terrible mess of a life I had created for myself.

I was finally able to acknowledge what I knew for over six years, but didn't have the courage to say or act upon— my relationship with Pierre wasn't right for either of us. So many times, I'd berated myself for marrying him, asking, *Why? WHY did I walk down the aisle when I so clearly knew what we had was not mutual love and respect?*

One of my mentors, who I'd placed on a pedestal, told me that in order to be successful, I needed to find someone who would go to any length for me and my dreams. Clearly, Pierre was that for me. He'd stuck with me through all of the pain of my unfaithfulness, sneaking around, and lying. I could practically hear his heart break when he synced my text messages to show up on my iPad and caught me in my lies. And yet, he had stayed. He continued to support me by helping me prepare for competitions, and continued to revere my dreams of conquering the fitness industry. I figured someone who cared for me enough to endure my lack of respect and my fowl temper (undoubtedly worsened by carb depletion) must be worth keeping around.

I also felt like I owed him for everything I'd put him through—the cheating, the lying—although I never begged him to stay. My marriage to Pierre was my warped way of paying my debt to him. From that day forward I was faithful, in hopes that me not cheating or lying would be enough to make a broken relationship happy, healthy, and whole again. But I brought the same lack of respect and love for him into the marriage.

Just because you suddenly stop being an asshole doesn't mean the relationship will repair itself. I'd done damage Pierre would never be able to forget, even though he was willing to forgive.

It's unsettling for me to look back on the way I treated Pierre, especially after *I* had been mistreated by others before him. I had a nasty underlying belief about relationships that locked itself in after my parents' messy divorce: *Hurt, or be hurt.*

Pierre had wounded my ego repeatedly in the beginning of our relationship, so once I had the upper hand, I abused the power I had over him. Through my healing journey I would come to understand that relationships don't *have* to be a constant battle over who has the power. Mutual respect, unity, and teamwork can exist in a partnership.

Each week of the marriage seemed to get progressively worse. Both of us were crumbling under the weight of committing to something that was so toxic to begin with. Back in New York, I lacked the support system to feel secure enough to end the relationship. I felt trapped. But when I moved back to Milwaukee, I realized I needed to ask Pierre for a divorce. And so, I did. I had never felt more free to be myself than I did in that moment.

I moved into a gorgeous one-bedroom apartment on the east side of Milwaukee, with stunning views of Lake Michigan. For the exact same rent I'd been paying for my dismal, outdated apartment New York, I now lived in a place I was proud to call home.

My new place had shiny, dark cherry hardwood floors, sparkling granite countertops, and floor-to-ceiling windows that let sunlight pour in. My backyard was the massive blue lake, and my front yard was the heart of downtown, steps away from lively restaurants, cafés, bars, shops and entertainment. It made me feel reinvigorated, and excited about *life* again.

My parents donated furniture, glassware, dishes, and towels, because nothing I'd had in New York was really worth taking. I'd never bothered to invest in myself in that way. My "dishes" had been cheap Tupperware containers and Ziploc bags. I mean, who has the energy to decorate a home when you're working out for three hours a day, every day?

But now I had time. With the intention of healing my adrenals and my thyroid, I'd scaled way back on my workouts, from my extreme contest-prep regimen to just taking daily walks, as Dr. Grant had advised. I thought this would drive me insane, but I really didn't have the energy to berate myself for missed workouts.

Moving to Milwaukee changed my health seemingly overnight. Almost immediately the color started coming back to my face, and a little sparkle came back to my eyes, which had been weary and hopeless for a few years now.

I lived six blocks from Whole Foods, and I'd go there on my daily walk and nourish my body with giant kale salads filled with chickpeas, roasted vegetables, nuts, and whatever other toppings I was craving. I even put wonderful, delicious *cheese* on my salads, which I hadn't done in five years.

What an *experience*, eating what I wanted, without measuring my food. The more I continued to "eat like a normal person," as Dr. Russo had advised, the more my body rejoiced. I'd been so fearful of not following a meal plan or having a coach to tell me what to eat, when to work out, and how to treat my body. I thought surely I'd gain weight and get fat if I wasn't dieting, restricting, weighing, and measuring. But miraculously my body was much leaner than it had been earlier in the year when I'd been in contest prep, on a crazy strict diet and punishing workout plan.

What I'd first discovered that summer, that I could eat what I wanted, workout less, and *not* gain weight, continued to ring true my first year in Milwaukee. I bought a giant floor length mirror from IKEA for my new place, and for the first time in a long time, I'd look in that mirror and really, truly *like* what I saw—a confident and capable young woman taking her life back.

I loved being near my family, and being able to enjoy food with them again. For the past five years, it was always feast or famine, to the extreme, when we got together. Either I'd show up to Easter dinner with a slimy, bland, pre-cooked meal, weighed and measured, shooting death stares at everyone enjoying freshly baked bread or chocolate egg-shaped candy, or I'd be "on a break," gorging myself on all the things I was normally forbidden to eat, all the while hating myself more and more with every bite, completely missing out on being present. I didn't make for a very fun dinner guest, if you catch my drift.

My parents were delighted to have me home, and even happier that competing was no longer on the table.

One night my dad and I went to a Milwaukee Bucks basketball game, and when we grabbed dinner beforehand, I ordered a cheeseburger, side salad, and two hoppy IPA's. I savored the meal, but even more, I savored being able to spend time with my dad, without being hindered by obsessive thoughts about calories and weight gain. We got to talk, laugh, and enjoy the game, without the company of my inner demons spoiling all the fun.

Moving to Milwaukee lifted the veil from my eyes and let the light in. Piece by piece, every part of my life went on the chopping block. And piece by piece, things started to get better. I began to make choices for my own health and happiness, which I hadn't factored into my decisions for a very long time.

April 2015; age 28

In January of 2015, my Facebook Fan Page hit 1 million followers, with zero sign of slowing down. By April, it was at 1.5 million.

I had been so fearful that not competing would be a death sentence for my Internet fame, but it was quite the opposite. Echoing the way my body looked better and healthier the further I distanced myself from competing, my following exploded when I changed the page name from "Justine Moore: NPC Bikini Competitor" to simply "Justine Moore." I realized that no one but me really cared whether or not I was competing, or whether or not I was an IFBB Pro. To the average person, that title I'd practically sold my soul for is meaningless.

Moving out of New York was the end of my corporate training position at MET-Rx headquarters, and my athlete endorsement had been centered around competitions. I attended the Arnold Sports Festival again in March of 2015, and negotiated a deal for four times the amount I'd been getting paid, on account of my impressive social media presence. Unfortunately, before the new contract was signed, the brand did some massive house cleaning, and the executives I'd struck a deal with were let go. My contract never went through. The abrupt way things ended left a bad taste in my mouth, but looking at the big picture, I have so much gratitude for my experience working with MET-Rx.

Without these streams of income, I'd grown to depend on, I leaned into my entrepreneurial side. I published an eBook of fitness-friendly recipes, co-authored with my mom. I launched the Justine Moore Fitness app, with workout programs and motivational tips. I focused more on my online fitness programs and serving new clients. Learning how to build my own brand and market myself, after spending years being a face for someone else's brand, proved to be way more challenging than I expected.

I made a lot of mistakes in those ventures, but I also received a crash-course education on running my own business.

***

The lab results of my blood work came back with positive news in January. After six months of working to repair my hormones naturally, my thyroid was almost in a normal range. *Hallelujah.*

I was able to start working out again. With a brand-new appreciation of my body, I ventured into a small boutique gym and fell in love with fitness all over again—but this time, in a very different way.

The gym wasn't even open on Sundays, sending a strong message advocating for days off to rest, which had been a foreign concept while training for shows. The workouts were 45 minutes tops— including a dynamic warm up and foam rolling, to avoid injury and improve recovery. At first, I was paranoid that 45-minute workouts wouldn't be enough, but I kept an open mind knowing my adrenals were still in a delicate place.

Workouts varied daily, ranging from kickboxing to strength training, to something called "Metabolic Cardio."

"What's Metabolic Cardio?" I asked Elise, the bubbly, redheaded manager at the gym.

"We do high intensity intervals that rev up your metabolism for up to 72 hours! It's intense, but fun! I love doing those workouts on Fridays— it's the perfect way to go into the weekend. I usually take Saturday and Sunday off, and get back to training on Monday," she explained.

Mind = blown. *Weekends off training? How balanced. How smart. How sustainable!*

Elise and the other instructors were knowledgeable, and regularly explained fitness concepts based on cutting-edge science, rather than outdated bodybuilding myths. They taught members how to work out safely and effectively to create a metabolism that works *for* you, focusing on strength and health, versus being as "tiny and tight" as humanly possible. They even referred to treadmills as "dreadmills," and explained how to make cardio more effective (and more enjoyable!)

I became stronger, fitter, and happier than I'd ever been in any gym. So naturally, I applied to work there, following my passion the way I had years ago at XSport Fitness. Only this time, the environment was helping me thrive. I found that 45-minute workouts 5 days a week suited me far better than The Plan ever had. My muscles popped, my energy soared, and my skin glowed. I was working out less, enjoying burgers and beers, and learning to love what I saw in the mirror. Cue: A choir of angels singing from the heavens.

The gym was predominantly female, both the members and the staff, which was a far cry from the male-dominated weight rooms I was used to, where everyone called everyone "Bro," or "Brah." Without any "Bros" in sight, I started showing up to the gym without makeup on— something I wouldn't be caught dead doing back in New York. I no longer felt a sense of desperation to get attention from guys, and no longer felt the need to compare myself to or compete with other women.

Even on social media, I was more interested in posting pictures of my daily outfits instead of my abs and cleavage. For years I hadn't been able to enjoy fashion—something I'd always loved—because I never *went* anywhere besides the gym. I hardly even owned "normal clothing," during the years I was competing, because I was exclusively in workout gear or competition bikinis. I had a body I worked so hard for, but I never really *rocked it*. Inside

I'd still felt too insecure and "not good enough," to show off my shape with fun outfits. Distorted body image really robs you of your ability to enjoy the even smallest things in life.

Now I was having the time of my life, focusing on what made me feel good.

This was a turning point in my relationship with exercise and my body, and also a turning point in my relationships with other women. I bonded with the other instructors at the gym, and, to this day, I'm still extremely close to a few of them. I also befriended two women at a salon I'd been going to, who would later be bridesmaids in my second wedding.

These true, supportive, female friendships were brand new territory for me. Women who wanted to build me up, instead of compete or tear me down, were a breed I wasn't familiar with. I was especially thankful to have them in my corner as I ventured back out into the dating world, single, for the first time since college.

July 2015; age 28

Dating as 28-year-old-me, with over 1.5 million followers and 19 fitness competitions under my belt, was remarkably different from dating as 20-year-old-me, insecure and ravenous for attention and acceptance from anyone who would give it to me. At 28, I knew the world was my oyster.

Along came Caleb. Caleb was a former NCAA football superstar, a first-round draft pick who'd tragically injured himself in his first season playing for the NFL, terminating his dreams of football glory. We'd met multiple times at the Arnold Sports Festival, introduced through a mutual acquaintance. When he found out I was no longer married, he asked me to come visit him in Las Vegas, and our whirlwind romance began.

Overnight I fell crazy, head-over-heels, deliriously in love with him. By the end of our first weekend together, we were talking about marriage, children, where we'd spend our Christmases, the whole nine yards (pun intended.) I didn't even want kids, but Caleb was dead set on it, and I was dead set on being with him, so I made it work in my mind.

It was euphoric to experience the blissful feelings of being *in love* with someone— something I had denied myself for years, believing I needed to settle. And he loved me back, or so he told me, morning, noon, and night.

But then things started to feel off. Caleb's mother had been an abusive drug addict when he was growing up, and gradually his disdain for women became obvious through the language he'd use. He'd make subtle comments that made my insides squirm. He also had a beastly chip on his shoulder, enraged at life by the cards he'd been dealt.

After Caleb's initial politeness and charm wore off, I started feeling sick to my stomach every time we'd finish a FaceTime, phone call, or get into a minor disagreement via text.

One night I addressed my concerns and he exploded.

"You need to relax! There is nothing wrong with us. You're just letting your mind run wild!" he insisted.

"I just feel like you are talking down to me—"

"Oh my god, Justine! *Again* with your feelings! You need to relax, this shit is getting old. I need you to toughen up and stop with your feelings bullshit," he barked at me.

The more I tried to defend my point of view and my desires in the relationship, the more he'd shout over me and put me down. Finally, my own temper kicked in, and I hung up on him. He called back immediately and I picked up.

"Did you just hang up on me?"

"You wouldn't let me get a word in and—"

"If you ever, ever hang up on me again, Justine, it'll be your last phone call." Click.

I wanted to throw up. The next 24 hours my stomach was in knots. I confided in one of my girlfriends over dinner and martinis, showing her some of Caleb's texts to me. It was the first time I'd opened up to a female friend about the unsettling way a guy was treating me.

"Justine, this is emotionally abusive behavior. I don't like it at all. And him threatening you like that? That's not okay," she told me.

I could have defended his bad temper. I could have made his behavior okay, justifying his reactions based on his traumatic past.

I could have made excuses and accepted the apologies that would always follow a nasty quarrel. I could have focused on all of his positive qualities, and the great times we shared, arguing he was just "going through some things," and maybe he'd change.

My heart wanted to, badly. My old pattern of settling for less than I deserve in relationships was banging at the door, tempting me to give in and do the easy, comfortable thing.

But I had to agree with my friend—the way he made me feel was not okay. I refused to be talked down to, insulted, or disrespected by men—or by *anyone*, for that matter—anymore. I'd gotten a glimpse of self-respect and happiness, and I wasn't about to give it up, no matter how strong my feelings for this guy were. I had to make a choice between being who I'd always been, or showing up as the newly empowered Justine.

I broke it off with Caleb the next day. For the first time in my life, I took a stand for myself and said no.

No, you can't speak to me like that. No, I am not available to be treated this way. No, I am not settling for anything less than I deserve.

Caleb's reaction was erratic, angry and terrifying, leaving me very thankful he lived in another state. I blocked his number and blocked him on every social media channel, hoping his feelings would simmer down as quickly as our love affair had initially started.

I knew I had done the right thing, but the breakup left me feeling like a tidal wave had swallowed me up in a sea of heartache. The week after, I couldn't follow the choreography or keep the beat in kickboxing class. It was like my brain wasn't working.

After class, I called Dr. Grant out in New York. We were still in touch to make sure my health continued to improve. I explained my "symptoms," and Dr. Grant asked a series of questions to gather more information. When he asked about my stress levels, I divulged the details of my breakup with Caleb.

"Oh, Justine. I am so sorry," Dr. Grant said. His tone changed from knowledgeable doctor to sympathetic fellow human being. "There's nothing wrong with your brain or adrenals. You're just heartbroken. I know it hurts like hell right now, and you don't feel like yourself, but I promise, it'll get better. Just give it some time. And be sure to surround yourself with people who love and support you."

I took his advice and kept myself busy, and in good company. As the weeks passed, my heartache subsided, and eventually I let my friends talk me into dating again.

"Date everyone you can right now. If someone asks you out, say yes, even if you don't think they're your type. Just go meet people and have fun," they advised.

So, I did. I went on a dating spree the rest of the year—going out with 15 different guys—usually just one or two dates before deciding it wasn't a match for me.

I did have fun. Lots of fun. I got to dress up, be wined and dined, and discuss topics other than the fitness industry—things I had missed out on for years in my 20s.

I learned what I liked and what I didn't. If I didn't feel a spark, I'd politely say so and keep it moving. I made my theme song, "On To The Next One" by Jay-Z. I highly recommend this approach to dating, because in the process of meeting other people, I learned so much about myself. Answering a stranger's questions about who you are, what you like, and what you want in life is an excellent way to get to know these answers intimately.

But by the end of 2015, I decided I was burnt out with dating and meeting new guys. It required a lot of energy, and I was ready to direct it elsewhere. I made a vision board, complete with my order to the Universe of my ideal partner. I decided to set it and forget it—and focus on myself, my health, and my business in 2016. I knew it was better to be single than to settle in anyway, and I trusted the right person would come along at exactly the right time.

February 2016; age 28

"I'm taking a break from dating," I announced to my friends, my parents, and anyone else who'd listen. "2016 is all about my business and taking care of my body. No guys!"

Five weeks later, I got a Facebook message from some guy named S.p. Sloan.

I had a digital ad for my fitness website running at The Bradley Center, which was Milwaukee's premier concert venue and the NBA arena for the Bucks at the time. The ad also spilled over into nearby bars. So, this S.p. guy was using the men's room when he saw my ad and worked up the nerve—or had the right amount of vodka—to message me.

"Every time I see your ad at Loaded Slate, I don't know whether to eat clean, work out, get ripped, and then ask you out, or just ask you out now and bring you down to my level," he wrote.

Cute, right? So, I bit.

Two hours of messaging back and forth later, I told him he could text me, and gave him my cell number.

"Hey, it's Scott," he texted, filling me in on what the "S" in S.p. stood for. His text was a green bubble— ew! Still, I *felt* something.

We made dinner plans for the following Friday, then continued talking nonstop.

"I know we said next Friday, and this is a long shot for a girl like you, but is there any chance you're free to get together sometime this weekend?" his text read.

I was supposed to see my dad that weekend, but we didn't have concrete plans yet, and I knew he wouldn't mind. *Sorry, pops!*

I texted my dad, "I know I said I wasn't dating, but I feel like this one is different. I can tell he's smart, and I feel like he has the same sense of humor as me."

"Well, then you'd better go out with him," my dad gave his blessing. "There probably aren't too many of those in the world!"

Scott and I met at Distil, a hip, dark, cozy little cocktail lounge in downtown Milwaukee. He was already there, waiting in a booth when I slid out of my Uber and glided through the front door wearing a black and white plaid blouse, the tightest skinny jeans you can imagine (but dang they looked *good*!), and these high heeled Timberland-looking booties.

I sat down and I can't remember the exact words he first said to me, I just remember falling in love with his voice. It was deep and sexy, and it gave me little butterflies and made my heart pitter patter faster.

Three hours, lots of laughs, and a couple of cocktails later, we decided to share an Uber home. Well, *he* suggested it, to be fair. I would've gladly stayed out for who knows how many more drinks with this tall, charming, green-eyed creature, but I'll forever appreciate that he made the move to end the night long before things got sloppy.

We discovered my apartment was only two short blocks away from his, so he set the app to have me dropped off first, then have the driver take him home. I climbed into our Uber and planted myself in the middle seat. *I know! How saucy of me!*

He slid in after me. His side was pressed up against mine and our fingers felt for one another's at the same time. We locked hands.

Then we kissed. And kissed. And kissed, the entire five-minute drive to my apartment. Pure magic coursed through my body.

We were still kissing when the driver pulled up to the entrance. Scott got out to hold the door open for me.

"Are you still free tomorrow?" I asked, giving him an *I'm-so-sexy-and-irresistible* smile.

"I am!" he replied in that deep, dreamy voice. "I'll see you then?"

I nodded. We kissed one more time. I peeled myself off of him and went up to my apartment. As soon the door shut, I did a happy dance, spinning around and basking in the joy of falling for someone new. Seriously, is there any better feeling?

Three minutes later my phone lit up.

"Get in safe?" Scott's text read.

"Yes! Thank you for tonight."

"It was my pleasure. I can't stop thinking about you and smiling. Sweet dreams, beautiful. I'll text you in the morning."

Eight days later, Scott and I said "I love you," for the first time, and we've said it to one another every day since.

I wish I could tell you it was all "happily ever after" from that point on. But not quite.

Just because the right person shows up in your life doesn't mean you're going to be fully ready for them. Nothing highlights your own neurosis like meeting the person you want to spend the rest of your life with, then wondering if you'll screw it all up and reinforce those fears that you aren't good enough somehow. I had come a long way in terms of confidence, loving myself, and respecting my body, but I still had a lot of healing and personal growth to do.

The truth is, the first ten months of dating Scott were kind of a shit show. He moved into my apartment after just four months of dating. We were insanely in love, and also drinking our faces off, partying three or four nights every week. I hadn't been out regularly since college, so it was fun to experience the nightlife scene from a more confident, secure-with-myself place.

Many nights, we had the time of our lives— loading jukeboxes, singing, dancing, kissing, talking, laughing, and planning our future wedding. But some nights, the booze would make my old insecurities rear their ugly heads. His, too.

We each brought our old, relentless demons and nasty baggage into our new love affair. We'd get into brutal fights that still hurt my heart looking back. I think we were *so* crazy for one another that deep down we were terrified of breaking up. So naturally, when you *don't* want to break up, you do all kinds of horrendous things to sabotage the relationship, right?

We took a cruise at the end of the year and we were plastered pretty much the entire trip. We fought *four* of the five nights of our "vacation." The day we spent traveling home, we barely spoke. I was so afraid we were going to break up. Then I could go back to my old type— guys who didn't respect me, value me, or treat me like an equal.

Sometimes it's so much easier to tell yourself you are damaged goods and don't deserve better.

We think*, certainly something this good can't happen to a fucked-up human like me. Certainly, I'm not really, truly worthy of happiness, love and respect! Certainly, fairy tales and happy endings happen for other people, but not me!*

By the grace of God, Scott and I managed to not blow it.

Pierre, my ex-husband, used to repeatedly say, "No one else would ever put up with you!"

As mean as that is to say, he was right. I was a total monster in that relationship. We were so wrong for one another, and brought out the absolute worst in each other.

Ironically, all those years spent obsessing over perfecting my outside led to the ugliest *inner* side of me emerging and running the show. And I'd let myself off the hook, excusing my atrocious behavior with claims that I was just too messed up to do better. It was the same behavior exhibited at XSport Fitness where someone had a show coming up and was a terrible human being, blaming the awfulness on the meal plan and intense workouts. That's the easy way out. It's easy to wave a white flag and say your demons are just too strong, and this is just the way you are. It's easy to go back to old patterns and old ways of behaving.

It takes a deep, mountain-moving kind of love, for someone or something, to make you decide: I *must* do better. I must *be* better.

Scott was that catalyst for me. I was already on a path to healing, but meeting him kicked things into extra-high gear.

I decided I had to commit to doing better. I had to check myself before I wrecked myself. I could no longer use my anxiety or other neurosis as an excuse to act like an asshole. I loved Scott too much to sit back and allow myself to hurt him. And I understood that hurt people hurt people. So, I had no choice but to get un-hurt. And the opposite of hurt is healed.

I first struggled to write this section because the last thing I want to tell you is that it takes someone else to heal, and truly love yourself. I don't believe that's true at all, and I also don't believe we can will others to change. To make a transformation you have to truly want it for yourself.

What has been so healing about my relationship with Scott is not the way he sees me, accepts me, loves me, and respects me. All of those things are powerful beyond measure, but even the deepest love from someone else won't heal your self-worth. A love coming from outside of you will never be enough. Any amount of outside praise and adoration will never make you feel completely whole.

What has been so healing about Scott is not the way he loves me, but the way I love him. Getting to love someone to the extent that I love Scott has been the single most greatest blessing in my life.

He has been a catalyst for me to continue working on myself, to be the best partner I can be. And that means loving and accepting myself, fully. All of me. The good, the bad, and the ugly. The stretch marks, jiggly bits, and other Problem Areas, which I no longer view as problematic at all.

I dove head first into an exploration of the deepest, darkest parts of myself—the parts I had deemed unlovable in the first place. I took a good, hard look at my self-hatred—where it came from and how it had driven me for so many years.

This kind of work is not for the faint of heart. But your heart, my darling, is hardly faint. And it is the greatest gift you can ever give yourself, and everyone in your life.

September 2017; age 29

My lack of direction complicated the first year of my relationship with Scott. I realized a career in fitness no longer felt fulfilling. I could give someone an effective, top-notch workout blindfolded. I could write a dynamite training program in my sleep. But I had this menacing, ever-present feeling: *There has to be something more for me.*

Some refer to this questioning period of your late twenties as a "quarter life crisis," but I refer to it as my Saturn Return phase. The Saturn Return is when the planet Saturn returns to the exact place it was in when you were born, usually right around 29.5 years. This astrological occurrence is said to bring about feelings of uncertainty and doubt, while highlighting existential questions like, *who am I? Why am I here? What's my purpose? What do I really want to do with my life?*

I had to sit with these unanswered questions for a whole year, which felt excruciating for someone who has always identified with her goals, vision, and ambition. I felt a sense of belonging in my relationships, but in the areas of my career and life purpose, I felt utterly unsure of where I was supposed to be.

One week in March of 2017, two things happened that showed me exactly where I was supposed to go next. After a boot camp workout I led with a small group, one of the women in the group plopped herself down next to me and began to spill her guts about stressors in her life, I listened and we talked it through. After ten minutes, she left feeling encouraged and more sure of herself

"Thank you for letting me vent tonight. I feel so much better!" she texted me later that night. I was amazed because I hardly knew this woman, yet in a short amount of time, I'd managed to calm her fears and help her step into a more empowered place.

The next day one of my private training clients texted me, shortly before our session was scheduled to start.

"Can I take you for coffee for our session today, instead of working out? I really need someone to talk to," she asked.

I said of course, and we spent an hour sorting through some things that had been troubling her. As we were wrapping up, she thanked me for my willingness to listen and process with her. I mentioned that I'd been considering transitioning into a career more focused on psychology, which had been my major in college.

"You know Justine, you wouldn't have to go back to grad school to help people in that way. You could get certified as a life coach," she said.

A lightbulb went off in my head. I suddenly knew this was my next step. *Of course! That's it! Why didn't I see this sooner?*

I had always adored helping clients get stronger and healthier, and had also served as a therapist during many sessions over the nine years I'd been a personal trainer. By now, I understood that for someone to really make a lasting transformation, mindset is crucial. You can eat the right foods and workout consistently, but if you don't deal with your old crummy beliefs and negative thought patterns, you will always be fighting an uphill battle with your body. I knew this firsthand.

With Scott's support, I immediately enrolled in the Become A Health Coach program through Health Coach Institute, and began this new venture just two weeks after that "A-ha!" moment.

To graduate, I was required to act as both coach and client, going through a 12-session program with another student. I partnered up with a wonderful woman named Amy. Amy and I coached one another through a series of specific sessions designed to help you break through in not just your health, but in all areas of your life.

This holistic program changed my life forever. It laid the foundation for me to learn how to eat intuitively. It eradicated emotional eating for me, once and for all.

I still had that nasty habit of chewing a whole pack of gum every day that I'd developed back in high school— a side effect of depriving myself from the actual food I wanted to eat. Overnight, that habit fell away, because I began to give myself full permission to actually eat what I wanted. Having a full understanding of why I was doing harmful things to myself in the first place, and how I could meet my needs in a more supportive way, made any leftover bad habits around food start to dissolve from my life forever.

Health Coach Institute endorsed a 14-Day Detox protocol, suggesting we use it with clients. As a trainer and now, as a coach, I've always had a rule that I try everything first, before having a client go through it. Without testing out my own workouts, it was hard to know how my clients would feel—so it was important to me that I also try this Detox program if I was ever going to share it with anyone.

The program seemed harmless enough—cutting out dairy, gluten, alcohol, caffeine, and processed foods for 14 days, while focusing on nourishing the body with nutritious, unprocessed foods.

By day four, I was marching myself up the block to Whole Foods to buy pints of ice cream, which I promptly devoured as soon as I got home. It was college all over again: giving up on a diet, binging 'til I was in a food coma, and hating myself for a perceived lack of willpower. Only this time, I was wiser, and more self-aware. Instead of berating myself, I got curious about what had triggered my old binge eating behavior. I realized I wasn't weak, broken or defective. The *diet mentality* is. I sorted through my feelings and then dove into studies around this, realizing that deprivation physically and mentally leads people to overeat and binge.

Eureka! I was onto something. I discovered diets have an insanely high failure rate, with a whopping 83 percent of dieters gaining back more weight than they lost in the first place! (Wolpert, 2007) Yet we blame *ourselves* when diets don't work.

I'm proud to say my failed attempt at a 14-Day Detox was my very last diet, ever.

After over 20 years, I retired from dieting, reclaimed my life, and vowed to help other people do the same. It was a process to get comfortable letting go of tracking calories, counting macros, and weighing every gram of food on a scale. It was a process to get over my insecurities about weight gain. It felt scary, like riding a bike without training wheels for the first time, but eventually I realized I was doing it. I could coast!

Turns out, my body, like all bodies, knew how to eat innately all along. I realized I'd never need another book, magazine, or coach to tell me how to eat again. I tuned out the noise of diet culture once and for all, and tuned into the miraculous wisdom of my magnificent body.

March 2018; age 30

I married Scott Patrick Sloan on March 11, 2018. It sounds so corny and cliché, but our wedding day was one of the happiest days of my life. I had a permanent grin on my face, and all of my family and friends told me they'd never seen me so happy. The first picture I posted on social media was of the two of us, beaming as we walked down the aisle as husband and wife. Of course, the beautiful diamond engagement ring and wedding bands were on my ring finger, but I was more focused on our loving relationship.

Two days later, we newlyweds went on a "Mini-moon" to Lake Geneva, a nearby vacation town in Wisconsin. We had a more extravagant trip booked to Jamaica two months later, but we wanted to get away and enjoy some downtime post-wedding.

Our first night there, we went to a restaurant friends had raved about. The menu was small, and the standout option was the "Chef's Special," which consisted of three types of meat, (chicken, steak, and house made sausage) plus three types of seafood (salmon, shrimp and lobster tail!) It came with a side of sauteed spinach and mashed potatoes. *Sign me up!*

When the waiter came to take our order, we ordered the calamari appetizer, and then I went for the Chef's Special, while Scott got something boring and basic like the chicken dish, as usual.

"That's a *lot* of food for one person," the waiter said, cautioning me. He raised his eyebrows and paused, waiting for me to change my order.

A hundred thoughts went through my mind.

Um, excuse me? Would you say the same thing to my husband? Am I supposed to switch my order to a salad? Can you just write down my fucking order, kind sir?

I looked him right in the eye and smiled.

"Perfect. I'm really hungry," I responded.

I shared half of the appetizer with Scott, then cleaned my Chef's Special dinner plate. Then, I ordered three scoops of house-made gelato that I'll never forget. I cleared that plate, too. Well, to be fair, I let Scott have *one* bite of each flavor. Marriage means sharing— even food.

The waiter cleared my empty dinner and dessert plates without a word. He looked a little sheepish, as I sat there, belly full of delicious food with a smug little smile on my face.

After dinner we went for drinks, and I had a few beers and an Irish coffee. I did all of this wearing a stunning red strapless jumpsuit that I felt amazing in, without any trace of food guilt to be found. I'm sure the caloric value of all of this was high, but I can't really say, because I didn't bother to mentally tabulate it. I simply enjoyed myself, math-equation free. It was like those evil voices in my head had vanished, through years of working on my self-love game. It was glorious.

That night, only I could fully appreciate the victory that was mine, but I can tell you it felt a million times more rewarding than any night I'd been given a trophy onstage. Not all victories require an audience to feel triumphant.

Two months later, on our honeymoon in Jamaica, I enjoyed wonderful food and sugary, blended beach drinks with the same glorious, guilt-free satisfaction.

While walking down Seven Mile Beach with Scott, I handed him my phone and asked him to take a picture of me. I posed naturally, hands on hips, confident but relaxed, smiling in my strapless two-piece black bikini.

My husband does not enjoy taking pictures, so he pulled his classic move of snapping *one* single photo then handing my phone back to me. Normally I'd protest and insist he take 20 more, so I can choose the one I despise the least. "Best of 30!" is my joke when it comes to iPhone pictures, which is both amusing *and* true.

I looked at the photo my husband took of me in a bikini on the beach and, son of a gun, I *liked* it. I really, truly liked what I saw.

For a moment, time stopped, and it was as if cherubs were sprinkling glittering angel dust down on me from the heavens. Another silent victory. A victory no one else could appreciate or understand, because no one else really knew what it took for me to get there.

There being free from the critical voices that had governed over most of my life.

There being happy in my body, happy in my own skin, happy in my marriage, and happy in my life.

There being at peace, loving myself, respecting myself, and living life to the fullest.

I posted the photo taken on that beach in Jamaica as a side-by-side comparison with a photo of me from a shoot I'd done after a competition in 2013. Both of the women in the photos are posing in bikinis, but the energy behind the photos could not be any more different.

Whenever I post comparison photos, naturally someone will comment, "You look great now, but WOW. You looked amazing then!"

At other points in my life, this would have triggered the heck out of me. Now I just laugh, and send that person so much love. Years ago, I would have thought that way, too.

To me, there is no comparison. I know what it was like to live *inside* of that body, and it was hell on earth. Now life feels like freedom and peace. I'd never for one second trade places with the person I used to be.

June 2018; age 31

As I opened myself up to healing, I was guided, time after time, to the next right book, podcast, modality, or healer.

After posting about my inner critic on social media, a friend reached out to tell me about a hypnotherapist she'd been seeing, who used a technique called "tapping," which she found to be helpful in breaking up negative thought patterns. Willing to try anything at least once, I made an appointment right away.

I worked with the hypnotherapist a handful of times, and each time I walked out of her office feeling like a ton of bricks had been lifted off my shoulders.

"Tapping" is another name for EFT, or Emotional Freedom Technique, first discovered by Dr. Roger Callahan in 1979. The technique involves tapping on the body's meridian points while making a series of statements out loud to release stored negative emotions.

Of all of the techniques and modalities I've tried, EFT has been one of the most effective for me, which is why I got certified as a practitioner myself. I've included a deeper explanation and how-to video in the resources for this book, which can be found at www.JustineSloan.com/book

Sometimes we have no idea what is weighing us down until we are truly willing to face our stored pain and trauma. It can feel like exploring a dark, spooky, cobweb-filled basement— part of your brain will shout, *NO! Don't go down there!* and you'll desperately want to comply.

But unlocking and understanding the shadowy parts of ourselves is the path to true self-acceptance, and it's also incredibly liberating. It provides the bridge of being able to choose forgiveness and compassion, for ourselves and others, rather than operating from a reactive, wounded place, and being the puppet of old shadows we are too afraid to face.

Remember the "saus-eeege" pants? I had no clue what pain those comments caused me until 23 years later, when the memories came up during a session with my hypnotherapist. For the entire 90-minute session I bawled, soaking tissue after tissue with tears and snot as we worked to release the stored trauma from the "saus-eeege" incidents.

The word trauma might sound excessive here, but the Merriam-Webster dictionary defines trauma as "an emotional upset." In the world of psychology, we now recognize that it's not as much about the context of what happened to us, as it is the meaning we made of it. As children we are meaning-making machines, and not all of the meanings we create are helpful, or true.

We tend to brush things off that happened in childhood. We might say, "Oh, that person didn't intend to hurt me. I'm okay now," or, "That friend I had was really nice until she wasn't, but it was a long time ago, so it's okay."

Lodging your pain away and carrying it around is not okay. It's never okay.

Doing this over and over again and not giving yourself permission to say aloud, "That incident actually *wasn't* okay" is why you're carrying heavy-ass bags of pain and stored trauma around. It's why random, seemingly trivial things can set you off. It shows up in those moments where you hear a song in a grocery store, or an instructor makes a comment in spin class, and suddenly, out of nowhere, you feel like you're going to cry. Or in those moments where a loved one says or does something relatively insignificant that makes you go 0 to 100, losing your temper and lashing out.

You say things like, "I don't know why I'm so emotional right now." You blame your hormones. You wonder why you feel so messed up, so unworthy, and so downright exhausted all the time. It's from all that pain you bottled up for the sake of making others comfortable. For the sake of *not* stirring the pot—not speaking up and saying, "Actually this is not okay."

Stop and consider your true feelings. Were you actually okay?

If you are ready to shine light on those shadowy parts of your past, I highly recommend enlisting the support of a trained professional, counselor, coach, or therapist to do the deeper work. You might find there are events from 10, 20, 30, 40 years ago blocking you from being able to receive true joy, love, and acceptance. You don't have to let your past dictate your present.

You are not the things people said or did to you. You are not the mistakes you or others have made. You are not the beliefs formed by a younger version of you. You deserve to be free of the chains of your past.

February 2021; age 33

Have you ever watched a physical wound heal? It's mind blowing. Truly miraculous. Day by day it gets better, without you having to do anything. It knows what to do and it goes to work. It heals itself and gets the job done, without any of your meddling, controlling, obsessing, or overthinking.

That's how it is when you surrender your life to something greater than you. Call it God, the Universe, Source Energy, The Holy Spirit, or simply the power of choosing Love over Fear. Whatever floats your boat. When you allow yourself to trust in something beyond your physical human self, everything starts to organize itself in your favor.

When I stop and look at where I am today compared to where I was in 2014, and prior, I realize it is nothing short of a miracle.

Today, I am able to eat whatever I want, whenever I want, and however much I want, without any nagging voices telling me "eating that is bad," or "you're eating too much," or "you're going to get fat." That voice is gone. And food has never tasted better. Side note: If you're wondering, I've never touched another piece of tilapia again, but shockingly, I still enjoy eating asparagus.

These days I move my body with tremendous reverence, appreciation, and love. I honor my energy levels, my monthly cycle, and my body's signals. I push when it feels awesome to push, and I rest when it feels best to rest. When I rest, I feel zero guilt. There's no need to "make up for it" the next day. There's no need to eat less to compensate for not working out. It's just me honoring my gorgeously spectacular body.

I no longer think about burning fat or calories during workouts. I think thoughts like, *Thank you, body! You're so amazing! Thank you for all you do for me!*

I strongly encourage you to try thinking this way.

I am married to my soulmate, Scott, who is my best friend. The love we share continues to be my greatest teacher. He treats me with so much respect, adoration, and never-ending acceptance that it unceasingly reinforces the way I should treat myself. I still wake up in the morning grateful beyond words for the person next to me.

I have so many incredible women in my life supporting me, too, which is a far cry from several years ago. I have an abundance of friends I can go to with absolutely anything, who make me feel truly seen and heard. In 2018, I co-founded Boss Ladies MKE with my dear friend Diana. Boss Ladies MKE is a networking and mastermind group for women in the greater Milwaukee area (for details visit BossLadiesMKE.com!) I've put my heart and soul into serving that community, allowing me to practice what I preach in terms of truly supporting other women, rather than competing.

I really don't know where I'd be without the amazing women in my life. I wouldn't be writing this book, for starters. Humans are wired for connection, and I believe women need a tribe of other supportive women to reach their full potential. I'm eternally thankful for my tribe.

I'm in a career that doesn't feel like work or a job, because it's not. I'm living my soul's purpose a little more every day, and I get the extraordinary honor of sharing my gifts, wisdom, and knowledge with others. Whether it's in a coaching session with one of my 1:1 clients, a social media post that shares powerful insight that helped me transform, or a random heart-to-heart conversation, my intention is always to help others feel good about themselves, and to help them know their tremendous power. This was my inspiration to create Empowered 365, a membership program for women that contains the resources, tools and philosophies that changed my life (available at JustineSloan.com/membership).

After over two decades of struggling with food and body image, I developed my unique, balanced approach to eating and exercise, which I call the Empowered Eating Method. I teach this method in my 1:1 coaching, group programs, and my membership.

My true goal is to leave people better than I found them. To help them know their magnificence. To be a mirror to reflect that no matter where you are, no matter what you've been through, you can change. You can heal. Things can be so different for you. I believe I'm living, breathing proof of that, and I want people to know that healing, transformation, and miracles are available to them.

When I look in the mirror, or look down at my body, I love what I see. Unconditionally. Every single day.

Loving what I see in the mirror isn't about believing every single detail is aesthetically perfect. Believe me, I still have my days where I struggle with that. After all, I'm an imperfect human, floating around in a culture that tells women thinner is better, aging is ugly, and looking perfect equals love.

I buy into some of these messages, and some part of me probably always will. I notice the stark contrast between what my husband does to get himself ready in the morning, and what I do. There is daily, weekly, and monthly maintenance that goes into my appearance, and I would never want anyone to think otherwise. In other words, I do not wake up like this.

I tell myself I really love these things I do—I'm obsessed with makeup, fashion, skincare, fabulous hair, and I genuinely prefer smooth, shaved legs, hairless underarms, and a groomed bikini line—but I can't help but to wonder how much of that is inherently me, and how much is from decades of cultural programming.

Loving what I see in the mirror isn't about believing every single part of me perfect. It's about appreciating this vessel that has been with me since birth. It's about being thankful for this physical body that has put up with years of abuse and disrespect, and still, she stands strong, healthy, and resilient. It's about honoring the soul within my body, who has fought like hell to get here. I'm so fucking thankful for her.

Since I hit my personal rock-bottom in 2014, I've been in the process of unlearning all the destructive, dysfunctional behaviors and beliefs I had taken in since childhood.

I've gone on a personal journey of waking up and learning how to trust my body, my feelings, my decisions and my desires, for the first time in my life. I've learned how to honor myself in every way— physically, mentally, emotionally, and spiritually. I've learned I get to say no to anything that doesn't feel loving, joyful, or respectful. I've learned I get to ask questions and not just accept what's handed to me.

Most importantly, I've learned how to take care of myself in a way that says, "SOMEONE I LOVE LIVES HERE."

When I think of how grateful I am to be where I am today, how could I *not* love that person I see in the mirror?

Empowering Truths of Being A Woman

Empowering Truth #1: Self-love will make you feel happier and more confident than weight loss ever will.

Empowering Truth #2: Your perfect size is whatever size you are while living the healthiest life you truly enjoy living.

Empowering Truth #3: When you care for yourself from the inside out, you look different. You glow. You're magnetic. Self-love looks gorgeous on everyone!

Empowering Truth #4: We all innately have the skill of eating intuitively. Our bodies know what to do; we've just tuned that wisdom out. It's a process, but no matter your background, it is 100% possible to learn how to tune back in and create a positive, drama-free relationship with food.

Empowering Truth #5: Nothing is more important than your health and well-being.

Empowering Truth #6: Exercise—or movement—should be a celebration of what your body can do (not a punishment for what you ate.)

Empowering Truth #7: Your value is not negotiable. Your worth does not need to be proven. You always have been, and always will be, inherently worthy of love and respect.

Empowering Truth #8: You become like the people you surround yourself with. Choose wisely. The world is filled with kind, supportive people, but only if you look for them.

Empowering Truth #9: It is better to be single than to settle for anything less than you deserve. And, my darling, you deserve to have it all!

Empowering Truth #10: There's no such thing as competition when you're showing up as your most authentic self. No one can ever be YOU, and that is your superpower.

Empowering Truth #11: You matter. Your voice matters. Your feelings matter. You are here on purpose, and you are not here to stay quiet and play small. Your power lies in owning your story and speaking your truth from a place of love.

Goodies + Resources

Book Goodies:

If you feel inspired to dig in deeper, I've created some free resources related to the book, including:

-an online photo album

-a Spotify playlist

-EFT Tapping how-to video

-printable PDF of the 11 Empowering Truths of Being A Woman

-journal prompts

-a guided meditation for self-love and body acceptance

To access these, visit: www.JustineSloan.com/book

Social Media:

Instagram: @thejustinesloan

Self-Love Club Facebook group: https://facebook.com/groups/selfloveclubforwomen

YouTube: https://youtube.com/JustineMoore

TikTok: @justinemooresloan

Empowered 365:

I feel incredibly blessed to have had access to the coaches, mentors, books, podcasts, programs, and retreats that helped me learn how to fully love myself. It is now my mission to empower other women to do the same. Enter: Empowered 365.

Empowered 365 was created to be your one-stop shop to feel empowered in your body, around food, and in every area of your life! I truly believe you deserve to have it all. My darling, if you are ready to own your power and create a life that FEELS good, this is the place for you!

Join me at https://www.justinesloan.com/membership

Thank you, thank you, thank you!

If you loved this book, I would be SO incredibly grateful for a review. Positive reviews are basically the equivalent of sending fresh flowers (or a chocolate cheesecake) to an author!

Acknowledgements

I am deeply grateful for everyone who helped me bring this book into existence.

To my husband, Scott, for being my #1 supporter through this process. Thank you for believing in me and my vision enough to help me make it a reality.

To my parents, Janet and Kelly, for never once asking me what details would be in the book, or discouraging me in any way from sharing openly, honestly, and fully. Your faith in me brings tears of joy to my eyes.

To my coach Sara Connell, for holding my hand through every step of this process, and for creating Thought Leader Academy to support the voices and visions of women everywhere.

To my editor Danielle Perlin-Good, for helping me develop and shape this book into something I am proud of.

Kaleigh Atkinson, Elise Albers, Renee Natzke, and Katherine Dorman, my beautiful beta readers, thank you for your time, energy, and support in providing feedback on the manuscript.

To Meena Zia and Nicole Moza, my spiritual mentors, thank you for being the inspiration and driving force behind me committing to this project. You have changed my life in ways you'll never fully know!

Melissa Makeiff, thank you for being my ride-or-die through this process. You are the sister I never had.

To Lori Harder, for the endless inspiration you provide, and for supporting this project. You have empowered me to shine my light, simply by shining yours.

To all of the incredible women in my world— my friends, my clients, the Boss Ladies MKE community— thank you for the opportunity to know the beauty of women supporting women.

Last but certainly not least, to my community near and far, thank you for sharing so much excitement and enthusiasm throughout this entire process. ILYSM.

Works Cited

Bijlefeld, M. &. (2003). *Encyclopedia of Diet Fads.* Westport: Greenwood Press.

CBSnews.com. (2011, March 2). *Survey: 97 percent of women have negative body image*. Retrieved from CBSnews.com: https://www.cbsnews.com/news/survey-97-percent-of-women-have-negative-body-image/

Miller, K. (2015, January 26). *Study: Most Girls Start Dieting By Age 8*. Retrieved from Refinery29: https://www.refinery29.com/en-us/2015/01/81288/children-dieting-body-image

NEDA. (2014). *Something "Needs Improvement," But It's Not Your Body*. Retrieved from NationalEatingDisorders.org: https://www.nationaleatingdisorders.org/blog/something-needs-improvement-its-not-your-body

Oldenhave, A. J. (2002). Center of Excellence for Eating Disorders. In *Characteristics and treatment of patients with chronic eating disorders.* (pp. 15-29). Retrieved from UNC School of Medicine: https://www.med.unc.edu/psych/eatingdisorders/learn-more/about-eating-disorders/statistics/

Wolpert, S. (2007, April 3). *Dieting does not work, UCLA researchers report*. Retrieved from UCLA Newsroom: https://newsroom.ucla.edu/releases/Dieting-Does-Not-Work-UCLA-Researchers-7832

CPSIA information can be obtained
at www.ICGtesting.com
Printed in the USA
LVHW081539181021
700762LV00013B/526

9 781662 907784